The Palestinian Catastrophe

The Palestinian Catastrophe

The 1948 expulsion of a people from their homeland

MICHAEL PALUMBO

faber and faber
LONDON · BOSTON

First published in 1987 by
Faber and Faber Limited
3 Queen Square London WC1N 3AU

Typeset by Goodfellow & Egan Ltd Cambridge
Printed in Great Britain by
Mackays of Chatham Ltd Kent
All rights reserved

©Michael Palumbo 1987

British Library Cataloguing in Publication Data
Palumbo, Michael
The Palestinian catastrophe : the 1948
expulsion of a people from their homeland.
1. Jewish–Arab relations——1949– ——
Political aspects
I. Title
956'.04   DS119.7
ISBN 0-571-14864-6

dedicated to
Israel Shahak

Table of Contents

List of Illustrations — vi
Prologue — vii

Chapter

I Land Without a People — 1
II Plan Dalet — 34
III Deir Yassin — 47
IV The Haifa Tragedy — 58
V The Fall of Jaffa — 82
VI The City of Peace — 95
VII The Road to Safed — 105
VIII The Lydda Death March — 126
IX The Troubled Truce — 139
X Operation Hiram — 163
XI There Could Have Been Peace — 175
XII Theft of a Nation — 194
Epilogue — 209
Sources — 214
Acknowledgements — 227
Index — 229

List of Illustrations

The United Nations Partition plan	30
Exodus: 1948	121
Captain Zeuty's sketch of the Elabun massacre	165
The final armistice partition	197

Prologue

And the Philistines were humbled and they did not come any more into the borders of Israel.

1 Kings 7:13

The atmosphere was tense as four UN observers arrived for a meeting in the Negev with a team of Israeli liaison officers. A cease-fire several months before in July 1948 had left most of the Negev under Egyptian control, and there had been constant truce violations, including several pitched battles. The principal mission of the UN on the southern front was to prevent a renewal of all-out warfare. But on this morning of 13 October, the four UN officers of the so-called 'Special Investigating Team for the Negev' were visiting the Israeli-controlled sector in order to check on the status of any Arab civilians who might be left in the villages occupied by the Jews.

When the Israelis arrived for the conference, their leader Major Michael Hanegbi asked whether the UN team had investigated his complaints of Egyptian truce violations. Colonel Gerald De Greer who headed the UN delegation replied that he could give no answer on that subject but instead asked the Israelis why they had expelled so many Palestinian civilians. 'We emptied the villages where the population had hostile attitudes towards us,' remarked Major Hanegbi.

The UN observers asked to visit several villages where Arab refugees reported that the Israelis had committed atrocities. Major Hanegbi replied that it was impossible to enter these villages since they were blocked by mine fields. The Israeli officer claimed, however, that those Arab civilians who remained under Israeli control were well treated. When Colonel De Greer expressed a desire to see a village where the Palestinian inhabitants were living peacefully under Israeli rule,

Major Hanegbi agreed to take the observers to Huzaify, thirty kilometres away.

As they drove along the road, the UN officials could see the desolation of the villages. The inhabitants had been driven out, leaving the harvest rotting on the vine. They also saw many homes that had been demolished by the Israelis. It was the same in other parts of the new Jewish state. The Israelis had placed field mines all over the Negev area. When Colonel De Greer asked why so many mines had been put around the abandoned villages, the Israeli major answered, 'It's necessary to stop the Arab population from returning at night.'

Colonel De Greer saw signs that the area was already being populated with Jewish immigrants. In some cases settlements had been newly formed and in other cases, the Israelis had moved people into abandoned villages. Before the war there had been few Jews living in the area but, as in other parts of the country, Prime Minister David Ben-Gurion wished to change the demographic character of the region as soon as possible.

When they arrived at Huzaify, Major Hanegbi showed the UN observers what he called an example of close and peaceful collaboration between the Arabs and Jewish colonists. From a distance of almost two kilometres, the Jewish officer pointed out people living in tents next to an Israeli settlement. Hanegbi claimed that the people in the tents were Arab Bedouin. De Greer and his party were not allowed to get any closer to the settlement nor would the Israelis give any more information. The Belgian officer was later told by another UN observer that the people who were pointed out to him living in tents were really Jews.

Colonel De Greer asked if the Arab refugees would be allowed to return to their homes and whether UN observers might be permitted into the Jewish-controlled districts on a permanent basis, as in the Egyptian-controlled areas. The Israelis would agree to neither request. The UN officers left with an unfavourable impression of the Israeli treatment of Arab civilians. They concluded unanimously in their report that 'lands have been taken quite unlawfully from the Arab population which was compelled to leave their villages.'[1] Colonel De Greer noted, 'we did not meet one Arab civilian.' It was obvious that the Israelis had used force to drive out the Palestinians and were prepared to use force to keep them from returning.

After leaving the Jewish officers, the UN team re-entered Egyptian territory in order to visit the refugee camps. There were 175,000 Arab civilians in these camps, a figure which UN mediator Ralph Bunche found 'astoundingly high'.[2] Despite aid from various sources, there were not nearly enough facilities to care for such a multitude. When Colonel De Greer visited the camps at Majdal and Gaza, he noted, 'The people in these areas are living in shelters dug out of the ground and with burlap bags covering them, branches from trees and any makeshift shelter available.' He described how the death rate among the refugees, particularly child mortality, was exceedingly high. Most of the bodies of the youngsters were covered with sores and they were all suffering from exposure.

There was no doubt in Colonel De Greer's mind that the refugees had been *'driven from their areas by Jewish mortar, machine gun and rifle fire.'*[3] Many civilians had been killed during the expulsions. In their report, the UN observers stressed, *'This Jewish action happened when no armed resistance was offered to their forces.'* Indeed, during their investigation, the 'Special Investigating Team for the Negev' found that many of the Palestinians had been driven from their homes in southern Palestine during the first truce at the end of June and early July. The Arabs were robbed of their land and cattle and forced to flee to the coastal areas and the refugee camps at Majdal and Gaza. Colonel De Greer was very concerned about the welfare of the refugees. He predicted that 'numerous Arabs will die due to their lack of food and exposure to the elements unless they are permitted to return to their homes or unless relief is given to them.'

Colonel Vermeulen, the senior UN official in Gaza, made his own report on the refugees. He agreed with Colonel De Greer and his team about the cause of the Arab exodus on the southern front. Colonel Vermeulen wrote, 'According to the observers, and we are able to state it also, in this area Jewish action obliged the Arabs to withdraw from many villages.'[4] Vermeulen believed that, 'the exodus of the native Arab population from the Negev' was caused by the Jews who frightened many Arabs by 'destroying villages' and killing many people and cattle. Like Colonel De Greer, Vermeulen was worried since, 'winter is coming and the refugees live in unbearable conditions'.

There was a final meeting between Colonel De Greer and the Israeli liaison team which was now headed by Colonel Baruch. Colonel De Greer asked Baruch about permitting the Arabs to return to their homes in peace, 'without being shot or driven out by Israeli forces'. Baruch flatly refused. He asserted that it was the Egyptians who had expelled the Arab civilians. This claim was not taken very seriously since Baruch's predecessor, Major Hanegbi, had admitted that the Israelis had driven out the indigenous population. The UN observers pleaded with Baruch to take back the refugees. 'The Egyptians have a hostile mob of hungry people on their hands,' the Jewish colonel answered. Baruch added that the Israelis had no intention of relieving the Egyptians of this problem by accepting the refugees back.

At the meeting the Israelis made it clear that they would not permit UN observers on their territory. They claimed that the land mines they had placed around the abandoned Arab villages made the area too dangerous for UN personnel. Another subject discussed at the meeting was the Israeli demand that they be allowed to send convoys across the Egyptian lines in order to supply Jewish settlements in the Negev. But Colonel De Greer told Baruch, 'The Egyptian army will not permit the convoys to pass through their lines until the refugees from the Negev are allowed to return to their homes.'

The dispute over the supply to the Jewish settlements in the Negev which were behind Egyptian lines was to provide a convenient excuse for the Israelis to resume fighting on the southern front and occupy more territory. On 15 October, an Israeli convoy of sixteen trucks heading for the Jewish settlements was fired on as it passed through the Egyptian positions. Several of the lead vehicles burst into flames. The Israelis promptly blamed the Egyptians although UN reports indicate that the Jews themselves had blown up the trucks, so as to have a pretext for renewing combat.

Ben-Gurion had approved Operation Ten Plagues against the Egyptians at a Cabinet session on 6 October. In view of their overwhelming military power, the Israelis were gambling on the fact that they could overrun the Negev before they could be restrained by the Truman administration in America. Ben-Gurion believed that with the presidential election only a few days away, Truman would not risk alienating the American Jewish voters by putting pressure on Israel to halt the offensive.

The Israeli attack against the poorly equipped Egyptians was launched by their numerically superior army. The new Israeli Air Force took a heavy toll of the Egyptian positions in the Negev and the Sinai Desert. Israeli forces stationed in the Negev outposts behind Egyptian lines also attacked enemy supply lines and other strategic positions. Israeli Commander Yigal Allon's principal goal was the Faluja crossroads, the junction controlling the highway net into the Negev Desert. Here, however, under their Sudanese commander, Taha Bey, the Egyptian 4th Brigade held out against an encircling Israeli force.

Elsewhere in the Negev, Egyptian resistance collapsed. In town after town, the Arab civilian population was expelled by the advancing Israelis. At Beersheva, the IDF (Israeli Defence Forces) drove out thousands of Arabs and looted the town. The official report for the operation notes that the population of Beersheva had been transferred to Egypt 'at their own request'.[5] Prime Minister David Ben-Gurion who had his own sources of information knew that the official report was false. Ben-Gurion approved of the expulsion of Arab civilians (he later told his colleagues, 'Land with Arabs on it and land without Arabs on it are two very different types of land') but he was annoyed by the looting and excessive brutality, which was bad for discipline. Ben-Gurion noted in his diary that at Beersheva 'the army failed to control its men.'[6]

The UN made an attempt to halt the Israeli offensive. On 19 October, a resolution was passed by the Security Council requesting a cease-fire. The Egyptians immediately agreed but the Israelis wished to keep the offensive going until they had taken all of their objectives. By the time a truce finally settled over the desert during the last days of October, the Israelis had conquered almost the entire Negev region.

The Egyptians charged that the Israelis had used considerable brutality in order to drive out the Palestinian civilians. There is in fact a great deal of evidence from a variety of Israeli, American, UN and Palestinian sources to support the claims that mass murder took place in many of the towns on the southern front during the October offensive. The Israelis knew from previous experience that news of the atrocities would hasten the flight of the Palestinians.

Mahmoud Abu Ghalyon, a farmer living in a village that lay in the path of the Zionist assault, recalled that when the attack began most of the people were in the village mosque. 'The Jews entered the mosque and slaughtered without mercy 100–150 people including old people, women and children.'[7] The rest of the village fled and they were pursued by the Israelis. According to Chalyon, 'Some twenty to thirty families sought shelter in a cave. The Jews found them there and shot them all.' One woman who was left for dead survived among the pile of bodies.

One of the worst but best-documented massacres during the offensive took place at Dawayma. This town was taken by a company of the 89th Commando Battalion which was composed of former Irgun and Stern Gang terrorists. A veteran of the unit has published an account of the massacre. He notes that in order 'to kill the children they fractured their heads with sticks. There was not one house without corpses.'[8] After murdering the children, the Jewish soldiers herded the women and men into houses where they were kept without food or water. Then the houses were blown up with the helpless civilians inside.

The Israelis were particularly sadistic in their treatment of Arab women. One Zionist soldier in Dawayma, 'prided himself upon having raped an Arab woman before shooting her to death. Another Arab woman with her newborn baby was made to clean the place for a couple of days and then they shot her and her baby.' The conscience-stricken Israeli veteran who revealed these events stressed that they were committed by 'Educated and well-mannered commanders who were considered good guys.' They became 'base murderers and this was not in the storm of battle but as a method of expulsion and extermination. The fewer the Arabs who remained, the better.'

PROLOGUE

At the end of the offensive on the southern front, the UN requested that the Israelis allow a team of observers to visit Dawayma to investigate Egyptian charges that a massacre had taken place there. After three previous requests were denied, on 8 November the Israelis finally allowed Colonel Sore and Warrant-Officer Van Wassenhove to visit the village. As he walked through the town, the Belgian Van Wassenhove saw that many of the houses were still smoking. Some of these houses, the Belgian officer noted, 'gave a peculiar smell as if bones were burning.'[9] But he was not allowed by the Israeli officer to investigate further. When he asked about a house which was about to be blown up, Van Wassenhove was told 'The house has vermin in it and that's why we are blowing it up.'

The UN team requested to see the village mosque in Dawayma but an Israeli officer replied, 'we never go into the mosque because this is not correct and we must follow tradition in such things.' But when the UN officials did get a brief look inside they found that there were quite a few Jewish soldiers in the Islamic holy place, which had obviously been desecrated.

Sore and Van Wassenhove wanted to see the other side of the village, where they suspected there might be more incriminating evidence. The Israelis would not let the UN team go there because they claimed that the area was mined. But Van Wassenhove remarked, 'I haven't noticed any place where there could be mines or where mines could have been taken out.' He also observed that the road that the Israelis claimed had been mined by the Arabs faced the Arab lines, which is not the side of the village where mines would be placed.

When Sore and Van Wassenhove asked about the evacuation of the village by its inhabitants, they were told that the whole population had fled when the Arab forces left the region. The Israelis denied that they had used force to expel the villagers but they were greatly disturbed when the UN observers came upon the body of an Arab civilian and they refused to allow Sore and Van Wassenhove to examine it. Despite the hostile attitude of the Israelis, the UN team had little doubt about what had taken place at Dawayma.

The American Consul in Jerusalem, William Burdett, had heard about the visit of the UN team to Dawayma. After making inquiries, on 6 November, he reported to Washington, 'Investigation by UN indicates massacre occurred but observers are unable to determine number of persons involved.'[10] Estimates vary considerably but probably about 300 Arab civilians were slaughtered in the town.

Members of the Israeli government knew what had happened at Dawayma and other towns in the Negev but most were unconcerned. However, one Israeli leader had a conscience. On 17 November, Agriculture Minister Aharon Cizling told the Cabinet, 'I feel that things are going on which are hurting my soul, the soul of my family and all of us here.'[11] Probably referring to Dawayma, he added, 'Jews too have behaved like Nazis and my entire being has been shaken.'

Those who survived the Dawayma massacre as well as thousands of other Arab civilians from the Negev, crowded into Gaza, the last Egyptian stronghold in Palestine. They were joined by the tens of thousands of Arabs from Majdal who were pushed out when the Israelis seized the large refugee camps there. Conditions in Gaza had been extremely bad but with so many additional refugees the situation became acute.

Dr P. Descoudenes of UNICEF visited Gaza after the Israeli offensive. He reported that 'the living conditions of this large number of refugees can hardly be described.'[12] According to the UNICEF physician at least ten children a day were dying of starvation in the Gaza refugee camps. But many were not able to get into the camps. 'The largest number of refugees are living under trees or just along the road.' Dr Descoudenes estimated that there were 213,000 refugees in Gaza.

In all, according to American estimates in 1948, about 750,000 Arabs from all parts of Palestine fled in terror from their homes in what is now the State of Israel. Many fled to the West Bank or Gaza (where they again came under Israeli rule in 1967) while others went to Lebanon, Syria, Jordan or Egypt. For all of them the tragedy of the great exodus, which they refer to as al-Nakba (the catastrophe) has made an indelible impression. Their expulsion from their homeland has embittered many Palestinians and made them eager for revenge. The world still suffers from the spiral of reprisals and counter reprisals which began in 1948.

PROLOGUE

The official Israeli version of the Palestinian exodus places the blame for their exile on the Palestinians themselves. As early as 10 August 1948, Israeli Foreign Minister Moshe Sharett informed UN Secretary-General Trygve Lie that the Palestinians had 'left partly in obedience to direct orders by local military commanders and partly as a result of the panic campaign spread among Palestinian Arabs by the leaders of the invading Arab states.'[13] A recent pro-Zionist author claimed that the great majority of Palestinians fled, despite Israeli pleas for them to stay, 'on orders from the Arab High Command'[14] and because of the 'fiery propaganda of Arab League orators' which was broadcast over radio programmes beamed into Palestine from the surrounding Arab capitals. The charge is made that this was all part of an Arab plan to evacuate Palestine.

Various reasons have been offered as to why the Arab leaders ordered the Palestinians to leave their homes, including the suggestion that they wanted to provide 'a clear field of fire' for the Arab armies that were being sent into Palestine, as well as to show that the Arabs refused to accept the UN partition plan. Some pro-Israeli writers go as far as to suggest that the Arab leaders ordered the Palestinians to leave their homes because they feared that they might help the Israelis fight the Arab armies that were being sent to rescue them.

It is not difficult to understand why the Israeli government and its supporters have clung tenaciously to their story. They feel that if they can show that the Palestinians are responsible for their own exile, it will justify their policy of forbidding the refugees to return home and their refusal to recognize a Palestinian state on the West Bank. The official Israeli view of the Palestinian exodus has been widely accepted, particularly in the United States where the news media is so intimidated by the powerful Zionist lobby. But no one has presented any evidence that the Arab leaders encouraged the Palestinians to leave. Nor has any proof been offered to show that there was a serious Israeli effort to encourage the Arabs to remain within the borders of their new Jewish state.

Many pro-Israeli writers have ignored abundant evidence that in parts of Galilee, the Negev and Jerusalem, as well as in the Lydda–Ramle region, the Arab population were driven from their homes with extreme violence, especially during the later stages of the war. They have also ignored conclusive evidence that shows that rather than encouraging the Palestinians to leave, the radio broadcasts from Cairo, Beirut, Baghdad and Damascus encouraged the Palestinian Arabs to remain in their homes, and on several occasions threatened that those who did flee would be punished as traitors. In some towns there was an effort to evacuate the civilian population during periods of intense combat particularly because the Arab women and children were the targets of Israeli terrorism. But in each of these towns evacuation was a last-minute decision reluctantly arrived at and was not part of a premeditated Arab plan to evacuate Palestine.

The only town where the Israelis made any effort at all to encourage a few Arabs to remain was Haifa. The sincerity of these pronouncements can be doubted, however, in view of the rather extensive and sophisticated campaign of psychological warfare that the Israelis waged against Arab civilians in Haifa and elsewhere during the course of the conflict. Using sound-trucks, Arabic language radio broadcasts, rumours, sound effects and handbills, the Israelis carried on one of the earliest and most effective campaigns of psychological warfare against the Arab civilians of Palestine aimed at forcing them to leave their homes.

The story of the Palestinian exodus is of great significance to anyone wishing to understand the Middle East situation, but surprisingly little research has been done on this subject, with the notable exception of several important articles written a quarter of a century ago by Erskine Childers and Walid Khalidi. Their work strongly suggests that the official Israeli view of the Palestinian exodus is largely inaccurate. Childers and Khalidi wrote, however, at a time before the United Nations, American, British or Israeli archives for this period were open.

Recently, several articles on the Palestinian exodus by Israeli historians have appeared.[15] Although they add some interesting details, their work is flawed by their almost exclusive reliance on the Israeli archives, which are not reliable with regard to the expulsion of Arab civilians in 1948. In particular, the Israeli military records offer a distorted picture of how the IDF treated Palestinian non-combatants. Israeli diplomatic and political records are noticeably better but many of the most important files are still closed and those that are open have been heavily censored. The American, United Nations and British archives which are largely ignored by Israeli historians are far more objective in describing the flight of Arab civilians in 1948.

Most United Nations field reports were made by American, French, Belgian and Swedish staff members. They all came from Western countries that supported the creation of the Zionist state but this type of bias was not unusual in the United Nations of 1948 in which Third World countries had no real voice. Nevertheless, the United Nations observers were very honest in their reports, which leave no doubt that the Israeli campaign of atrocities was the principal cause of the Arab exodus. It is a pity that these valuable reports have not previously been utilized. American State Department personnel also made objective reports on the expulsion of Arab civilians but their dispatches were ignored by a Truman administration which was anxious to please the Zionist lobby in Washington.

It is of course an article of faith among many Zionists that the British openly favoured the Arab side in 1948 just as most Arabs are convinced that British policy favoured the Zionists. The truth is that British military and diplomatic personnel in the Middle East had equal contempt for both Arabs and Jews; the British sometimes favoured one side and then the other in pursuit of purely British interests. However, most British soldiers, diplomats and administrators were thoroughly professional and there is no reason to doubt the accuracy of their secret reports, which are a valuable source for the early months of the conflict.

Among other important sources are the CIA and BBC records of Middle East radio transmissions, which include all broadcasts originating in or beamed into Palestine. Also of great interest are the candid memoirs of Jewish veterans of 1948 that have appeared in recent years in the Israeli press. This testimony is particularly important in view of the unreliability of the Israeli military records.

But besides being a historical controversy, the Palestinian exodus is also a human tragedy. For this reason the reminiscences of some Palestinian refugees have been used. One of the most remarkable aspects of this fascinating drama is the consistent accuracy of these Palestinian memoirs in the light of American, United Nations, Israeli, British and other non-Arab sources. Frequently, poorly educated Arab peasants interviewed years after the events recall facts that are substantiated by recently available archive documents. There is also verification for the testimony of many Israelis who have spoken honestly about the expulsion of Arabs in 1948.

Most of the American, United Nations, British, Israeli and Palestinian sources make clear that refugees left their homes as the result of Israeli terror and psychological warfare. Of course other factors were also important in explaining the Arab exodus. Some historians have stressed the early flight of Palestinian doctors and other professionals as a major cause for the subsequent exodus. Others blame the lack of co-operation among Arab factions or the wave of fear that swept the Arab community after the slaughter of 250 Palestinian civilians by the Irgun and Stern Gang at Deir Yassin in April 1948. All of these factors did weaken the resolve of the Arab community in Palestine. However, no amount of pseudo-academic argument about an 'irrational panic syndrome' or the 'loss of community infra-structure' can obscure the fact that most Palestinians did not leave their homes until their town or village was invaded by an Israeli army that subjected them to a reign of terror.

In a recent interview, the Israeli historian Meir Pa'il has given a generally accurate estimate of the reasons for the Palestinian exodus. 'Around one third fled out of fear. One third were forceably evacuated by the Israelis, for example, from Lydda and Ramle. About one third were encouraged by the Israelis to flee.' Despite his admission that most of the Palestinians were either forced or persuaded by the Israelis to leave, Pa'il blames the Arabs for the exodus, because according to him they were responsible for a 'premeditated conspiracy'[16] to start the war. However, the intervention of the Arab states in Palestine was not the cause of the exodus, but in large measure, a reluctant response by the Arab governments to the expulsion of the

Palestinians that had already begun. Most Israelis are unwilling to recognize the responsibility of their country for the expulsion of so many civilians.

The situation in which the Israelis find themselves with regard to the Palestinian exodus is not unique. Most countries have periods in their history that they would prefer to forget. It took about a century before Americans were willing to recognize the injustices committed against the Indians in the expansion of their country. At present it seems it will be well into the next century before the Israelis as a nation are willing to face up to the manner in which the Jewish state in Palestine was created.

And yet from the very beginning there were those Israelis who realized that by the expulsion of the Palestinians, the new State of Israel was planting the seeds of future hatred. S. Yizhar, one of the greatest Hebrew writers who fought in Israel's 'War of Independence' wrote a poignant short story in 1949 that describes the reaction of a sensitive young Jewish soldier who is ordered to expel Arabs from a small village. Although his comrades did not doubt the necessity of the mission, the central character of 'The Story of Hirbet Hiz'ah' foresaw the end result of his assignment:

> It was impossible for me to come to terms with anything, so long as tears were springing from the eyes of a sobbing child, walking by the side of a mother tense with the fury of silent tears, and going out into the exile carrying with him such an anguished cry of complaint against evil that there could not fail to be found in the world someone to hear it in due season – then I spoke to Moshe: 'Moshe, we have no right to send them away from here.'

But hundreds of thousands of Arabs were sent away from their town or village to face exile, their only consolation being a forlorn hope of someday returning to a home that had long since been occupied by Jewish immigrants from Yemen, Iraq, or Romania. In order to understand how this could come about we must see the expulsion of the Palestinians for what it is – the fulfilment of the destiny that was implicit in Zionism from the very beginning.

CHAPTER I

Land Without a People

I shall not expel them from the land in one year for fear that the land will become a desert. . . I shall expel them slowly before they multiply and possess the land.

Exodus 23, 29–30

'There is no hope that this new Jewish state will survive, to say nothing of develop, if the Arabs are as numerous as they are today.'[1] So spoke Menahem Ussishkin, at seventy-five, one of the oldest and most respected Zionist leaders. His audience on the afternoon of 12 June 1938 was the Executive Committee of the Jewish Agency, which was considering a plan by the British administration to divide Palestine between Arabs and Jews. For decades there had been strife between the two ethnic groups in the mandate territory and now the British administration was considering partition as the best way to end the conflict between the Jewish colonists and the indigenous Arab population. But partition would leave over 200,000 Arabs in the proposed Zionist state, and the leadership of the Jewish community in Palestine was grappling with the problem of how best to get rid of them.

None of the members of the Executive disagreed with Ussishkin when he stated: 'The worst is not that the Arabs would comprise 45 or 50 per cent of the population of the new state but that 75 per cent of the land is owned by Arabs.' This land was desired for the waves of Jewish immigrants who would populate the Jewish state. There were many other reasons why the Zionists wished to get rid of the Arabs. Ussishkin claimed that with a large Arab population the Jewish state would face enormous problems of internal security and that there would be chaos in government. 'Even a small Arab minority in parliament could disrupt the entire order of parliamentary life.'

For Ussishkin the solution to the problem of the large Arab

population in the proposed Jewish state was for their removal by the British army before the state was established. 'For this two things are required, a strong hand by the English, and Jewish money. With regard to money, I am sure that if the first requirement is met the Jewish money will be found.' Like most other Zionists at the time, Ussishkin believed that the Palestinians could be coerced into leaving their homes and settling on land that would be purchased for them in Trans-Jordan, Iraq or Saudi Arabia. He made it clear that he did not favour sending the excess Palestinians to the Arab state that the British planned to create on the West Bank. 'If you wish ever to expand you must not increase the number of Arabs west of the Jordan,' Ussishkin reminded his colleagues.

Ussishkin seems to have had no moral scruples about dislocating tens of thousands of Arab families at gunpoint and moving them out of villages their people had occupied for centuries. He firmly believed in the Jewish right to all of Palestine; a belief he based on the Bible and the promises made by the British. For Ussishkin, the Palestinians were usurpers who deserved to be expelled. 'I am ready to defend this moral attitude before the Almighty and the League of Nations,' he said.

All the other speakers at the Executive Committee meeting voiced similar sentiments. Berl Katzenelson of Ben-Gurion's Mapai party saw only disaster in a Jewish state with a large Arab minority. 'There is the question of how the army will function, how will the police, how will the civil service. How can a state be run when part of its population is unloyal to the state.'[2] As a 'liberal' Zionist, Katzenelson had a relatively tolerant attitude toward the Palestinians. 'I am willing to give the Arabs equal rights,' he said, 'if I know that only a small minority stays in the land.' He proposed for the new state a development plan that would include a provision to eliminate thousands of Palestinians. He made the position clear: 'A development plan means evictions.' The Mapai party official urged negotiations, with neighbouring Arab states that might be persuaded to receive the expellees.

The proposal to partition Palestine and to transfer the Arabs out of the resulting Jewish state came from a Royal Commission under Lord Peel, which had been appointed in November 1936, in the wake of widespread Arab disturbances. Peel and his colleagues decided that the only solution to the Palestine problem was to divide the country, thus forming a Jewish state that would include Galilee and most of the coastal plain. Though small in area, the Jewish state would have most of the fertile regions of the country. The Peel Commission suggested that, if necessary, force should be used to eliminate the Arabs living in the proposed Jewish state. For several decades the Zionists had favoured the removal of the Palestinians and so they attempted to persuade the British to carry out the transfer. On 19 July 1937, Chaim Weizmann, President of the World Zionist organization, spoke with Ormsby-Gore, the British Colonial Secretary. Weizmann told the British minister that the whole success of the partition depended on whether the removal of the Arabs was accomplished. Weizmann later noted, 'The transfer could only be carried out by the British government and not by the Jews. I explained the reason why we considered the proposal of such importance.'[3] It would serve the purpose of the Zionists to have the British carry out the expulsion for them.

But many British ministers, while favouring partition, had serious reservations about the transfer of Arabs. At a Cabinet meeting, the Secretary of State for India, 'pointed out the great difficulty which lay in the transfer into Arab territory of some 250,000 Arabs now located in territory proposed for the Jewish state. It was clear from the report of the Royal Commission that land was not available for them in the proposed Arab state. What was to happen to the quarter million Arabs in the interval?'[4]

In January 1938, the British government appointed a second commission under Sir John Woodhead to consider the technical implementation of partition. Sir Stephen Luke, a British official in Palestine, noted that when the Peel Commission had originally proposed the transfer, it had in mind the 1922 'vast exchange of population between Greece and Turkey. They had hoped a similar situation could be found in Palestine but even before the [Woodhead] partition commission left England, the Secretary of State had ruled out any possibility of compulsory transfer of population and the Woodhead Commission concluded after investigating the situation that the prospects for a voluntary transfer were slight indeed.'[5]

But despite the equivocal attitude of the British, most Zionists were determined to implement the transfer of the Arabs. David Ben-Gurion, head of the Jewish Agency Executive, believed that the Zionists had to exert pressure to force the British to act. But if necessary, he wrote in his diary, 'we must ourselves prepare to carry out'[6] the removal of the Palestinians.

A plan had been developed by Joseph Weitz, director of the Jewish National Fund, who served on the Population Transfer Committee of the Jewish Agency. He wrote in a report that the transfer of the Arab population from the Jewish areas, 'does not serve only one aim – to diminish the Arab population. It also serves a second purpose by no means less important, which is to evacuate land now cultivated by Arabs and thus release it for Jewish settlement.'[7] Weitz believed that the transfer of the rural Arab population should be given preference over the removal of the city Arabs. In all he calculated that 87,000 Arabs could be removed from the rural areas along with 10–15,000 Bedouins. Most would go to Trans-Jordan while the remainder would go to Gaza and Syria. Weitz realized that the British would not remove the Arabs by force, so he hoped to persuade the Arabs to leave by economic inducements. For this he calculated that over two million Palestinian pounds would be needed.

The Weitz plan was thoroughly discussed by the Zionist leaders, all of whom favoured the removal of as many Arabs as possible. Dr Yakov Thon also served on the Population Transfer Committee. Thon had been a founding member of Brit Shalom, the 'ultra-liberal' group composed of Jewish intellectuals who sought reconciliation and accommodation with the Arabs. But his remarks in the secret committee meetings made it clear what type of reconciliation he had in mind. 'Without transferring the Arab peasants to neighbouring lands,' he said, 'we will not be able to bring into our future state a large new population. In short without transfer there can be no Jewish immigration.'[8] Thon noted that the British would not use force to implement the removal of the Arabs but he urged that all other possible measures be taken.

Another member of the transfer committee, Dr Mendelsohn, suggested that once the Jewish state was formed, 'a certain amount of pressure could be used to encourage transfer – such as agrarian reform or government measures.'[9] At a later meeting of the Executive, Isaac Ben-Ziv proposed that, 'supervision of citizenship'[10] might provide an opportunity to force the Palestinians to leave.

The British, however, soon abandoned the idea of partition and with it the plan to transfer the Arab population. But a decade later, the idea of partition would be revived in the form of a resolution by the United Nations General Assembly, which proposed a Jewish state with an even larger Arab population. The Arab–Jewish conflict which followed the passage of the UN resolution would provide an opportunity for the Zionists to achieve their goal of a Jewish state in Palestine that was largely free of Arabs.

In the early years, the political Zionists, including the founder of the modern movement, Theodore Herzl, were not particular about where their Jewish state would be located. In 1896 when Herzl wrote *Der Judenstaat*, he was undecided as to whether the new Jewish nation would be in Palestine or Argentina. At various other times he considered Cyprus, Kenya, and the Sinai peninsula. Some early Zionists even proposed that wealthy Jewish bankers purchase several of the western territories of the United States as a site for a Jewish nation. In the end Herzl chose Palestine because of its strong emotional appeal to the Jewish masses of Eastern Europe. But he was opposed by practically every rabbi in Europe, many of whom denounced political Zionism as a vile heresy since religious Jews at that time believed that only the Messiah could resurrect the Kingdom of Israel. It was not until well into the twentieth century that the majority of religious Jews were converted to political Zionism. As Herzl, Max Nordau and many of the other early Zionist leaders were non-believers, the religious objections to political Zionism did not concern them.

An even more disturbing feature of the early Zionists was

their close relationship with anti-Semites, who Herzl believed were the most useful allies for the Zionists because no one could doubt the sincerity of their desire to see the Jews leave to found their own homeland. Herzl wrote, 'Anti-Semitism has grown and continues to grow and so do I.'[11] He referred to anti-Semitism as a great force which, 'if rightly employed is powerful enough to propel a large engine and dispatch the passengers and goods' – to Palestine or anywhere else the Zionists desired.

Herzl did not hesitate to negotiate with the German Kaiser (who made anti-Semitic remarks in his presence to which the Zionist leader offered no objection) as well as the dreaded Russian Minister Wenzel von Plehve, the most notorious Jew hater of his age. Although no concrete agreements emerged from Herzl's negotiations with anti-Semites, he set a precedent, which was followed by many Zionist leaders of subsequent generations who had extensive relations with all manner of Jew haters.

This tendency to deal with anti-Semites is more easily understood if we consider the anti-Semitic mentality of many leading Zionists. Herzl remarked on the lack of 'ethical seriousness in many Jews' and the 'crookedness of Jew morality'.[12] He looked down on the Jewish masses of Eastern Europe and admired the haughty Prussian aristocracy. Other Zionists called Jews 'parasitic' and 'fundamentally useless people'.[13] They criticized their own people for being a commercial urban race who they claimed worshipped the Golden Calf. The Zionists bemoaned the fact that few Jews were farmers or workers who created with their own hands. This they believed was the source of the hatred which many gentiles felt towards Jews.

The answer to this problem, the Zionists believed, was the establishment of a Jewish state in which all functions of society, including the working-class jobs, would be performed by Jews. The Zionist ideologue A. D. Gordon insisted that 'There is only one way that can lead to our renaissance – the way of manual labour. . . a people can acquire a land only by its own efforts.'[14] Unlike other European colonies in Africa and Asia, where the manual labour was done by local people, the Zionists were determined that in Palestine Jewish labourers would work the farms and industries of the new state. Thus there was no place for the Arabs, since Zionist ideology dictated that Jewish farm owners and capitalists could not employ non-Jewish workers.

Herzl foresaw that the Arabs would have to be removed from a Jewish state in Palestine. This is clear from long-suppressed entries in his diaries. 'We shall try to spirit the penniless population across the border', Herzl wrote, 'by procuring employment for them in the transit countries while denying any employment in our country.'[15] Herzl believed that the 'expropriation and removal of the poor [Arabs] must be carried out discreetly and circumspectly.' As for the richer Arabs of Palestine, Herzl urged that they should be bought out even if they demanded very high prices for their land. He wanted the Jews to buy up every parcel of land in Palestine. The Arabs, Herzl observed, 'will believe that they are cheating us, selling things for more than they are worth. But we are not going to sell them anything back.' As with so many of Herzl's ideas, his plan that the Zionists buy up as much land as possible while denying employment to any Arabs on this land was to become standard procedure for Zionist colonies in Palestine.

The Zionists spoke of making Palestine 'As Jewish as England is English'. They also used the slogan 'A land without a people for a people without a land' to describe their attitude toward Palestine. The Zionists considered Palestine uninhabited, despite the fact that in 1881 almost half a million Arabs lived in Palestine, forming almost 95 per cent of the population.

Although the early Zionists made a considerable effort to organize a mass movement to the Holy Land, few Jews actually emigrated to Palestine. Most Jews who left Eastern Europe went to America, where there was considerable economic opportunity. By 1914, there were still only 85,000 Jews in Palestine, many of whom were religious people who strongly opposed the political Zionists in their aim of establishing a Jewish state. Those who ventured to Palestine before the First World War found a land that was not 'without a people' but a province of the Turkish Empire which was inhabited by an Arabic speaking race (85 per cent Muslim, 15 per cent Christian) most of whom traced their ancestry in the country back for many generations.

7

Ahad Ha'Am (né Asher Ginzberg) was a religious Jew who recorded many prophetic observations on the way in which the political Zionists were treating the indigenous Arab population of Palestine. Ahad Ha'Am deplored the fact that many Jewish settlers in Palestine believed that 'the only language that the Arabs understand is that of force.'[16] He observed that many Jews 'behave toward the Arabs with cruelty, infringe upon their boundaries, hit them shamefully without reason and even brag about it.' He believed that the main reason the political Zionists treated the native population so badly was that they were 'angry towards those who reminded them that there is still another people in the land of Israel that has been living there and does not intend at all to leave.'

During this period many Zionists were already setting up their own banks, schools and businesses. Although Palestine was still part of the Turkish Empire, Jews often flew their Star of David flag and were preparing for the day when they could create a Jewish state. As a young man, Moshe Menuhin studied at the élite Herzlia Gymnasia. He later recalled, 'It was drummed into our young hearts that the fatherland must become *goyim rein* [free of Gentiles–Arabs].'[17]

In the years before the First World War, political Zionism continued to be rejected by many Jews. Although most religious Jews supported spiritual Zionism, which saw Palestine as the cultural centre of Judaism, they remained convinced that political Zionism, which favoured the establishment of a Jewish government in Palestine, was heretical. Assimilated Jews were offended by the suggestion that their loyalty must be divided between a Jewish state and the land of their birth. But Zionism had surprising support among the non-Jewish population in most Western countries.

Besides anti-Semites, Evangelical Christians are another large and influential group that to this day remains as a strong base of support for Zionism. Evangelicals believe that the return of the Jews to Palestine is a necessary prerequisite to the second coming of Christ. The Zionists have not been reluctant to exploit the theology of fundamentalist Christians for their benefit.

In England in the early part of this century, many Christians believed that the millennium predicted in the Bible would occur when the Zionists achieved their goal of founding a Jewish homeland in Palestine. In his conversations with government officials, the leader of the British Zionists, Chaim Weizmann, often used religious arguments to gain support for his cause. Other arguments were used as well. When the First World War broke out, Weizmann suggested that if the London government sponsored Zionism, Jews all over the world would rally to the British war effort. Thus in November 1917, the British issued the famous Balfour Declaration which proclaimed: 'His Majesty's Government views with favour the establishment in Palestine of a national home for the Jewish people.'[18] But the document also made it clear that, 'nothing shall be done which will prejudice the civil and political rights of existing non-Jewish communities in Palestine.'

Prior to the Balfour Declaration the British had given written promises to the Arabs implying that Palestine would be among the territories in which Arabs would enjoy their independence after the war. Much has been written about whether the British promises to the Jews or Arabs took precedence. While not devoid of interest, this debate misses the central point that Palestine belonged to the people who had lived there for over 1,000 years and the British had no right to promise away another people's country. This nineteenth-century tendency to ignore the rights of an indigenous population was widely accepted in 1917 (and still greatly influences the Zionist treatment of the Palestinians). But even during the First World War, there were some who raised serious objections to the Balfour Declaration.

Among the most vocal critics were English Jews who served in high positions in the British government. Edward Montagu, a Cabinet minister, called Zionism a 'mischievous political creed'. He believed that the creation of a 'Jewish state' in Palestine would make citizenship dependent on a religious test, which he strongly resented. Montagu did not want to see the Jews 'driving out the present inhabitants'[19] of Palestine, which would earn them the enmity of both Christians and Muslims. Indeed, he asserted that the Jewish claim to Palestine on religious grounds was no stronger than that of Muslims or

Christians. The Jewish Cabinet minister pointed out that most of the British-born Jews opposed Zionism and that the Christian leaders of England were wrong if they believed that their espousal of Zionism would gain much support from Jews for the British war effort.

The severest critics of Zionism were its victims – the Palestinians. As early as 1891, Arab notables in Jerusalem sent a petition to Constantinople protesting against the intrusion of European Jews into Palestine. The most serious complaint was that these early 'proto-Zionist' settlers were buying up land and creating a class of landless Arab peasants. Also, the failure of the European Jewish colonists to respect local customs and their tendency to insulate themselves against the Middle Eastern environment aroused the enmity of many local inhabitants. By the turn of the century leaflets were widely distributed which warned Arabs not to sell land to the Zionists and demanding that the Turkish government halt Jewish immigration. The newspaper *Al Karmel* was established at Haifa in order to arouse the Palestinians against Zionism.

The Arab members of the Turkish parliament often spoke out against Zionism, especially against Jewish land purchase and immigration. They also accused Turkish officials of ignoring the separatist tendencies of the European Jewish settlers, in particular the Zionist establishment of paramilitary organizations, the open display of the Star of David flag and the singing of Zionist national songs.

The Christian Arab Naguib Azouri wrote *Le reveil de la nation Arabe*, in which he warned of the 'effort of the Jews to reconstitute on a very large scale the ancient kingdom of Israel.'[20] In 1911, an anti-Zionist association was founded in Jaffa. There were protests and several anti-Zionist demonstrations in various cities. But this early movement dissipated before it could play any real role.

Many Zionist settlers tended to ignore the unrest among the Palestinians, but some took note of the 'Arab problem'. It was suggested that increased Jewish immigration was necessary to secure Zionist control of Palestine against Arabs, Turks or other possible settlers. But when one Zionist physician was told that there must be an acceleration of Jewish movement into the country before others took it over, the doctor, mindful of the high Palestinian birth-rate replied, 'No one will take it, the Arabs have it and they will stay the leading force by a wide margin.'[21]

Indeed the birth-rate among the Palestinians, which was one of the highest in the world, ensured that the Arabs would remain the majority in Palestine even with a massive programme of Jewish immigration. To several Zionist leaders, the only solution appeared to be an implementation of Herzl's plan to deport a large part of the Palestinian population. In May 1911, Arthur Rupin suggested a 'limited transfer' to northern Syria which would be financed by the Jews.

Others took up the idea. In 1912, Leo Motzkin, in a speech at the annual conference of German Zionists, suggested that those Arabs who sold their land to the Jews should be resettled on uncultivated land in neighbouring Arab states. But during this period it was the Anglo-Jewish author Israel Zangwill who did most to popularize the idea of an 'Arab trek' by the Palestinians to a new state, which would be created for them in Arabia.

Zangwill believed that the migration could be initiated peacefully. After all, he reasoned, other peoples, such as the Boers of South Africa, had been relocated. Why shouldn't the Palestinians welcome an opportunity to make a magnanimous gesture by giving up their homeland to be used by the Jews who had been so badly treated in Christian Europe? Of course it did not dawn on Zangwill that the Palestinians were no less attached to Palestine than the Zionists. If the Arabs did not leave, Zangwill believed that a Jewish state could not arise and there would be only an endless conflict between Jews and Arabs.[22]

After the First World War, the British, who had driven the Turks out of Palestine, ruled the country as a League of Nations mandate. The territory east of the Jordan River was separated from Palestine and formed the Kingdom of Trans-Jordan with King Abdullah as monarch. In the Palestine mandate English, Hebrew and Arabic were regarded as official languages, while provision was made for Jewish immigration into the colony.

After the establishment of the Jewish 'national home' under the British mandate, the residents of the Yishuv (Jewish community) in Palestine had to decide on their long-term goals.

THE PALESTINIAN CATASTROPHE

Some Jews, not very many, rejected the idea of creating an exclusively Jewish state in Palestine but instead preferred a 'binational' country in which the religion, language and customs of both Jews and Arabs would be respected. Such people as Judah Magnes, Chancellor of the Hebrew University in Jerusalem, and the distinguished philosopher Martin Buber argued that the future government of Palestine need not be Jewish dominated in order to secure the rights of its Jewish citizens. Buber wished that the Jews would recognize the Arabs as their brothers and hoped that they would avoid the temptation of seeing themselves as emissaries of Western culture, which Buber regarded as decadent. Unfortunately, the size and influence of the binational group remained negligible.

Most Zionists desired the creation of an exclusive Jewish state in Palestine but differed on how best to achieve this goal. The Revisionist movement consisted of a group of Zionists who wanted immediate action on the formation of a Jewish nation that would include not only all of Palestine but Trans-Jordan as well. As for the Arabs, the leader of the Revisionist party, Vladimir Jabotinsky, regarded them as 'alien minorities who would weaken national unity.' Jabotinsky argued that there were many neighbouring states to which the Palestinian Arabs could emigrate.

In 1916, before he had established the Revisionist movement, Jabotinsky had met Israel Zangwill, who convinced him that the evacuation of the Palestinians was a prerequisite of the implementation of Zionism. Jabotinsky believed that if possible the Arabs should be removed from Palestine peacefully. But he suspected that military force would have to be used. As early as 1925, in a letter to Senator O. O. Grusenberg, Jabotinsky proposed that the establishment of a Jewish majority in Palestine would 'have to be achieved *against the will* of the country's Arab majority. An "iron wall" of a Jewish armed force would have to protect the process of achieving a majority.'[23]

Jabotinsky was surely one of the most interesting if sinister figures in the history of Zionism. An impatient man, he was honest enough to say publicly what Ben-Gurion and the other Zionist leaders plotted secretly. Greatly influenced by Italian Fascism, Jabotinsky and his followers introduced into Zionism a strident chauvinism, militarism and authoritarianism that had previously been absent from the Jewish *Weltanschauung*. Mussolini had proclaimed a desire 'to change a nation of lambs into a nation of wolves'; Jabotinsky also wished to alter the image of his people, whom he criticized for being effete and passive. Like Herzl, Jabotinsky had a basically negative attitude towards the Jewish people. He engaged in negotiations with anti-Semitic governments in the 1920s, especially the authoritarian regime of Poland, which was anxious to get rid of its Jews. The Revisionists wanted to transport the mass of East European Jewry to Palestine and took for granted the hostility of the Palestinian Arabs. But since they believed that the relocation of Eastern European Jewry to nowhere else but the Holy Land was a moral imperative, Jabotinsky concluded that the Arab opposition to this massive colonization was immoral and should be crushed.

Jabotinsky had utter contempt for the Arabs. He believed that they had contributed nothing to civilization and were not ready for independent nationhood. To the Revisionists, the Arabs of Palestine were decidedly inferior to Europeans and unworthy of a place in the Holy Land. In contrast to Martin Buber, Jabotinsky saw the chief aim of Zionism in classical nineteenth-century terms; thus he suggested that the Jews must come to Palestine in order to 'push the moral frontiers of Europe to the Euphrates.'[24]

The 'superior culture' that the Revisionists planned to bring to the Middle East contained a large measure of European racism. It is one of the tragic ironies of history that what the Revisionists and other Zionists wrote and said about the Palestinian Arabs closely resembled the calumnies that the Nazis were making against the Jews. Indeed, in their writings the Revisionists often used the same terminology as the Nazis.

An extreme example of this can be found in *The Rape of Palestine*, a book written by William Ziff, an American representative of the Revisionist movement. Ziff described the Palestinian Arabs as a 'sickly and degenerate race'[25] that was 'low on the scale of human development'. In explaining the origins of the Palestinians, Ziff noted that 'from the steppes, mountains and deserts an agglomeration of primitive and savage man has swarmed in successive waves over Palestine and left their seed.'

Since to Ziff the Palestinians were the result of a 'churning stew of races', it should not be surprising that he believed that they had 'virtually no creative gifts'. He also charged that 'the ruling passion of an Arab is greediness of gold.' Ziff suggested that an Arab's 'love of money is such that he loses all sense of proportion whenever currency is discussed.' Similar remarks directed against the Jews could easily be found in any number of anti-Semitic propaganda sheets then being published in Germany.* Considering the inflammatory nature of the Revisionist attitude toward the Arabs, it was inevitable that Jabotinsky's followers would provoke violence in Palestine.

One sweltering afternoon in August 1929, the American author and journalist Vincent Sheean sat in his room at the Austrian Hospice in Jerusalem when a servant burst in to say that a lady was waiting to see him. Downstairs Sheean found a Jewish-American woman whose acquaintance he had made some time before. She informed him that there was going to be serious trouble at the Wailing Wall, since hundreds of Jabotinsky's followers were coming into the city 'ready to fight' to protect the sacred monument. Many of the right-wing extremists were armed and Sheean's visitor looked forward to a bloody confrontation with the Arabs since it would 'show that we are here.'[26]

Trouble had been festering over the religious shrines in Jerusalem for quite some time. It is unfortunate and ironic that the Wailing Wall, the holiest Jewish shrine, lies directly below Al-Aqsa Mosque, which is the holiest Muslim shrine in Jerusalem. In September 1928, the Jewish sextant at the Wailing Wall placed a screen on the pavement in order to separate men and women according to Orthodox Jewish custom. The Muslims complained that this action violated the ancient agreements that regulated Jewish and Islamic worship in the area of the sacred

---

*Not surprisingly Ziff's book was endorsed by many of the leading members of the 'American liberal establishment' of the 1930s. Like their equivalent in our own day, they saw no inconsistency in condemning anti-Semitism while supporting Zionist anti-Arab racism.

shrines. The British colonial administration agreed and ordered the Jews to remove the screens. The Zionists objected to the decision, complaining that the ruling represented 'wanton interference' with Jewish religious liberty.

Most British officials in Palestine did not take the escalating crisis over the Wailing Wall very seriously. Indeed, one senior bureaucrat in a report on 29 July 1929, wrote that it was 'much to be deplored'[27] that he and his colleagues were required to concern themselves with 'the dimensions of wash basins and the position of water containers.' He lamented, 'but this is typical of Palestine and its sectarian pettiness.'

Within a few weeks this 'sectarian pettiness' was to erupt into violence. When Sheean went to the Wailing Wall, he saw religious Yemenite Jews observing the ancient rituals, oblivious to the fact that Jabotinsky's followers were attempting to provoke a conflict with any Muslims they could find. Sheean wrote in his diary, 'If I were an Arab, I should be angry, very angry and I don't think for a minute that this is over.'

On 23 August, came the inevitable Muslim reaction. Angered by rumours that the Islamic holy places in Jerusalem were in danger, thousands of Arab peasants poured into the Holy City. Vincent Sheean again found himself in the midst of the mêlée. As the Arabs approached the Jewish section of the city, the American journalist saw a Jew throw a grenade into the crowd, killing two people. These were the first fatalities of the day. Fighting raged in Jerusalem and spread to other parts of Palestine with several hundred Arabs, Jews and British being killed before order was restored.

In the wake of the disturbances, the British set up the Shaw Commission to consider the underlying causes of the rioting. Before the outbreak the Colonial Office had considered a plan to give a measure of self-government to Palestine. The Zionists greatly feared home rule while there was still a large Arab majority in the country. Indeed they may have provoked the disturbances so as to persuade the British that Palestine was not yet ready for any degree of independence. The Arab reprisals, however, greatly exceeded expectation. Although religion was the initial cause of the fighting, economic grievances motivated many of the Arab rioters. In Hebron, for example, where many

Jews were killed, the Muslim peasants of the region resented being exploited by Jewish speculators who they feared wished to drive them off their land.

While condemning the Arab excesses, the Shaw Commission recognized that the main reason for the Muslim violent reaction was the 'Arab feeling of animosity and hostility towards the Jews consequent upon the disappointment and fear for their economic future.'[28] The British investigators recommended that the Palestine mandatory administration respond to the justified Arab grievances by limiting Jewish immigration, protecting Arab peasants from eviction by Jewish land purchases, and preventing the 'Jewish Agency' from assuming governmental powers in Palestine.

In another report on 30 October 1930, Sir John Hope Simpson, an authority on agricultural economics, concluded that the root of the problem was the policy of the Jewish National Fund, which was driving the Arabs off the land by buying up farming plots and refusing to employ Arabs on the Jewish-owned estates. Like the Shaw Commission, Hope Simpson urged that both Jewish immigration and land purchases should be limited. On the same day as the Hope Simpson report was released, the British Colonial Secretary issued a White Paper in which he ratified the recommendations of the experts with regard to Jewish immigration and land purchase.

It appeared that the Zionist strategy (based on Herzl's plans of three decades earlier) of driving the Arabs out of Palestine by land purchase and denial of employment was about to be curtailed by the British Colonial administration. But the Zionists were able to negate the findings of the legal and economic experts by applying political pressure in London. Chaim Weizmann, the Zionist leader, had great influence with members of the British government. After having lunch with Weizmann, British Prime Minister Ramsay MacDonald made public an official letter to Weizmann in which he repudiated all of the reforms approved in the Passfield White Paper. MacDonald asserted, 'The obligation to facilitate Jewish immigration and make possible dense settlement of Jews on the land is still a positive obligation of the Mandate.'[29] He also upheld the right of the Jewish Agency to prohibit the use of Arab labour on

Jewish land. After the publication of the letter the Arabs of Palestine realized that they could expect no justice from the British administration. During this period the Zionists were emboldened to make their intentions to the Palestinians quite clear.

On a spring evening in 1933, David Ben-Gurion, then a newly elected member of the Executive Council of the Jewish Agency in Palestine, visited the home of his associate Moshe Shertok.* The two members of the council, which acted as a quasi-legal governing body for the Yishuv, were planning a secret meeting with Musa al-Alami who served as Attorney-General in the British administration. Ben-Gurion requested the meeting in order to discuss with Musa al-Alami, the scion of a distinguished Arab family, the ultimate fate of Palestine after the British left the troubled mandate territory. The official position of the Jewish Agency in Palestine was that 'neither of the two peoples shall dominate or be dominated by the other.' In reality, however, many of the Zionist leaders, including Ben-Gurion, had a somewhat different view.

During the discussion at Shertok's Jerusalem apartment, Musa emphasized the pessimistic feeling that prevailed among the Arabs of Palestine because they were gradually being ousted from all of the important positions, while the best land in the country was passing into Jewish hands. For the Arabs of Palestine, according to Musa, the future seemed 'bleak and bitter' since both their economic and political position in the country was deteriorating.

Shertok had soothing words for Musa, likening Palestine to a crowded hall 'in which there is always room for more people.' There was space in Palestine for the Jews who wanted to move in, Shertok claimed, since they had no intention of inflicting any real harm on the Arabs. At this point Ben-Gurion interrupted the conversation snapping at Shertok, 'It is useless to talk like this to a realist like Musa al-Alami.' Ben-Gurion considered Musa to be a 'sincere, straightforward and sensible man' so he spoke plainly to him. The Jews had nowhere else to go but

---

*In August 1948, he would change his name to Sharett.

Palestine, Ben-Gurion insisted, whereas the Arabs of Palestine could move to any of the neighbouring Arabic-speaking countries. Ben-Gurion posed the crucial question, 'Is there any possibility at all of reaching an understanding with regard to the establishment of a Jewish state in Palestine including Trans-Jordan?'[30] In return for the displacement of the Palestinian Arabs, Ben-Gurion offered Zionist support for an Arab federation which would include the remaining Arab countries. Alami would give no commitment.

Ben-Gurion had subsequent conversations with other Arab leaders with whom he was equally frank. On 18 July 1934, he met with Auni Abdul Hadi, head of the Palestinian Istiqlal (Independence) party. Ben-Gurion later recalled, 'Auni asked me, "How many Jews do you want in Palestine?"' To which Ben-Gurion replied, 'During a period of thirty years, four million.' In view of this candour, the Arabs could have little doubt that the real aim of the Zionists was to displace them with a flood of Jewish immigrants.

The fears of the Palestinians were greatly exacerbated in the mid-1930s as a result of the increased Jewish immigration, which reached a peak of over 60,000 in 1935. Many of these Jews came from Nazi Germany. Their immigration was the result of a Nazi–Zionist agreement that permitted departing Jews to withdraw their savings in the form of German-made goods at a time when Jews all over the world were attempting to organize an economic boycott of the Hitler regime. A recent study indicates that, 'the anti-Nazi boycott did have an excellent chance of toppling the Third Reich.'[31] However, the dealings between the Zionists and the Nazis severely undercut the effect of the boycott. Indeed, some Zionists showed a liking for the Hitler movement.* Of course most Zionists hated the Nazis but they saw co-operation with them as the best opportunity to bring fresh waves of Jewish immigrants to Palestine.

---

*Jabotinsky on 17 May 1933 sent a letter to Dr Hans Block in Germany complaining about the fascination which some members of the Revisionist youth movement had for the Nazis. 'I do not know what has happened,' Jabotinsky wrote, since Nazism 'impresses our youth so much in the manner which communism impresses other Jews.'[32]

The Arabs of Palestine believed that they were receiving an unfair proportion of the Jewish refugees who could better be accommodated in America or in the underpopulated states of the British Commonwealth. They demanded not only a halt to immigration but also the establishment of democratic institutions in Palestine based on majority rule. This was staunchly opposed by the Zionists who realized that they had greater influence under the prevailing system through the political pressure they could put on the British Cabinet in London.

When it became clear that the Arab demands would not be granted, violence erupted in Palestine. On 25 April 1935 the Grand Mufti Haj Amin, the political and spiritual leader of the Palestinians, joined with other Palestinian notables in establishing the Arab Higher Committee (AHC). Shortly after its formation, the AHC urged all Palestinians not to pay taxes to the mandate government and organized a nationwide general strike which lasted seven months. During this period there was considerable fighting between the Palestinians and the British army in which thousands of Arabs were killed.

On 11 November 1936, the Peel Commission arrived in Palestine with instructions to determine the fundamental cause of the unrest. The Arabs who testified before the Royal Commission demanded the formation of an independent Palestine which would be ruled by proportional representation. But, as already noted, the Peel Commission recommended the partition of Palestine, which was not implemented.

With the failure of the Royal Commission, the Arab resistance intensified. Mahatma Gandhi believed that the justice of the Arab cause was obvious. He wrote, 'Palestine belongs to the Arabs in the same sense that England belongs to the English or France to the French;'[33] the Indian leader added, 'according to the accepted canons of right and wrong, nothing can be said against the Arab resistance in face of overwhelming odds.' But the Palestinians were gradually defeated because they foolishly dissipated their strength in open combat with the British army. The Jewish community worked closely with the British during this period. The Yishuv organized Haganah (The Defence) to combat the Arabs. Thus the Jews began to develop the fighting machine that would perform so well in 1948. The

Haganah organized 'pre-emptive' tactics, including raids on many Arab villages that were sanctioned by the British. By August 1939, the Arab resistance finally collapsed. The rebellion had fatally weakened the military potential of the Palestinians and decimated their leadership.

As war in Europe appeared increasingly unavoidable, the British government felt a need to make some gesture on Palestine that would pacify the Arab world and prevent the further increase of Axis influence in the Middle East. On 17 May 1939, a White Paper was published in which the British government ruled out the establishment of either a Jewish or Arab state in the Holy Land but instead announced that eventually both groups would share power in Palestine. During a ten-year interim period, Jews and Arabs would be given the opportunity for increased participation in government. With regard to immigration, the White Paper provided that 75,000 Jews would be permitted to enter Palestine over a five-year period but there would be a limitation on Jewish land purchases, particularly in predominantly Arab areas.

The Zionist response to the White Paper was immediate and violent. The headquarters of the Department of Migration was set on fire and government offices in Haifa and Tel Aviv were stormed by crowds bent on destroying all files on illegal immigration. In Jerusalem Arab shops were looted. A British policeman was shot during a demonstration. A few days later the Rex Cinema in Jerusalem was bombed, killing five Arabs and injuring eighteen. This was followed by the attack on the village of Adas in which five more Arabs were killed. So began a reign of terror against both Arabs and British that came to be known as 'Gun Zionism'.

The Zionists fought violently against the White Paper. However, they saw no reason to give up their plans for an exclusively Jewish nation. Not long after the White Paper was issued, Weizmann explained to Winston Churchill the Zionist intention to build up a state in Palestine with three or four million Jews. 'Yes, indeed I quite agree with that,' Churchill replied.[34]

Most Zionists were determined that their Jewish state should be free of Arabs. In December 1940, Joseph Weitz wrote in his diary:

Between ourselves it must be clear that there is no room for both peoples together in this country. . . We shall not achieve our goal of being an independent people with the Arabs in this small country. The only solution is a Palestine, at least Western Palestine (west of the Jordan river) without Arabs. . . And there is no other way than to transfer the Arabs from here to the neighbouring countries, to transfer all of them; not one village, not one tribe, should be left. . . Only after this transfer will the country be able to absorb the millions of our own brethren. There is no other way out.[35]

On the eve of the Second World War, Nazi Germany and Fascist Italy signed an agreement that provided for the transfer of thousands of German-speaking residents from the Italian South Tyrol to the Reich. The Revisionist leader Vladimir Jabotinsky was greatly impressed by the accord which had been negotiated by his mentor Benito Mussolini. Jabotinsky believed that the agreement could serve as a model for the transfer of the Arabs out of Palestine. With regard to the Nazi–Fascist accord, Jabotinsky wrote, 'This precedent may perhaps be fated to play an important role in Jewish history.'[36] Indeed, other Zionist leaders tried to negotiate an agreement for the transfer of the Arabs out of Palestine.

On 8 October 1939, Chaim Weizmann, along with Moshe Shertok, Political Secretary of the Jewish Agency, conferred with H. St John Philby, a British explorer, orientalist and friend of King Ibn Saud. A few days before, 'Philby of Arabia' had met Professor Lewis Namier, an historian and confidant of the Zionist leaders. Namier had arranged the meeting between Philby and Weizmann because the British adventurer had suggested that King Ibn Saud might be persuaded to take a position on the Palestine question that would be favourable to the Zionists.

At the conference with Weizmann, Philby revealed that King Ibn Saud would agree to the creation of a Jewish state in all of Palestine and the transfer of considerable numbers of Palestinians to Arabia in exchange for Zionist help in the unification of the Arab world under Ibn Saud and a subsidy of twenty million pounds. (Saudi Arabia was not yet oil rich.) Shertok suggested that the Zionists might pay the twenty million provided that at least part of the money was used for the 'transfer of the Palestinian Arabs to other Arab countries.'[37] But although Shertok favoured the scheme, he doubted whether Philby had sufficient influence to carry it out. Weizmann put a great deal of stock in Philby. For years afterwards the Jewish leader remained confident that a bargain could be made to transfer the Palestinians to Saudi Arabia.

In his memoirs Weizmann claims that he had 'never contemplated the removal of the Arabs.'[38] It is clear, however, that like all other Zionists, Weizmann saw the elimination of the Palestinians as a necessary prerequisite to the creation of the Jewish state. On 25 May 1941 Weizman told a conference of American Jewish leaders that the Zionists planned to acquire a great deal of land in the Arab states and would tell the Palestinians: 'We shall see that you are colonized [relocated] and you get five dunans of land for every dunan [in Palestine] that we get.'[39]

Although there is no evidence that he ever received the acquiescence of a single Palestinian leader, Weizmann believed that the Arabs of Palestine would agree to the transfer plan. When Colonial Secretary Lord Moyne asked Weizmann if the relocation of the Palestinians could be accomplished without bloodshed, the Zionist leader replied, 'It could be done if Britain and America talked frankly to the Arabs.'[40] For decades Weizmann had believed that Britain could be a valuable ally for the Zionists. During the Second World War, not only Weizmann but the whole Zionist movement began to focus its attention on America as their most logical and valuable ally.

It is hardly a coincidence that Ben-Gurion chose a conference of American Zionists in May 1942 at the Biltmore Hotel in New York to formulate his demand that 'Palestine be established as a Jewish commonwealth.' There is no doubt that the Zionist programme developed during the Second World War provided for the removal of the Palestinians from this Jewish commonwealth.

In 1943, General Patrick Hurley, the personal representative of President Roosevelt, visited Palestine on a fact-finding mission. He reported that many of the Jews in Palestine preferred to settle eventually in the United States or Western Europe after the war. He noted, however, that in contrast the Zionist leadership was determined to create a Jewish state that would include all of Palestine and 'probably Trans-Jordan'.[41] According to General Hurley, the Zionist leaders also desired 'the eventual transfer of the Arab population to Iraq.' Not all Zionists believed that the transfer of the Palestinians could be accomplished without strife. When an American diplomat told a group of Zionists that the relocation of the Arabs should be accomplished peacefully, Dr Nahum Goldmann, a Zionist representative replied, 'Justice can be enforced only if there is force behind it.'[42]

But Weizmann believed that the Palestinians could be removed via an agreement with King Ibn Saud. Eventually it became clear that Philby had greatly exaggerated the Arab monarch's interest in the transfer agreement. Ibn Saud told Colonel Harold Hoskins, a personal representative of President Roosevelt, that he refused to meet Dr Weizmann, 'owing to the dishonourable and insulting suggestion conveyed through Mr Philby.'[43]

Even after Colonel Hoskins reported on Ibn Saud's negative attitude, Weizmann still retained hope for the Philby plan. On 13 December 1943, in a letter to United States Secretary of State, Sumner Welles, Weizmann indicated the Zionist intention, 'to carry out a Jordan development scheme suggested by the Americans,'[44] which would, 'facilitate the transfer of population.' Weizmann felt that the Zionists could use the help of, 'an outstanding personality in the Arab world such as Ibn Saud.' The Jewish leader added, 'I therefore feel that despite Colonel Hoskins' adverse report that properly managed Mr Philby's scheme offers an approach which should not be abandoned without further study.'

Nothing came of the Philby plan, but the idea of solving the Arab-Jewish impasse by expelling the Palestinians from their homeland was to re-emerge in April 1944 when the British Labour party's national executive urged the removal of the ban on Jewish immigration into Palestine and recommended that, 'the Arabs be encouraged to move out as the Jews move in.'[45] The Labour party announced that all of Palestine should be given to the Zionists and proposed that 'we should re-examine also the possibility of extending the present Palestine boundaries by agreement with Egypt, Syria and Trans-Jordan.'

The Arabs were outraged by the position taken by the Labour party, particularly since it was generally expected that the Socialists would come to power in England after the war. Zionist opinion as expressed in several newspaper editorials was favourable but an effort was made to avoid gloating. Zionist policy on the removal of the Palestinians had always been based on the hope that the British and/or the Arab states would do their dirty work for them. This of course would make the British and the leaders of the Arab states, and not the Zionists, the focus of Muslim world resentment. While in private meetings Ben-Gurion strongly favoured the removal of the Palestinians, in public he did not during this period reveal his true intentions. In a newspaper article the Zionist leader claimed, 'Jewish plans do not entail the displacement of a single Arab.'[46] Ben-Gurion wrote that if the Arabs wished to emigrate to other lands it was their own affair. Like every other Zionist, Ben-Gurion hoped that after the war, when, as expected, the British Labour party came to power, they would carry through their pledge to expel the Palestinians.

But when the Labour party did come to power, they found that in the post-war world, British hopes of maintaining her status as a world power depended in part on her retaining her traditional influence in the Middle East. There seemed no rational reason for Britain to antagonize the Muslim world by taking a pro-Zionist stance on Palestine. Meanwhile, the United States with Harry Truman as President had emerged as the champion of the Zionist cause. Truman greatly desired Jewish votes if he was to win a full term as President in 1948.[47] Besides, there was widespread pro-Jewish sympathy in the United States in view of the revelations about Nazi atrocities.

In late 1945, the British, who were concerned about Jewish immigration into Palestine, invited the United States to form a joint commission to study the future of the Jewish displaced persons (DPs) who had survived the Holocaust. After some negotiation the Truman administration accepted the proposal to form a commission. In January 1946, the Anglo-American

Committee began hearings in Washington, after which it travelled to England, Germany and the Middle East. Although a disproportionate number of witnesses who appeared before the Committee espoused the Zionist party line, the record of the proceedings contains some interesting testimony.

Most of the Zionists stressed the need for Jewish immigration to Palestine, which they urged should be turned into a Jewish state. They pledged that the rights of the Arab minority in the new Zionist nation would be protected. But the testimony of the expert witnesses made it clear that no Jewish state could be created in Palestine without the removal of the Arab population.

Dr Frank Notestein, director of the Population Research Institute at Princeton, revealed that even with massive Jewish immigration, the Arabs would soon outnumber the Jews because of the unusually high Palestinian birth-rate and the low natural population increase among the Jews. In London, Notestein's testimony was supported by Dr D. V. Glass, another demographic expert. He estimated that the Muslim Palestinians (85 per cent of the total) had an annual population increase of 30 per 1,000 which was, 'among the highest recorded in the world'.[48] The Jewish annual population increase was less than 18 per 1,000. It was obvious that unless the Arab population was somehow reduced, the viability of any Zionist state would be questionable since it would always face the danger of an Arab majority.

When the Anglo-American Committee arrived in Palestine, a visit to several Arab villages was on their agenda. The commission toured an Arab school where they asked the students about their future plans. The British and American committee members were surprised that they so often heard, 'work on the land',[49] as a reply. Richard Crossman, a staunchly pro-Zionist member of the Committee, wrote about the Palestinians, 'They cling to the soil even with education.' Indeed an acute sense of belonging to their soil was one of the most characteristic traits of the Palestinian Arabs. Earlier a British report on the Palestine mandate had noted: 'The bulk of the Arab community is composed of peasants and small landowners, hard-headed and stubborn, with a profound attachment to the land.'[50]

The Anglo-American Committee issued its report on 1 May 1946. With regard to the future government of Palestine, the report was vague, but it urged that 100,000 Jewish immigrants be immediately allowed into the country. It is ironic that the United States government strongly urged the British to allow large-scale immigration into Palestine, but only 4,767 Jewish refugees were permitted to enter the United States in the first eight months of 1946. There were many reasons why the United States permitted so few DPs into the country, not least of which was the apathetic attitude of the American Jewish community leadership to a liberalization of US immigration law.

By 1946 most American Jewish organizations had been converted to Zionism. As such they viewed the immigration of the Jewish DPs to the United States or anywhere else besides Palestine as a diversion from their goal to establish a Jewish state in the Holy Land. The Jewish DPs in their detention camps in Europe were subjected to intense propaganda by Zionist agents. But according to General Frederick Morgan who ran the camps for the United Nations Relief and Rehabilitation Agency (UNRRA), if the Jewish displaced persons had been allowed to make their own decision, few 'would have gone elsewhere than to the USA.'[51] But the Zionists used the Jewish refugees as propaganda for their cause and as cannonfodder in the struggle to create a Zionist state in Palestine. After the horrors of the Holocaust, these unfortunate survivors deserved a better fate.

During this period, Palestine was suffering as a result of Jewish terrorism perpetrated by the Irgun and Stern Gang, which directed their attacks against British installations. The terrorists hoped to persuade the British, who had 100,000 troops in Palestine, that continued occupation would be too costly. Both the Irgun and the Stern Gang came out of the right wing of the Zionist movement.

The Stern Gang had originally been formed early in the Second World War by Abraham Stern, who like Jabotinsky, greatly admired Mussolini. Stern had studied classics at the University of Florence and had been influenced by the extreme Anglophobia of Italian Fascism. Stern believed that no effort should be spared to drive the British out of Palestine. Indeed in

1941, the Stern Gang even contacted Otto von Hentig, the German emissary in Syria, in the hope of making a Nazi–Zionist alliance against the British. In their proposal the Stern Gang (which included as one of its leaders the current Israeli Prime Minister Yitzhak Shamir) offered to co-operate with the Nazis on the formation of a Jewish state, 'on a national and totalitarian basis which will establish relations with the German Reich'[52] and protect Nazi interests in the Middle East. The Jewish terrorists also proposed to recognize the Nazi 'New Order in Europe' which was then planning the murder of millions of Jews. These overtures were ignored by the Nazis but do no credit to the Stern Gang.

Although Stern was killed in a gun battle with police in 1942, his group continued their operations, including the murder of British officials. Their best-known victim during the war was Lord Moyne, whose 'crimes' included a statement that the European Jews were not the descendants of the ancient Hebrews and therefore had no claim to Palestine. Lord Moyne had further displeased the Stern Gang because he refused to co-operate with Adolf Eichmann in a trade of Auschwitz inmates for Allied goods. The murder of Lord Moyne greatly angered the British public.

The other Jewish terrorist group, the Irgun, was an offshoot of Jabotinsky's Revisionist movement. During the Second World War, the Irgun had come under the command of Menachem Begin, who proved to be a ruthless and resourceful leader. After the war the Irgun directed its terrorist activities against the British, killing scores of soldiers and police in bombing raids on British installations. On 22 July 1946, the Irgun carried out their most spectacular raid when they blew up the King David Hotel, killing ninety-one Britons, Arabs and Jews.

It is ironic that the news media laments PLO terrorism but fails to mention that it was the Zionists who first used political terrorism in the Middle East. Many of the victims of the Stern Gang and Irgun were innocent civilians, since the terrorists often planted bombs in Arab markets or other crowded areas. But in 1946, their principal target was in fact the British. The government in London, however, feared that the Americans would retaliate against a firm anti-terrorist campaign by holding up a much-needed loan. The British army was not allowed to use the tough tactics required to halt the Irgun and Stern Gang. Execution of captured terrorists was rare, house searches were limited and round-ups unusual.

The British army Chief of Staff, Field Marshal Montgomery, was outraged by the restrictions placed on the army by the politicians in London. While on a fact-finding mission in Palestine he reported, 'the whole business of dealing with illegal armed organizations in Palestine is being tackled in a way which will not produce any good results.'[53] He recommended, 'If we are not prepared to maintain law and order in Palestine it would be better to get out.' There were many in Britain who agreed with him. The British taxpayers were supporting an army of 100,000 men in the troubled mandate territory with no end in sight. The tactics of the Irgun and Stern Gang, designed to bomb the British out of Palestine, brought quick results.

On 14 February 1947, British Foreign Secretary Ernest Bevin announced that he was turning the Palestine problem over to the United Nations. On 13 May, the General Assembly set up the United Nations Special Committee on Palestine (UNSCOP). The purpose of the Committee was to investigate the Palestine problem, including the question of the Jewish DPs in Germany. The Arabs made repeated but unsuccessful attempts to have the DP issue divorced from the Palestine problem. This failure put the Arab Higher Committee in a difficult position since consideration of the Jewish refugees in connection with Palestine practically assured a UNSCOP report favourable to the Zionists. Many nations (including the US) which had done little or nothing to relieve the plight of the DPs were sure to vote on 'humanitarian grounds' for the creation of a Jewish state in Palestine to rescue the refugees. Thus the Arabs declined to give testimony before the UN Committee. But the refusal of the AHC to work with UNSCOP cast the Arabs in a most unfavourable light from a propaganda point of view as the Jewish Agency extended full co-operation to the Committee.

After extensive hearings, the eleven-nation committee

announced on 31 August a majority report (supported by seven members) which recommended the partition of Palestine and the creation of a Jewish state, an Arab state and the internationalization of Jerusalem. After some modifications were made, the partition plan provided that the Jewish state would include the coastal plain (except for Arab Jaffa), part of Galilee, and most of the Negev. There would be 538,000 Jews in the Zionist nation. The total number of Arabs in the Jewish state was in dispute since the AHC pointed out that the UN estimate of 400,000 failed to take into account the large Bedouin population in the Negev. Thus the Arab population nearly equalled the Jewish population of the proposed Zionist state.

When the UNSCOP report was announced, there was little stir among the Arab community in Palestine. On 8 September, Sir Henry Gurney, the Chief Secretary of the Palestine government informed the British Secretary of State for the Colonies that, 'the absence of any immediate reaction of the Arabs [to the UNSCOP report] can be attributed to their incredulity.'[54] According to Gurney, the Arabs didn't take the partition plan seriously because, 'it seems very possible that the Arabs would have a majority population within quite a short time if the present rate of natural increase continues.'

Most Palestinians found it difficult to imagine that the UN General Assembly would be so irresponsible as to vote for a partition plan that would create a Jewish nation which lacked viability. In view of the demographic time bomb, it was obvious that in the state created by the UNSCOP plan the Zionists must either accept an eventual Arab majority or expel a large part of the Palestinian population. There was no other possible choice. Even if the entire 250,000 DPs were admitted, because of the exceedingly high Arab birth-rate, there would be a Palestinian majority in the Zionist state within a few decades.

But long before that there would be massive chaos in view of the Zionist desire to seize Arab lands for Jewish colonization. During the debate in the General Assembly on the partition plan, Ambassador Camille Chamoun of Lebanon quoted from the constitution of the Jewish Agency to show that discrimination against the Arabs in employment and land ownership had

THE PALESTINIAN CATASTROPHE

been Zionist policy for decades. The Lebanese delegate made a telling point: 'If such had been Zionist policy under the [British] mandatory administration, it could be asked what the fate of the Arabs would be under the regime of a Jewish state.'[55] The Arabs realized that discrimination in employment and land ownership would be used by the Zionists to push out the Arabs and make room for new Jewish immigrants. Such a development could only lead to war between Jews and Arabs.

The Jewish state created by UNSCOP was also likely to have border disputes with the Arabs. Jaffa was completely surrounded by Jewish territory, so was the Arab portion of the Negev. About 100,000 Jews in Jerusalem were cut off from the Zionist state. This could also be the cause of friction and the rise of irredentist agitation in the Jewish state.

Despite its huge Arab population and its unstable borders, on 29 November 1947, the Jewish state in Palestine was created when the General Assembly approved the UNSCOP majority report by a vote of thirty-three to thirteen. The necessary two-thirds majority in the General Assembly had been achieved because the United States had supported the Zionists by putting great political and economic pressure on the many governments that had originally opposed partition. President Truman needed Jewish votes if he hoped to win the 1948 presidential election. Acting against State Department advice, during the last crucial days before the UN vote, Truman ordered American officials to make an all-out effort to support partition. The Liberian Ambassador later complained that the US delegation at the UN had 'carried on a high pressure electioneering job in which they were assisted by the Jewish agencies and organizations which had not hesitated to bring pressure on many countries.'[56] Some nations were threatened with financial reprisals by the US if they voted against the partition resolution.

In view of the inviability of the Jewish state, the Zionists might have been expected to oppose the UNSCOP majority report. The reason why the Zionists supported the partition resolution was explained by Sir Mohammed Zafrullah Khan of Pakistan: 'If the Jewish Agency was prepared to accept the majority plan, it was probably because it considered it as the thin end of the wedge and not the final irrevocable culmination of Jewish hopes and ideals.'[57]

Ten years before, when the Peel partition plan was being considered, a Foreign Office report noted that partition, 'will mean the creation of a new jumping-off place for the Jews from which they will inevitably spread their influence over a much larger area. The Jews make no secret of this and it has become clear that it is the main objection of the Arabs to the partition proposals.'[58] Indeed in 1938, Ben-Gurion had told a Zionist meeting: 'I favour partition of the country because when we become a strong power after the establishment of the state, we will abolish partition and spread throughout all of Palestine.'[59] Even the 'moderate' Weizmann had a similar view. In 1944, he told Richard Meinertzhagen, a pro-Zionist British official that he had favoured the Peel partition plan because, 'he knew that war was inevitable and he thought that if there was only a small Jewish state, the Jews might have gained by conquest what they wanted.'[60]

It was obvious to Arabs, Jews and British that once a Zionist state was established, it would engage in territorial expansion. It was equally clear that the extension of Zionist influence would necessitate the removal of large numbers of Arabs. The Palestinian historian George Antonius wrote, 'no room can be made in Palestine for a second nation except by dislodging or exterminating the nation in possession.'[61] Some Zionists believed that the Palestinians could be persuaded to relocate to Saudi Arabia, Iraq, Trans-Jordan and other Arab states.

But many Zionists had serious doubts as to whether the Palestinians could be removed by negotiation. In 1937, Ben-Gurion had written to his son that when the Jewish state was created, 'We will expel the Arabs and take their places.'[62] The Zionist leader boasted, 'our army will be among the world's outstanding' and would be used to intimidate the Palestinians into fleeing. Ben-Gurion left no doubt that if the Palestinians did not succumb to threats, they would be dealt with firmly. 'Then we have force at our disposal,' he wrote. Ben-Gurion accepted the Jewish state created by the UN resolution since he believed that eventually it could be turned into a sizeable nation that would be largely free of Arabs. With the outbreak of war, the opportunity for Ben-Gurion and his associates to expand their state and make it *goyim rein* would come sooner than they expected.

CHAPTER II
Plan Dalet

Fight in the way of Allah against those who fight against you, but begin not hostilities. Lo! Allah loveth not aggressors.

Koran II, 190

One Saturday in mid-December 1947, the men of the Arab village Yehidya met at the local coffee house to discuss the events of the day. Violence was erupting all over Palestine and because they were near the Jewish town Petah Tikva, the people of Yehidya felt particularly vulnerable. So far, any major conflict with the Jews of Petah Tikva had been avoided but no one in Yehidya knew how long their tranquillity would last.

The crisis in Palestine had begun on 2 December, at the start of the three-day general strike to protest the partition resolution. On the second day of the strike, there had been some looting and sporadic violence against Jewish shops. According to a British police official these incidents, 'had undoubtedly not been organized but were the acts of individuals and groups.'[1] The relatively subdued Arab reaction to the partition resolution contrasted sharply with the Zionist reign of terror that had accompanied the announcement of the White Paper in 1939. It was clear that although the Palestinian leadership wanted a show of defiance against the partition resolution, they did not wish to fight a civil war.

However, the Irgun used the Arab rioting in early December 1947 as an excuse to launch a murderous terrorist campaign that claimed the lives of many Arab civilians in numerous towns and villages. The Irgun leader Menachem Begin later explained his attitude during this period: 'My greatest worry in those months was that the Arabs might accept the United Nations plan. Then we would have had the ultimate tragedy, a Jewish state so small that it could not absorb all the Jews of the world.'² Irgun terrorism however would make sure that no agreement would be possible.

On Friday, 12 December, Jewish terrorists had murdered nineteen Arab civilians in reprisal for the Jews killed in the Arab riots. But on the following afternoon the people of Yehidya were reassured when they saw a patrol of British army vehicles enter their village. The four cars stopped in front of the coffee house and out stepped men dressed in khaki uniforms and steel helmets. However, it soon became apparent that they had not come to protect the villagers. With machine guns they sprayed bullets into the crowd gathered in the coffee house. Some of the invaders placed bombs next to Arab homes while other disguised terrorists tossed grenades at civilians. For a while it seemed as if the villagers would be annihilated but soon a real British patrol arrived to foil the well-organized killing raid. The death toll of seven Arab civilians could have been much higher.³

Earlier in the day Jewish terrorists had tossed home-made bombs from a speeding taxi into a crowd of Arabs standing near the Damascus Gate in Jerusalem. Six Arabs were killed and twenty-three were wounded. In Jaffa another bomb was thrown into a café, killing six more Arabs and injuring forty.

Throughout Palestine twenty-one Arab civilians were murdered on Saturday, 13 December by Jewish terrorists. Added to the previous day's casualties it amounted to a declaration of war by the Yishuv against the Palestinian Arabs. Sir Alan Cunningham, the British High Commissioner, had the task of attempting to mediate between Jew and Arab in Palestine. Although Cunningham favoured partition and the establishment of a Jewish state, he had no sympathy for the terrorist tactics of the Zionists. On 13 December, he reported to London:

> The initial Arab outbreaks were spontaneous and unorganized and were more demonstrations of displeasures at the UN decision than determined attacks on Jews. The weapons initially employed were sticks and stones and had it not been for Jewish resource to firearms, it is not impossible that the excitement would have

subsided and little loss of life been caused. This is more probable since there is reliable evidence that the Arab Higher Committee as a whole and the Mufti in particular, although pleased at the strong response to the strike call were not in favour of serious outbreaks.⁴

On 15 December, in an equally revealing dispatch, Cunningham told London the names of those in the Jewish community responsible for the reign of terror engulfing Palestine. 'The provocative action of the Jews and their admission that the Haganah is authorized to take what they call counter-action, but what is in effect indiscriminate action against the Arabs is hardly calculated to have a calming effect.'⁵ Cunningham denied the claim that the dissident Irgun and Stern Gang terrorist groups were acting independently of the Jewish Agency. 'This has not in fact been the case and in any event the Haganah and the dissident groups are now working so closely together that the Agency's claim that they cannot control the dissidents is inadmissible.'*

The offensive actions of the Haganah and Irgun not only helped to provoke the war but also stimulated the earliest indications of the Palestinian exodus. On 15 December 1947 the left Zionist newspaper *Al Hamishmar* published a report that stated that as a result of Zionist terrorism 'many of the Arabs who live near Hebrew settlements are moving to areas with large concentrations of Arab population.' As the violence in Palestine increased the flight of the Palestinians accelerated.

As Cunningham expected, the situation in Palestine worsened during the last days of 1947. On the morning of 18

---

*There is Israeli evidence to support Cunningham's assertion that the Zionists bear a large part of the responsibility for the outbreak of war in 1948. The Israeli historian Uri Milstein has published the text of a meeting between Zionist leaders in January 1948. At the conference Gad Machnes, an expert on Arab affairs, blamed the Mufti for starting the riots in December but revealed that 'if it was not for the open [Zionist military] preparations which had a provocative nature the drift into war could have been averted.'⁶ Milstein concluded that the Zionist leaders ignored their own Arab experts who 'estimated that the Palestinian Arabs were divided and thus the majority among them did not want a war.'

December, a group of Arabs attacked a Jewish settlement in the Negev but were driven off by the RAF. That evening the Haganah staged a raid against the village of Khisas near the Lebanese–Syrian border. The attacks started at 9 p.m. when two carloads of terrorists drove through the village firing machine guns and throwing grenades. Ten Arab civilians were killed in the raid. The following day at the village of Qazaza, five Arab children were murdered when Jewish terrorists dynamited the house of the village Mukhtar. By the end of the month, 450 people had been killed and over 1,000 injured in the violence.

It is often claimed that the Arabs initiated the 1948 war when they rejected the partition resolution. But to portray the Jews in Palestine as innocent victims of Arab aggression is ludicrous. Although the Zionists had publicly agreed to the partition resolution, they had no intention of accepting the borders or demographic composition of their new state. Yeshayahu Ben Porat was a member of the Haganah during this period. He noted that while he had been in the Zionist youth movement, he 'was trained to despise the Arab population.' He was taught that he must one day struggle for a Zionist state that would be *goyim rein*. 'They did not educate us in the perspective that there will be a Jewish state here where Arabs and Jews will live together. The hidden thought and sometimes the overt thought was: they will go away and we shall stay.'[7] Ben Porat later recalled that on the eve of the conflict most Jews believed, 'we needed a war with the Arabs. In the kibbutzim they looked at the Arab villages in the vicinity and they divided up their land in their thoughts.'

In point of fact the 1948 war was an 'irrepressible conflict'. There was no way to create a Zionist state in Palestine without displacing large numbers of Arabs, who would never leave voluntarily. At best an Arab–Jewish conflict could have been delayed, but not avoided. After the passing of the partition resolution both sides took steps that contributed to the escalating violence.

The Palestinian AHC made it clear to the UN Palestine Commission (which had been set up to administer partition) that they bitterly opposed the UN plan. On 6 February, the

AHC informed the UN Commission that, 'the Arabs of Palestine consider any attempt by the Jews or any other power or group of powers to establish a Jewish state in Arab territory as an act of aggression which in their own self-defence should be resisted by force.'[8]

The Palestinians realized that there could be no peace once a Jewish state was established because it would inevitably seek to expand and rid itself of the huge Arab population. Indeed, on 7 February, Ben-Gurion made a speech before the Central Committee of the Mapai party in which he predicted, 'it is most probable that in the next six, eight or ten months of the struggle many great changes will take place in this land and not all of them to our disadvantage and there surely will be a great change in the population of the country.'[9] Later, Ben-Gurion would make it clear to his Cabinet that he had no intention of respecting the boundaries indicated in the partition resolution. 'United Nations resolutions are not compulsory and we ought not to pin all our hopes and efforts on them.'[10]

For many years the Palestinian Arab leaders had realized that there would be a showdown with the Zionists but they were not prepared for the inevitable conflict. The 1936–39 Arab revolt had decimated the military potential of the Palestinians. At the beginning of 1948, they could barely muster a force of 2,500 men, who were poorly armed and organized. They were supported by the Arab Liberation Army (ALA) which consisted of volunteers from various Arab countries who served under the control of the Arab League Military Committee in Damascus. Between January and May, 4,000 ALA volunteers entered Palestine.

The policy of the Arab League states was that they would assist the Palestinians but that they had no intention of sending in their own regular armies. On 18 March, Damascus Radio announced that, 'it was not the intention of the Arab states to intervene in Palestine by force unless an international force was used to implement and foster Zionism.'[11] There were many reasons why the Arab states hesitated to send their regular armies into Palestine, not the least of which was their military weakness. All five Arab states together (Egypt, Syria, Lebanon, Iraq and Trans-Jordan) had less than 14,000 men available for service in Palestine in 1948. Even when these were combined with the ALA volunteers and the Palestinian irregulars in the later stage of the war, they would be no match for the huge force that the Zionists were gradually able to mobilize in 1948.

One of the most misleading Zionist myths about 1948 is the portrayal of the Jewish community of Palestine as a David who was attacked by a gang of Arab Goliaths. In every stage of the war the Zionists had forces that were more formidable than the Arabs. Moshe Shertok boasted that 'during the Second World War, the Jewish community of Palestine had mobilized 26,000 recruits for active service' as well as '7,000 for local defence.'[12] In 1948 the Yishuv had a high proportion of young men of military age, many of whom had training and battle experience. In addition, about 5,000 volunteers across the globe came to fight for the Zionist cause. Arms were brought in from around the world including large consignments from Czechoslovakia. Eventually the Haganah would have a front-line strength of 30,000 men plus 30,000 more in reserve and garrison units. (The Zionists also possessed the critical advantages of unity of command and interior battle lines that enabled them to switch men from one front to another more quickly than the geographically and politically divided Arab armies.)

The greatest Zionist advantage in 1948 was in the area of military planning. Neither the Palestinians nor the Arab states had done any strategic planning for a war against the Zionists. Indeed, this lack of planning was to become an even more serious problem in the latter part of the conflict when the contingents from the various Arab states seemed to work against each other. In contrast, the Zionists had made a number of detailed plans in anticipation of a war with the Arabs. Plan Dalet (D), which was implemented in April 1948, called for an offensive strategy against the Palestinians and their Arab allies. Among the principal aims of Plan D were the enlargement of the Jewish state and the expulsion of many Palestinians.

The Israeli staff officer Yigal Yadin remembered: 'I prepared the nucleus of Plan D in 1944 when I was head of planning in the underground and I worked on it further in the summer of 1947 when the Chief of Staff, Yaacov Dori, fell ill. The Plan was to take control of the key points in the country and on the roads before the British left.'[13] Among the key targets of Plan D, according to Yadin, were 'the main Arab villages'. In conjunction with Plan D, the Haganah command compiled a 'List of Arab villages'.[14] This document contained the names of every Arab town and village in Palestine along with its population, location, names of principal notables as well as the political tendency of the town's leadership. This document would prove of great value to the Zionists during the war.

On 19 December 1947, Ben-Gurion called for an aggressive policy in the developing conflict in Palestine. 'In each attack, a decisive blow should be struck, resulting in the destruction of homes and the expulsion of the population.'[15] In a newspaper interview which was published after his death, Yadin outlined the methods of Plan D, which was designed to fulfil Ben-Gurion's orders. Top priorities under Plan D were 'the destruction of Arab villages near the Jewish settlements and the expulsion of the inhabitants' as well as 'the domination of the main arteries of transportation that are vital to the Jews and the destruction of Arab villages near them.'[16] Plan D also called for the 'siege of Arab towns that are located outside the Jewish state created by the UN resolution [Acre and Jaffa].'

Since Plan D was offensive in nature, it provided for 'direct action against Arab targets in western Palestine, outside the border of the Jewish state.' A key role in these operations would be played by the isolated Jewish settlements which were deep inside Arab territory. According to Plan D, they would serve as 'forward bases whose main function was to hold out at all cost until the advance of the main body of troops.'

It is noteworthy that on 5 December, only a few days after the passage of the partition resolution, Ben-Gurion ordered 'immediate action to expand Jewish settlement in three areas assigned to the Arab state: the South-West (Negev), the South-East (Etzion bloc) and Western Galilee.'[17] If Ben-Gurion had any intention of respecting the boundaries created by the partition resolution, he would never have sent Jewish settlers to live permanently under Arab rule. His action in ordering the expansion of Jewish settlement in the proposed Palestinian state must be seen within the context of Plan D, since the Zionist leader wished to strengthen Jewish 'forward bases' in anticipation of conquering Arab territory in the Negev, Galilee and the corridor between Jerusalem and Tel Aviv.

The historian and veteran of the 1948 war, Meir Pa'il notes: 'It was the feeling of every Zionist in early 1948 that there were too many Arabs in the proposed Jewish state.'[18] But like most Israelis, Pa'il maintains that the expulsion of Arabs under Plan D was motivated solely by 'military necessity'. It is clear, however, that when Ben-Gurion and his associates drew up Plan D they were well aware that victory in the war with Arabs would be meaningless unless the resulting Jewish state was territorially and demographically viable. The claim that only 'hostile' Arabs were expelled is refuted by the UN and other neutral observers who reported that frequently considerable brutality was used to expel Palestinian villagers who offered no resistance. Each commander was left to decide which Arabs were 'hostile'. In view of the Zionist desire to reduce the number of Arabs in the proposed Jewish state it follows that orders to expel Arabs under Plan D were interpreted liberally by most Haganah officers.

According to Nataniel Lorch, 'Zero hour for Plan D was to arrive when the British evacuation had reached a point where Haganah would be reasonably safe from British intervention and when mobilization had progressed to a point where the implementation of a large-scale attack would be feasible.'[19] The Haganah leadership estimated that they would need 30,000 men to implement Plan D. It would take them several months to mobilize and equip such a force. Thus, during the first months of 1948, the Haganah operated Plan C, which was primarily defensive.

During this early period the first wave of Palestinians left their homeland. On 4 February, British High Commissioner Cunningham reported to the UN that 'throughout the Arab middle class there is a steady exodus of those who can afford to leave the country.'[20] This exodus, however, had not yet reached massive proportions. The Israeli historian Rony Gabbay notes, 'According to Jewish sources some 30,000 persons, members of the well-to-do families in Jerusalem and Haifa, together with the inhabitants of some of the villages in the Sharon greatly affected by the disturbance and riots departed for neighbouring Arab countries between January to March 1948.'[21] These 30,000 comprised about 4 per cent of the eventual total volume of refugees in 1948 and were fewer than the number of middle-class Palestinians who had fled the country temporarily during the strife of the 1930s.

Because the Arabs did surprisingly well in the early phase of the fighting, few Palestinians were motivated to leave their country. These early encounters consisted mainly of the 'battle of the convoys' in which Arab irregulars attempted to interdict Jewish convoys that were supplying Jerusalem and other outposts. Despite their small numbers and lack of equipment or training, the Arab forces destroyed many of the Jewish trucks since it required little organization or modern weapons to halt the vulnerable supply vehicles.

Because in the early months of the war the Zionists were operating under the defensive Plan C, there were not, as in the later stage of the conflict, the wide sweeps of the countryside that were to cause thousands of Palestinians to flee their homes. In early 1948 most Palestinians still cherished the myth of Arab military power. They could not imagine being defeated by a people like the Jews, who they believed lacked martial qualities. The Palestinians did not yet understand the superior organizational and technical capacities that would give victory to the Zionists, just as it had all modern Western armies that made war on a Third World people. The Palestinians spoke of 'sweeping the Jews away with a broom.' Even those wealthier Arabs who had left fully expected to return after the Zionists were overwhelmed by the Arab armies whose weakness the Palestinians could not contemplate.

Many Zionist historians claim that in the early months of the war the Arab leaders encouraged the Palestinians to leave their homes. Their only evidence, however, is a vaguely worded statement by the Arab League urging the member states to give shelter to 'women, the elderly and children'[22] who might flee if fighting broke out in Palestine. But this statement was made in September 1947 before the partition resolution was passed and before the exodus had begun. At that point none of the Arab leaders anticipated the mass flight of hundreds of thousands of

Palestinians. The Arab leaders believed that if as had happened in the 1930s, a few thousand Palestinians should flee, they should be provided for by the Arab states. But when it became clear that there might be a large-scale exodus, the Arab leaders took steps to halt the flight.

Thus on 1 March, the Jewish Agency's Political Department noted that 'the Arab Higher Executive has succeeded in imposing close scrutiny on those leaving [Palestine] for Arab countries in the Middle East.'[23] Indeed, on 8 March, Mohammed Amin al Husseini, the chairman of the Palestinian AHC, requested that the Egyptian government cancel the residence permits of those Palestinians who had fled to Egypt. The AHC asked that this migration be curtailed because 'the exodus will adversely affect the national movement.'[24] Later as the flight from Palestine reached alarming proportions, the Arab governments would make constant appeals in newspapers and radio broadcasts asking the Palestinians to remain in their homes (see pages 66, 96, 112).

During the period after the passing of the partition resolution the Jewish Agency proceeded with plans to set up a Zionist state. A major complication was that this Jewish nation would contain a huge Arab minority, which, in view of the Palestinian birth-rate, would always threaten to become a majority despite the expected influx of Jewish immigrants. An added problem was the Palestinian possession of most of the desirable farmland in the country, which would stifle Zionist plans to set up numerous agricultural settlements. All of the questions that were raised ten years earlier when the British-sponsored portion plan was considered, re-emerged in early 1948.

An Israeli historian has recently suggested that the Zionist leaders in early 1948 made plans for the 'integration of Arabs into the life of the state.'[25] There is, however, no reason to believe that Ben-Gurion and his associates had given up their ultimate plans for an enlarged Jewish nation from which most of the Arabs would be expelled. But it was not clear as to when and how the Palestinians would be driven out. Although the Zionist leaders took actions that increased their chances of a confrontation with the Arabs, in general they were not anxious for a war until they had consolidated their position. The Zionist leaders had drawn up Plan D with its provisions to expel many Palestinians and expand their state but they saw no need for immediate implementation. To Ben-Gurion, acceptance of the nation created by the UN was a stepping-stone to a larger state that would be *goyim rein*. But in the interim the Arabs could be tolerated as long as they accepted a subordinate position in the new Jewish nation. In many villages the Haganah threatened the Arabs to be docile, 'so that we shall not have to destroy you and your property.'[26] However, many Arabs continued to resist.

While the fighting escalated in early 1948, technical experts drew up their plans for the proposed state in which the Arab population would enjoy certain rights but would not be allowed any real power. A memorandum drawn up by A. Lotsky outlined the 'Principles and Aims of Our Policy toward the Arabs.'[27] According to this document the principal goal of Zionist policy towards the Arab minority would be to ensure the 'security of the state' by 'encouraging Arab collaboration and suppressing troublemakers.' Another aim would be to reduce Arab 'political identification' and 'prevent political and religious activism.' The ultimate goal would be to 'encourage the emigration of discontented Arabs.'

In 1938, it had been suggested that 'the supervision of citizenship' could be a useful tool to encourage Arab emigration. In January 1948, a legal committee was set up by the Jewish Agency to examine the question of citizenship in the proposed state. In their report the lawyers recommended a complex system which would make it more diffiult for an Arab to get citizenship than a Jew. The legal experts candidly admitted that 'this double standard is entirely desirable from the point of view of our national interest.'[28]

Of course some of the documents from early 1948 are contradictory with regard to the Arab policy that was proposed for the new state. The planning sessions were held while fighting was going on in many parts of the country. No one knew what the length or the intensity of the conflict would be or how many Arabs would be left in the Jewish state after the smoke had cleared. Some Zionist leaders favoured a more liberal attitude toward the Arab minority since they feared the negative foreign reaction if the Arabs were treated too harshly. But there was a general consensus of opinion that one way or another the Arab population in the Jewish state had to be reduced and that the remaining Arabs should be denied any real political or economic power. This consensus of opinion has characterized the Zionist attitude toward the Palestinians from the very beginning of the movement to the present day.

In early April there was a major intensification of the fighting in the Palestinian conflict when the Haganah implemented Plan D. This offensive strategy was required because of the apparent success of the Arab effort to defeat the Zionists by cutting off the vital supply-truck convoys. Besides, the Zionists felt political pressure for an offensive strategy. At the UN there were signs that American support for partition was waning. The State Department was attempting to persuade President Truman that partition should be abandoned in favour of a trusteeship plan that would postpone the creation of an independent Jewish state. Many American experts believed that this would be the only way to avoid a widening Arab–Jewish conflict.

Ben-Gurion ordered the implementation of Plan Dalet because he wished to recover the initiative for the Zionists in the conflict. He also wanted to show the Americans that the Jewish state was an established reality that did not depend on UN resolutions to ensure its existence. In accordance with Plan D the Jewish leader ordered offensives on several fronts outside the territory of the proposed Jewish state and deep inside areas which were exclusively Arab-inhabited. In the north, Operation Ben Ami was launched against Acre, a totally Arab city most of whose population would be expelled (see page 119). Several Zionist operations would be launched in order to conquer Jerusalem despite its status under the partition plan as an independent international zone. A key aspect of Plan D was Operation Nachson, which was designed to carve a corridor through Arab-inhabited territory in order to link Tel Aviv with Jerusalem.

Harry Levin, a pro-Zionist news correspondent joined in a Palmach attack during Operation Nachson. The élite Jewish troops struck at midnight on 12 April against Kalonia, a small Arab village several miles from Jerusalem. The attackers used, 'a medley of weapons, Sten-guns, rifles, machine guns and hand grenades.'[29] The battle did not last very long. Levin noted 'Arab resistance, feeble from the start, soon crumbled. When our men got to them many of the houses were empty. Others continued to spit fire but not for long.' According to the Jewish correspondent, 'In half an hour it was over. Most of the Arabs had fled into the darkness.'

In Kalonia, as in hundreds of villages throughout Palestine, the Zionist forces would make sure that the population which was expelled could not return. Levin witnessed the spectacle. 'When I left sappers were blowing up the houses. One after another the solid stone buildings, some built in elaborate city style, exploded and crashed. Within sight of Jerusalem I still heard echoes rolling through the hills.' With no homes to return to the people of Kalonia were condemned to become permanent refugees. But two miles away the population of another village had already suffered a far worse fate. The tragic story of this town would come to symbolize the agony of the Palestinian people.

CHAPTER III

Deir Yassin

And they utterly destroyed all that was in the city both men and women, young and old and ox and sheep and ass with the edge of the sword.

Joshua 6:21

Like most Haganah officials, the commander in Jerusalem David Shaltiel, had scant respect for the Irgun and Stern Gang since as a professional soldier he distrusted the independent tendencies of the 'dissident organizations'. In early April when the Haganah launched Operation Nachson, designed to open up a corridor between Jerusalem and Tel Aviv, the local commanders of the two terrorist groups wished to take part in the fighting. They came to Shaltiel with a proposal that they would attack Deir Yassin, an Arab village not far from the highway which connected Jerusalem and Tel Aviv.

'Why should you go to Deir Yassin?' responded Shaltiel, 'we have no trouble with them.' The Haganah commander suggested several other objectives which would be more helpful. But the Irgun and Stern Gang leaders insisted that each of the other villages proposed by Shaltiel would be too difficult. They insisted on going to Deir Yassin. Unable to talk them out of their militarily needless assault, Shaltiel relented. 'Okay you have permission but you should know that we've had no trouble with these Arabs till now.'

Yitzhak Levi, the chief of Haganah intelligence in Jerusalem, tried to prevent the attack on Deir Yassin. He told his superior David Shaltiel that on 20 January 1948, the Mukhtar and elders of Deir Yassin had agreed to 'inform on the movement of strangers in the area'[1] and to provide other intelligence information to the Jews. In exchange for becoming traitors to the Arab cause, the Zionists promised the people of Deir Yassin that their village would be spared. (Abu Gush an Arab village near Jerusalem, which still stands, made a similar agreement that was honoured by the Jews.)

Levi asked Shaltiel for permission to warn the people of Deir Yassin of the danger if they remained in their village. But Levi reveals, 'Shaltiel refused my request and said he could not endanger an operation of Jews by giving the Arabs a hint, even if we had an agreement with them.' Nor would Shaltiel forbid the Stern Gang and Irgun to attack since he claimed that they would launch the raid even without his approval. But according to Levi, 'If Shaltiel would have forbidden the organizations to attack the village because of the agreement with Deir Yassin, they would not have carried out their plans.'

The leaders of the two Zionist terrorist groups met to plan the attack. By their own admission, from the very beginning many of the terrorists were intent on a massacre. According to the Irgun officer, Yehuda Lapidot, the Stern Gang, 'put forward a proposal to liquidate the residents of the village after the conquest in order to show the Arabs what happens when the Irgun and Stern Gang set out together on an operation.'[2] One of the aims of the attack was 'to break Arab morale' and create panic throughout Palestine. Benzion Cohen, the Irgun commander of the raid, later recalled that at the pre-attack meeting 'the majority was for liquidation of all the men in the village and any others found that opposed us, whether it be old people, women and children.'[3]

Preparations were soon made for the attack. The Stern Gang provided explosives, while the Irgun contributed arms that had been manufactured in its clandestine arms shops. Rifles and hand grenades were provided by the Haganah. It was called Operation Unity because its goal was to demonstrate cooperation between the Haganah and the terrorist groups. There were over 120 men in the assault force, including a young Haganah soldier Meir Pa'il who went along so that he could 'get some estimate of these irregulars' combat capabilities.' The Haganah High Command was not sure how the terrorists would perform as combat troops so that Pa'il thought it would be useful to observe the attack.

After considerable debate it had been agreed that a loudspeaker would be used to warn the civilian population of the village to flee. This would soon become standard procedure in dozens of assaults on towns and villages all over Palestine, causing thousands of Arab civilians to flee their homes in panic. But unfortunately the loudspeaker van got stuck in a ditch and had to be abandoned. It was decided to attack without warning. At 4.30 a.m. on the morning of Friday, 9 April, Pa'il waited on the outskirts of Deir Yassin for the assault to begin.

Like many villages in Palestine, Deir Yassin was picturesque in a quaint Middle East fashion. Its flat-topped, sun-baked stone huts were mounted in tiers on the crest of a hill that was about a mile west of the suburbs of Jerusalem. The people of Deir Yassin cultivated apricots, olives and grapes in terraced fields that enhanced the beauty of the village.

But despite its picturesque location, Deir Yassin was not well situated in view of the developing war with the Jews. There were several large neighbouring Jewish settlements and Deir Yassin could easily be surrounded by Zionist forces. To prevent such a catastrophe a resident of Deir Yassin, Mohammed Aref Sammour recalls, 'There was a mutual agreement of non-aggression between us and the Jews'[4] of neighbouring Givat Shaul and Montefiore settlements. When Arab forces in the area had asked permission to use Deir Yassin as a base, the village Mukhtar had politely refused, pleading for the safety of the women and children in such an exposed location. The movements of these Arab forces were reported by the leaders of Deir Yassin to the Haganah.

On the morning of 9 April, sentries were posted around the perimeter of the village. They carried old Mausers and Turkish rifles that had only been used to hunt rabbits. When one of the sentries spotted the terrorists he fired his rifle and screamed, 'the Jews are coming!'

At first the Zionists made little progress. Though barefoot and half naked, scores of residents of Deir Yassin were able to reach neighbouring villages. Those who were unable to flee put up a valiant defence. Meir Pa'il noted the ineffectiveness of the terrorists. 'They just managed to occupy the eastern half of the village, they couldn't occupy the higher western half. About ten or twelve Arabs shot at them using only rifles, no automatic weapons and pinned them down on the eastern side.'

According to Pa'il, it soon became necessary for the terrorists to receive assistance from the Haganah. The young intelligence officer sent someone to a nearby Haganah base. A Palmach company commander named Yaakov (Yakki) Vaag answered the call for help. With a platoon of men he was able to occupy the rest of the village in a few minutes without a single casualty. After the victory Pa'il told the Palmach officer, 'Yakki, you know we have a saying in Yiddish "*Varf sich Avek*" – get away from here! Don't get mixed up with the Irgun and Stern Gang. Go home and go to sleep.' Pa'il didn't want to see the Palmach too closely associated with the terrorist groups. Yakki and his men who had already mounted a raid on another Arab village that night took Pa'il's advice and withdrew.

Had the story ended here, Deir Yassin would have become one of hundreds of forgotten Arab villages that were erased from the countryside of Palestine. But as Meir Pa'il observed, the terrorists wanted vengeance for the casualties they had suffered. 'And when the Palmach had gone away the Stern Gang and the Irgun began what I'd call an uncontrolled looting and massacre performance.' Yitzhak Levi agrees with Meir Pa'il that because of the few casualties the terrorists had suffered, 'their feelings of revenge were unrestrained.'[5]

Mohammed Aref Sammour witnessed the slaughter of many of his relatives and neighbours. In a house not far from his own, 'There were twenty-five people, twenty-four were killed and only one could escape through a window. They used grenades and after they stormed the house they used machine guns. In another house they captured a boy who was holding the knee of his mother. They slaughtered him in front of her.' Mohammed saw a family of eleven people attempt to surrender but the Jewish terrorists gunned them down, including a woman of eighty and a boy of three or four years old.

According to Mohammed the terrorists were guilty of terrible savagery. 'They ripped open the bellies of all the women they found straight away with bayonets.'[6] They also took all the jewellery from their victims: if those items did not come off easily 'they would cut off the arm to take the bracelet or cut the finger to get the ring.' Mohammed saw the terrorists pursue old people who recited the Koran as they fled. But this did not protect them. He later counted sixty-five bullet holes in the clothes of one of the elderly people who had been slain.

Mohammed was lucky since he escaped through the back door of his house with his mother, brother and sisters. The Sammour family escaped towards the western side of Deir Yassin along with many of their neighbours. Mohammed recalled, 'On our way a lady who worked as a teacher heard a voice calling for help. When she went back to offer assistance she was killed by the Jews.'

Many inhabitants of Deir Yassin were killed by terrorists who used explosives, their favourite weapon. More than fifteen houses in Deir Yassin were blown up by the Irgun and Stern Gang. A special target was the home of the village Mukhtar. When it was blown up many people trapped there were killed. More fortunate, however, was the Mukhtar's daughter who sought refuge in the village kiln. With its heavy iron door it survived the Irgun's dynamite. The terrorists tried to trick the people by calling, 'Come out! There is no risk!' but the Mukhtar's daughter recognized the accented Arabic. However, many residents of Deir Yassin were unable to protect themselves from the terrorists.

The British were still, technically at least, the rulers of Palestine. When High Commissioner Sir Alan Cunningham received news of the massacre he became extremely angry. He instructed Lieutenant-General Sir Gordon MacMillan, commander of British ground forces in Palestine, to send troops to Deir Yassin. But MacMillan was not eager to get involved in the widening Arab–Jewish conflict. MacMillan told Cunningham that there were no troops available. Intervention at Deir Yassin ran counter to MacMillan's policy of only using his troops in pursuit of British interests.

That afternoon when the commander of the area in which Deir Yassin was located, General Sir Horatius Murray returned to his office, he was told by a staff aide that his superior, General MacMillan, wished to speak to him on the phone. MacMillan told General Murray, 'There's been an affray amounting to a massacre at a place called Deir Yassin. It's in your divisional area so I am giving you a definite order. You will not interfere there in any event at any cost, you will leave it alone.'[7] Murray later recalled, 'I of course did what I was told.'

When questioned about Deir Yassin in parliament, the British Colonial Secretary announced, 'It must be realized that with the progressively reduced strength of our armed forces as our withdrawal proceeds, intervention in every instance of violence between Arab and Jew is not possible.'[8] The Colonial Secretary revealed that the High Commissioner had considered an air strike because a ground operation would probably have been 'very costly in British lives'. But before the air strike could be launched, 'it became known beyond the possibility of doubt that the members of the terrorist groups who originally occupied the village had left. In these circumstances it was decided not to proceed with the air operation.'

Since the British did not intervene, Meir Pa'il attempted to halt the massacre. He pleaded with the terrorist leaders who either couldn't or wouldn't stop their men (and women) from slaughtering the Arab civilians. According to Pa'il, the terrorists relented when the population of Givat Shaul arrived at Deir Yassin. 'They were just Jews, citizens who were ashamed. They began to shout and cry and the massacre was stopped.'

But the killing was not yet entirely over. As Meir Pa'il related, the Irgun and Stern Gang took some of the surviving men of Deir Yassin as prisoners. 'They were loaded into freight trucks and led in a victory parade like a Roman triumph through the Mahaneh Yehuda and Zichron Yosef quarters of Jerusalem.' The terrorist Yehuda Marinburg recalled the spectacle with pride. 'Our appearance encouraged the people very much and they received us with applause.'[9] Marinburg related that later, 'We executed the prisoners.' According to him there were eight prisoners; Meir Pa'il puts the figure at twenty-five. A soldier with Pa'il took photos but, like the official report made by the young Haganah officer, the photos are still kept secret by the Israeli government.

Meir Pa'il was not the only witness to the tragedy at Deir Yassin. On the morning after the attack Jacques de Reynier, a Swiss doctor working for the International Red Cross received a telephone call informing him of the massacre. De Reynier contacted the Jewish Agency and the Haganah, both of whom denied any knowledge of the atrocity and strongly urged de

Reynier not to make an investigation. According to de Reynier, the Jewish authorities were firm in their attitude. 'Not only did they refuse to help me but they also refused to be responsible for what they were sure would happen to me.'[10] But the Red Cross doctor would not be deterred. Dr de Reynier drove off, looking for the scene of the massacre.

The Red Cross physician grew apprehensive when he was stopped by two men armed with machine guns and large cutlasses in their belts. 'From their appearance,' de Reynier noted, 'I gathered that they must be the men I was looking for.' The Irgun terrorists were hostile to de Reynier and made threatening advances toward him. But then a very husky Irgun member pushed his comrades aside and took the Swiss doctor under his protection. 'He expressed his joy at seeing a member of the Red Cross because as he explained, its intervention had saved his life no less than three times when he was a prisoner in a German concentration camp.'

Dr de Reynier asked to see the Irgun commander. The Red Cross doctor waited anxiously for the arrival of the terrorist leader. 'At last he arrived, young, distinguished, and perfectly correct, but there was a peculiar glitter in his eyes, cold and cruel.' Dr de Reynier stressed that he had no desire to pass judgement on what had happened but he asked only to be able to look after the wounded and see to the burial of the dead. After a heated argument and the intercession of de Reynier's husky German-Jewish protector, the Irgun commander agreed to allow the doctor to remain.

As the Red Cross physician surveyed the remains of Deir Yassin, he was appalled. 'The first thing I saw were people running everywhere, rushing in and out of houses carrying Sten-guns, rifles, pistols and large ornate Arab knives. They seemed half mad. "We're still mopping up,"' de Reynier's German-Jewish friend explained.

According to de Reynier, '"the mopping up" had been done with machine-guns, then hand grenades. It had been finished off with knives, anyone could see that.' The Swiss doctor was particularly shocked by one of the terrorists who was holding a knife. 'A beautiful young girl with criminal eyes, showed me hers still dripping with blood, she displayed it like a trophy.'

The behaviour of the Zionist terrorists reminded the Red Cross doctor of his service during the Second World War. 'All I could think of was the SS troops I had seen in Athens.' The murdering continued in front of de Reynier's eyes. The Red Cross doctor saw, 'a young woman stab an elderly man and woman cowering on the doorstep of their hut.'

Dr de Reynier attempted to save the few survivors. Under a pile of bodies he found a little girl mutilated by a hand grenade but still alive. One of the terrorists tried to stop de Reynier taking the girl away but with the help of his friend, the Swiss doctor pushed him aside carrying his 'precious load'. Dr de Reynier eventually found two Arab women, one of them as old as a grandmother. They were hiding behind a heap of firewood where they had cringed without making a sound for twenty-four hours.

As for the murder victims, de Reynier attempted to arrange a decent burial. To the Red Cross physician, the condition of the bodies made it clear that they 'had been deliberately massacred in cold blood.' Indeed he saw the body of 'a woman who must have been eight months pregnant but the powder burns on her dress indicated that she had been shot point blank.'

Many of the survivors of Deir Yassin fled to Silwan, a nearby village. On 14 April, they were visited by a British team that included investigators and a doctor. The Arab civilians were interrogated and examined. The British, who had a translator with them from the Arab Women's Union, found great difficulty coaxing the female survivors into talking about the sexual assaults perpetrated on them. This reluctance on the part of the Palestinian women to speak is not difficult to understand in view of the Muslim attitude toward sexual matters. The investigation was further hampered by what the British called 'the hysterical state of the women who often broke down many times whilst the statement was being recorded.' But in their report the investigators concluded that, 'There is no doubt that many sexual atrocities were committed by the attacking Jews. Many young girls were raped and later slaughtered. Old women were also molested.'[11]

Rape would become a weapon used by the Zionists to terrorize the Arab civilians in Palestine. The rape of Arab women would be noted at several other Zionist atrocities after Deir Yassin. In view of the Arab sensitivity about rape, it is not surprising that many Palestinian civilians later remembered fear of rape as a prime motive for their exodus.

The chief British investigator also recorded other horror stories from the Arab survivors of Deir Yassin as they came out of their traumatized condition. 'Many infants were also butchered and killed. I also saw one old woman who gave her age as 104 who had been severely beaten about the head by rifle butts. Women had bracelets torn from their arms and rings from their fingers and parts of some of the women's ears were severed in order to remove earrings.' Looting would also become common practice for the Zionist forces in 1948.

After the massacre, Menachem Begin sent an order of the day to the attackers of Deir Yassin. 'Accept congratulations on this splendid act of conquest,' he announced. 'Tell the soldiers you have made history in Israel.'[12] The Irgun and Stern Gang held a joint press conference in order to publicize their victory at Deir Yassin. An Irgun representative told the newsmen, 'We intend to conquer and keep until we have the whole of Palestine and Trans-Jordan in a Greater Jewish state. This attack is the first step.'[13] The terrorists' public relations man was unapologetic about the massacre but he indicated that the Irgun and Stern Gang hoped to improve their methods so that in their future conquests fewer civilians would be killed.

But Deir Yassin had not been an undertaking of the terrorists alone. The Haganah had given permission for the attack and aided the terrorists in the conquest of the village. British intelligence was well aware of the involvement of the Haganah in the operation. On 20 April, the British government informed the United Nations Palestine Commission that the assault in Deir Yassin had been launched by the Irgun and Stern Gang 'with the knowledge of the Haganah'.[14] The British added, 'Haganah is unable to deny that it gave covering fire to the terrorists responsible for the outrage.'

The name Deir Yassin has for many years sparked bitter controversy. To this day, many Israelis, particularly those of the political right, deny that any massacre took place. In his memoirs the Irgun leader Menachem Begin asserts that, 'our officers and men wished to avoid a single unnecessary casualty in the Deir Yassin battle.'[15] Other terrorists have tried to excuse the high number of women and children killed by claiming that the village was defended by a large force of Iraqi troops who hid behind the civilians. Yehoshua Gorodentchik later gave his explanation of why his fellow terrorists killed so many innocent people. He asserted that some Arab civilians opened fire on those seeking to give them first aid and 'Arabs who dressed up as Arab women were also found, and so they started to shoot the women also.' Begin attributes the reports of an uncontrolled massacre to lies spread by 'Jew haters all over the world'.

But despite the continued withholding of important information on Deir Yassin by the Israeli government, the massacre must be considered one of the most thoroughly documented atrocities in history. The testimony of Meir Pa'il, Dr de Reynier and the British medical report, as well as the statements of numerous Arab survivors, all make it clear that a massacre undeniably did take place at Deir Yassin. The testimony of the terrorists themselves indicates that the massacre was premeditated by at least some of the attackers. Yitzhak Levi in his recent book was allowed to see but not quote the official reports on Deir Yassin. He contradicts Begin's version of the attack and asserts that published accounts of a premeditated massacre 'fit in with reports in the archives.'[16]

There still remains some question about certain details. Meir Pa'il recalls that at Deir Yassin, 'there was no rape or mutilation.' The former Haganah officer maintains, 'no bayonets or knives were used, the massacre was made with rifles and machine guns only.' But with regard to mutilation, there is substantial evidence that many of the victims at Deir Yassin were hacked to death with large knives, possibly after Meir Pa'il left the scene. The testimony of Mohammed Aref Sammour and other survivors indicating ghoulish conduct on the part of the Zionist terrorists is substantiated by Dr de Reynier and the British medical reports. Indeed, one of the terrorists, Reuben Grinberg, says that there was considerable torture and 'playing with the Arabs'[17] but he blames 'Yakki' and the Haganah people for the atrocities. Though it was common in 1948 for the

Haganah to torture Arab prisoners for information, it is probable that most, if not all of the atrocities at Deir Yassin were committed by the Irgun and Stern Gang.

The evidence for rape is not as strong as that for mutilation since the Arabs deny that any of their women had been sexually assaulted. But in view of the Muslim attitude toward rape their denials cannot be taken at face value.

The number of victims at Deir Yassin has also been disputed. The testimony of both Dr de Reynier and Meir Pa'il suggests that the generally accepted figure of 250 dead is correct. Several authors support Begin's claim of 116 Arab fatalities at Deir Yassin but this figure seems too low. Indeed, at the previously mentioned news conference on 11 April 1948, the Irgun spokesman cited Arab casualties as '200 killed, approximately half of them being women and children.'[18]

An even more significant controversy surrounding Deir Yassin concerns the effect of the massacre on the subsequent exodus of the Palestinians. Some observers tend to exaggerate its significance by claiming that Deir Yassin was the principal cause of the Palestinian exodus, thus ignoring the fact that most Palestinians did not leave until they were intimidated or forced to depart by the Zionists. Others tend to play down the effect of the massacre as a cause of the Arab flight. The historian and witness to Deir Yassin, Meir Pa'il, points out that the inhabitants of the surrounding region did not flee in panic immediately after the massacre. According to Pa'il the people of this region did not leave until 'the capture of these hostile Arab villages and the expulsion of the inhabitants.'

But the news of Deir Yassin was spread all over Palestine by radio and had its greatest effect in villages many miles away from the scene of the atrocity. Few Palestinians fled immediately. However, the fear generated by the news of the massacre made many Arab peasants vulnerable to intimidation when their village was invaded by Zionist forces. But it was in the Arab urban communities in Haifa and Jaffa that the first significant effect of Deir Yassin was felt.

CHAPTER IV

The Haifa Tragedy

The shuks in Haifa are deserted and the bazaars looted, the houses closed... It is another exodus, but the same desolation.

Arthur Koestler, 6 June 1948

'A group of Arab rebels left Deir Yassin today without expressing remorse for the abominable crimes which they had committed against their own people.'[1] With this bizarre announcement on the morning of 12 April, Haganah Radio made its first comment on the Deir Yassin massacre, adding that in order to protect property Haganah forces were compelled to enter Deir Yassin as soon as the 'Arab rebels' had left. But the Jewish Agency was not able to convince anyone with its initial cover story that the Arabs themselves were guilty of the slaughter perpetrated by the Irgun and Stern Gang terrorists. Several hours after the first Haganah Radio broadcast, the Jewish Agency issued a statement which acknowledged that 'dissident Jewish organizations' were responsible for the 'savage and barbaric' Deir Yassin massacre. The Jewish Agency cabled to King Abdullah apologizing for the crime.

The Arabs did not accept the apology, pointing out that terrorist groups could not have acted without the prior knowledge of the Jewish community leadership. When an American diplomat in Jerusalem went to see Hussein Khalidi of the Arab Higher Executive, he found him trembling with rage comparing the attacks to the 'worst Nazi tactics'.[2] For several days Arab radio stations broadcast all the gruesome details of the crime. Radio Cairo informed its listeners that by the Deir Yassin massacre the Zionists were 'thus gradually revealing their announced determination to exterminate the Arabs.'[3] Radio Damascus claimed that such Jewish crimes, 'are but what should be expected. In fact, we should expect more than this.'

THE HAIFA TRAGEDY

The effect of these radio broadcasts from the Arab capitals and from the Jewish Arabic-language stations was to devastate totally the morale of the Palestinians. The Arab governments expected that accounts about Deir Yassin would stiffen the resolve of the Palestinians, but instead they became convinced of the inability of their own forces to protect them from a similar massacre. Which Arab town or village would be next? In Akbara, a tiny Galilee hamlet, Mustafa Ahmad Ma'ari heard the broadcasts. As he later recalled, the tragic news encouraged the people of his village to arm themselves, '. . . but it also scared us.' Not far away in the village of Ein Zeitun, a retired policeman, Ahmad Hussain Harrid and his kinsmen also heard the broadcasts, 'Although we continued to ignore the Jewish threat, we were distressed about the massacre at Deir Yassin.'

In the port city of Haifa, during April 1948, a retired Yale professor Millar Burrows and his wife were staying at a hotel waiting for a ship that would take them away from war-torn Palestine. A noted scholar and Middle East expert, Burrows was more than a little apprehensive in view of the tension that seemed to mount every day. The ship for which he and his wife were waiting could not come into port since the dock space in Haifa was being used by the departing British army. The troops were anxious to leave Palestine before the British mandate terminated on 15 May. One day as he came out of his Haifa hotel, Burrows noticed a group of Arab boys sitting in front of a radio listening to the news about Deir Yassin. 'I shall never forget the serious worried look on their faces,' he later remembered.[4]

Even before Deir Yassin, the tension had been growing in the port city of Haifa which served as a terminus for Palestine's principal oil pipeline. With its thriving commerce and large population, Haifa ranked after Jerusalem as a major prize in the Arab–Israeli dispute. The side that lost the port city would have great difficulty creating an economically viable state. The Jews, however, had certain advantages. They constituted 55 per cent of the city's population of 146,000 and lived mainly on Mount Carmel, overlooking the Arab quarter and the approaches to the city. The Jews were solidly united. The Arab community was divided between Christians and Muslims. A great deal of distrust also existed between the community leadership in Haifa and the Arab Higher Committee because the city had long been a stronghold of the opponents of the Grand Mufti.

As soon as street fighting broke out in November 1947, the Jewish and Arab communities began a process of segregation. A local Arab National Committee was formed to supervise most of the usual government functions in the Arab sections of the city. The Arab military forces in Haifa were led by Muhammad Hamad al-Huneiti, a former Arab Legion officer who served with great distinction until he was killed on 18 March, while leading an important supply convoy from Lebanon. The failure of this and other convoys to get through greatly weakened the ability of the Arabs in Haifa to defend their position.

During the months after the adoption of the United Nations partition resolution thousands of Arabs left Haifa. There were various reasons for this early exodus. Yosef Varshitz, a Haganah expert on the Arabs who was in Haifa during this period believed that many people left since, 'there was nothing for them to do, a lot of work had stopped in many places and people who still had work sent their women and children away to Lebanon, Syria and other places because there was constant shooting.'[5]

There was in fact a great deal of violence in the Haifa area. The Greek Catholic Archbishop of Galilee who resided in Haifa indicated that in addition to Deir Yassin, there were several other incidents that had frightened the Arab civilians. He mentioned, 'the brutal throwing of bombs at a large group of innocent Arab workmen assembled at the outer gates of the refineries near Haifa, the dastardly night attack on Balad al-Sheikh village in the vicinity of Haifa, and other similar onslaughts.'[6]

Much of the violence in Haifa took the form of continual reprisals and counter-reprisals. After the Irgun wounded some Arab labourers in the oil refineries, the Arabs who comprised 80 per cent of the refinery work-force, rioted and killed thirty-nine Jewish workers.

The Haganah launched a 'punitive sortie' against Balad al-

Sheikh,[7] a village near Haifa. The massacre of civilians at Balad al-Sheikh, along with the other violent incidents, had a devastating impact on the resolve of the Arab population of the port city.

The Zionist campaign of psychological warfare was another major factor encouraging the Arab exodus in the early months of the war. Haganah Radio's clandestine transmissions in Arabic used a variety of techniques to undermine the morale of the Palestinian Arabs and persuade them that it was not safe for them to remain in their homes. It is significant that the Haganah's transmitter for its Arabic broadcasts was stronger than the transmitter it used for its Hebrew language service. The Zionist radio station placed greater importance on its campaign of psychological warfare against the Arabs than its supposedly primary mission to keep its own people informed.

The Jewish broadcasts in Arabic frequently warned the Palestinians that there were traitors in their communities gathering intelligence for the Haganah. On 25 March, the Arabs of Palestine were cautioned about turncoats who, 'spy on their own people and give information on the location of military stores.'[8] At other times, in what amounted to an almost comic opera performance, the Haganah station sent 'secret messages' in Arabic which the Palestinians were supposed to believe were intended for quislings in their midst. This type of propaganda was designed to make the Palestinians feel unsafe and that they could trust no one, even in their own town or neighbourhood.

Palestinian insecurity was exacerbated by the 'Arab Section' of the Haganah, which consisted of Arabic-speaking Middle Eastern Jews who wore Arab clothes that enabled them to move freely through Palestinian communities. They spread rumours and picked up useful intelligence, including facts that could be quickly broadcast in Arabic, so as to increase Palestinian fears that they were surrounded by spies.

Another common Zionist propaganda line was to try to convince the Arabs that they were in danger from their own military forces. On 2 March, Haganah Radio broadcasting in Arabic reported, 'looting committed by people encouraged to satisfy their inclinations thanks to having firearms in their hands.'⁹ Several days later the Arabs of Palestine were informed that, 'theft has spread to an unprecedented degree in Jerusalem.' A particular effort was made to sow discord between the Palestinians and the Arab volunteers who had come to assist them. The behaviour of the members of the Arab Liberation Army left much to be desired, but their tendency for misconduct was greatly exaggerated by Zionist propaganda. 'Iraqi and Syrian fighters don't mind if they destroy all Palestine,' Haganah Radio claimed. Supposedly their real goal was, 'to destroy as many homes and kill as many people as possible.' In view of the conduct of the ALA soldiers, the Palestinians were advised to follow the lead of the other Arabs who had already fled the country. Thus Haganah Radio reported that in Azoun and Miska, the population was evacuating because 'the Arab gangs were not attacking the Jews but their own Arab brothers.' (Jewish radio broadcasts invariably referred to their armed opponents as 'Arab gangs'.)

Haganah Radio constantly reminded the Palestinians that they had been deserted by their leaders and professional people. Here again the Jewish radio stations exaggerated a genuine problem for the Palestinians. Why should ordinary Arabs stay and fight when the community leaders had deserted them? Haganah Radio reported that many Arab physicians had fled to neighbouring countries, 'leaving their friends when they were in need.'[10] The Zionist broadcasts tried to convince the Palestinians that there was a particular need for doctors because the country faced the danger of severe epidemics including cholera and typhoid. Free Hebrew Radio, the Stern Gang's station, also cautioned its Arabic listeners 'to inoculate themselves against typhoid'[11] which it implied was being carried by ALA volunteers from Syria and Iraq.

Arab radio stations tried to counteract Zionist propaganda by portraying an optimistic picture of the Palestinian military situation. On 27 February, Cairo Radio announced, 'the Arab defenders of Haifa have been so strengthened that they will move from the defensive to the offensive.' It would be six weeks, however, before the Arabs of Haifa were ready to gamble on a near hopeless offensive.

On 13 April, there was a major escalation of fighting in the port city. According to British Consul-General Cyril Marriott, the Arabs launched an offensive the object of which was, 'to prevent the Jews from gaining complete domination of Haifa.'[12] But the Arabs lacked the leadership, experienced personnel or organization to mount a successful attack. They were unable to advance anywhere in the city, while expending much more of their strength than their adversaries.

The increased combat put General Hugh Stockwell, the British commander in Haifa, in a difficult position. It was his responsibility to prevent the Arab–Jewish conflict from interfering with the departure of the British through the port. As the fighting became more intense Stockwell decided to remove his forces from the residential and business area of the city and concentrate his troops near the dock facilities that were essential for the British evacuation from Palestine. He also decided to make an effort to bring about a rapid decision in the fighting.

It was British policy in Palestine to favour the stronger side in each town, in the hope that this was the best way of bringing about a speedy conclusion of the hostilities. In Haifa, the Jews were clearly stronger than the Arabs. Besides, Haifa had been assigned to the Jewish state under the partition resolution. On 18 April, therefore, General Stockwell informed the leaders of the Jewish community of his intention to evacuate most of the city, but he failed to give the Arabs any advance notice. As the British general expected, as soon as his troops left the key strategic positions in Haifa, Haganah forces were ready to occupy these strongpoints. With this decisive advantage, the Haganah, with some help from the Irgun, was able to gain complete control of the city by 22 April, only forty-eight hours after their offensive had begun.

During the fighting, the flow of civilians out of Haifa became a torrent. One reason for this was the unreliability of the Arab forces as both the commander in the city and his chief deputy fled during the battle. The cowardice of the military leadership affected the morale of not only the soldiers, but also of the Palestinian civilian population. But the chief reason for the exodus was the Haganah's campaign of psychological warfare, which greatly accelerated as the fighting increased.

Throughout the battle, a variety of methods was used to

encourage the Arabs to leave Haifa. The pro-Zionist author Arthur Koestler who was in the city during the war wrote that, 'Haganah was using not only its radio station but its loudspeaker vans which blurted their sinister news from the vicinity of the Arab shuks [markets].'[13] According to Koestler the sound-trucks warned the Arabs, 'to send their women and children away,' promising them, 'safe conduct and escort to Arab territory and hinted terrible consequences if their warning was disregarded.'

Leo Heiman, a Haganah officer, wrote honestly about the methods used by the Jews. According to him the Haganah brought up jeeps with loudspeakers that broadcast recorded 'horror sounds'. These included 'shrieks, wails and anguished moans of Arab women, the wail of sirens and the clang of fire-alarm bells, interrupted by a sepulchral voice calling out in Arabic: Save your souls all ye faithful! Flee for your lives.'[14] According to Heiman, Haganah loudspeakers warned the Arabs that the Jews were using poison gas and atomic weapons. In view of what had recently taken place at Deir Yassin, the Arabs took these warnings seriously. Indeed, the Irgun leader Menachem Begin relates that many of the Arab civilians were shouting 'Deir Yassin! Deir Yassin!' as they fled the city.

The Zionist sound-tracks and radio broadcasts were augmented by Davidka mortars which hurled sixty pounds of explosive at high speed about three hundred yards. Though very inaccurate and of little military value, the Davidka was useful in densely populated areas, particularly in view of its loud noise that horrified Arab civilians. 'Barrel-bombs' were also useful against civilians. These were barrels, casks and metal drums filled with a mixture of explosives and fuel oil, and fitted with two old rubber tyres containing the detonating fuse. These devices were then rolled down the sharply sloping alleys of the Arab sections of Haifa and other cities until they crashed into walls and doorways making 'an inferno of raging flames and endless explosions'. In addition to the Davidka mortar and barrel-bombs, the Zionist forces, according to Arthur Koestler, employed the 'ruthless dynamiting of block after block of bazaars and blind alleys until the panic had reached sufficient dimensions to end all resistance.'

THE HAIFA TRAGEDY

Abu Moussa, a policeman in Haifa, recalled the effect of the Jewish attack on Arab civilians. 'People could not bear this shelling for more than three continuous days.'[15] He remembers seeing 'people running through the streets unconsciously.' A British officer, Colonel John Waddy, also recalled the effect of the attack on Arab civilians: 'As the Jewish action against the Haifa Old Town stepped up from acts of terrorism to mortaring, then many of the Arabs started to evacuate the town, as indeed the Jews wanted them to do.'[16]

A disturbing aspect of Zionist military operations in Haifa and elsewhere in Palestine was the crimes committed by Jewish soldiers against Christian churches and other religious facilities. Various denominations filed numerous reports that their buildings had been desecrated. Many of these claims were verified by American, British and United Nations officials. On 21 April, Zionist soldiers expelled 'the Sisters of Saint Ann in Haifa with the shooting of bullets and grenades at the door of the house.'[17] Several days later the Vatican reported, 'the expulsion of the Sisters of Saint Charles from their hospital in Haifa.' The Catholics were outraged that many religious artefacts were covered with 'human dirt' and 'in the case of the Hospice of Terra Sancta in Haifa, a definite sign of particular hatred made to our sign of redemption.'

In view of the Zionist campaign of psychological warfare and terror tactics, the exodus of the Arab population from Haifa seems inevitable. Indeed, the Zionist historian Jon Kimche toured the Arab quarter in Haifa where he saw evidence that the civilian population had been terrorized into fleeing. 'The Arabs left in great panic,' Kimche wrote. 'I walked later through the shuks [markets] and saw the state of disorder in which they left their homes, often not bothering to pick up silver and valuables.'[18]

It has been suggested that the Haifa civilians were encouraged to leave by Arab propaganda. But in the days preceding the battle and during the fighting, the Arab leadership made every effort to encourage the Palestinians to remain in their homes. For example, Beirut Radio announced, 'no post shall be given to a foreigner who enters the Lebanon without the approved labour permit.'[19] The Lebanese station made it clear that able-bodied men would be returned to Palestine, 'in compliance with the request of the [Palestinian] Arab authorities.' Other governments including Syria and Jordan cooperated with the AHC effort to discourage the exodus.

The Palestinian press frequently carried stories that violently criticized those who fled the country. On 30 March, the Palestinian newspaper *al-Sha'ab* referred to the 'disgraceful exodus' of those who were quitting their villages 'bag and baggage'. Other stories referred to the refugees as a 'fifth column' and 'traitors'.

Palestinian radio stations urged the Arab population to remain at home. On 30 March, the AHC asked, 'All Arab employees in Palestine to continue at their posts and to take care of all furniture, property and documents entrusted to them.' The next day the AHC announced that it planned to move its headquarters to Palestine in order to prepare for the return of the Grand Mufti into his homeland. On 22 April, while the battle in Haifa was still raging, the Palestinian newspaper *al-Difa'a* carried a statement by the AHC fervently asking its readers to be patient and bear up and hold their ground, since 'The duty of the defence of the Holy Land rests upon us the people of Palestine first and foremost.'

Perhaps the bluntest appeal to the Palestinians to remain in their homes came from Fawzi al-Kaukji, head of the ALA, which consisted of volunteers from Syria, Iraq, and other Arab countries who had come to the aid of the Palestinians. Kaukji announced that 'cowards who desert their homes'[20] must be stopped because 'they contribute to the spreading of panic and chaos.' He recommended that 'everyone keep calm and be cautious of battle reports spread by enemies who want to create panic among the population,' and threatened to have no mercy with those who fled their homes. 'I shall even inflict the death penalty when security measures necessitate such a step.'

The Arab governments endorsed these stern measures because they believed that there was a Zionist plan to expel the Palestinians from their homeland and they wished to do everything possible to stop such a scheme. At the United Nations on 22 April, the Syrian representative cited 'current reports as evidence of a Jewish policy of either exterminating or driving out the Arabs in the area of the proposed Jewish state.'[21] On the same day British Ambassador Campbell in Cairo visited the head of the Arab League, Pasha Azzam, who said that he was convinced that there was 'a Jewish military plan designed to terrorize the Arab population inside the Jewish state so that by 15 May, they would be relieved of having to deal with a fifth column.' All the evidence suggests that the Arab belief that the Zionists were trying to expel the Palestinians was well founded considering the campaign of psychological warfare and intimidation that was being carried on throughout Palestine. The Arab governments hoped that the Palestinians themselves could defeat the Zionists and thwart their design, but this did not happen in Haifa.

In view of the Jewish victory in Haifa, a group of notables calling themselves the Arab Emergency Committee came to see General Stockwell. The delegation, which included the lawyer Elias Koussa, the banker Farid Sa'ad and the businessman Victor Khayat, handed the British general a memorandum which protested against the withdrawal of his troops from most of the city since, 'it was a flagrant violation of the declared policy of the British government to be responsible for the maintenance of order and peace.' They asked Stockwell if he would help roll back the Haganah offensive or at least allow Arab reinforcements to enter the city.

Stockwell took a firm stand. 'In the interest of humanity, I have issued orders that no reinforcements shall enter the city,' he told the Arab delegation.[22] Nor would he take any action against the Jews. 'I am not prepared to sacrifice the lives of British soldiers in this situation. My only suggestion to you is to begin negotiations with the Jews for a truce.'

Having satisfied themselves that there was no alternative the Arab delegation asked to see the Jewish terms. Stockwell slowly read the conditions. The Jews demanded complete Haganah control of Haifa, the surrender of all weapons and an immediate curfew in the Arab sections of the city. But the Palestinians were promised equal rights under Jewish rule. After hearing the terms, the Arab delegation departed, but at General Stockwell's request they agreed to meet with a delegation of Jews at the town hall at 4 p.m.

Elias Koussa proceeded to the Syrian Consulate from where he sent several telegrams to Damascus describing the flight of the Arab population from Haifa and the Jewish truce terms. Despite repeated requests for instructions Koussa received no reply.

At the appointed hour, the Arab committee entered the town hall where they met the Jewish delegation headed by Shabtai Levy, the Mayor of Haifa. At the outset, there was a great deal of cordiality as the two delegations greeted each other as old friends. General Stockwell assumed the chair as 'intermediary and unbiased President' of the meeting. Several other British officials attended, including Consul-General Cyril Marriott. A considerable amount of discussion took place, with the Jews making several changes in the truce terms at the request of General Stockwell.

With tears in his eyes, Shabtai Levy expressed the hope that those Arabs who had not already fled would stay in the city. Most of the conference participants were impressed with his sincerity although Consul-General Marriott noted that Mayor Levy 'regrets the violence now being adopted by his fellow Jews to fulfil the prayer with which he no doubt concludes all his prayers "Tomorrow in Jerusalem".'[23]*

As was inevitable, there was a great deal of conflict at the meeting. At one point Koussa snapped, 'One round has been lost but there will be others,' – a remark not appreciated by either the Jews or the British. General Stockwell who was becoming impatient, warned the Arabs, 'If you don't sign this truce, I shall not be responsible if three or four hundred more of you are killed by tomorrow.' Victor Khayat attempted to smooth ruffled feathers by suggesting that an agreement could be reached since, 'We are old friends.'

At 5.15 p.m., the Arabs asked for a twenty-four hour delay before signing the truce so that they could consult on the provisions which seemed very harsh to them. The Jews demanded that the Arabs sign immediately but at General

---

*Marriott's acid comments in his reports about both the Jewish and Arab participants at the conference reflect the 'plague on both your houses' attitude of most British officials in Palestine.

THE HAIFA TRAGEDY

Stockwell's insistence, they agreed to adjourn until 7 p.m. at the latest.

During the recess, Koussa sent several more frantic telegrams to Damascus, in which he described the crisis and the growing Arab exodus from the city. But once again he received no reply. He later explained that the Syrians failed to reply because they were, 'simply stunned by the gigantic magnitude of the flight which they did not foresee and which defied their ability to tackle.'[24] Although they present no evidence, Israeli historians reject Koussa's story, claiming that he must have received a message from Damascus ordering him to reject the truce.

But on 22 April, the British Ambassador in Damascus had a meeting with President Kuwatly who showed him a batch of telegrams which the Syrian leader had received from Haifa. The President told Ambassador Brosmead, 'Immediate instructions are asked for in view of the meeting between the Arab delegation, the British commander and the Jewish representatives.'[25] Kuwatly did not know what to reply. He told Brosmead, 'I am bewildered at the conditions of the truce which demand the delivery of arms to the Jews by the Arabs. I don't know what instructions to send. What do you suggest?' The Ambassador advised Kuwatly not to take any action, which is what happened.

Meanwhile Koussa and his associates had to make their decision on their own. Further resistance was impossible in view of General Stockwell's warning. Even if they accepted the truce, there was no guarantee that the Arab population would be safe. The Arab delegation could still hear gunfire around them. The American Consul in Haifa, Aubrey Lippincott, reported to Washington:

> Considerable Jewish looting in evacuated Arab areas. Two churches desecrated. Clinic stripped of equipment and furnishing demolished. Haganah claims that looting stopped with the imprisonment of forty Jewish looters. Constant visitors to Consulate, among them nuns and priests, claim looting continues.[26]

Despite Jewish promises that there would be no reprisals if they signed the truce, the Arab leaders in Haifa decided that it was safest not to sign the truce but to ask for British help to evacuate those civilians who wished to leave the city.

The conference at the town hall was resumed at 7.15 p.m. The members of the Emergency Committee made it clear that they would not sign the truce. General Stockwell called their action 'a foolish decision'. Mayor Levy begged them to reconsider. But the Arab leaders stood firm; they asked General Stockwell for assistance to effect the evacuation. At the end of the meeting the Arabs rose from their chairs, their faces tormented.

The next morning at 11 a.m., a joint Arab–Jewish committee under the chairmanship of Mayor Levy met to consider the evacuation problem. Most of the Arab population had already fled but an effort would be made to arrange an orderly evacuation for those who remained and wished to leave. Many of the Jewish civilian and military leaders opposed the evacuation of those Arabs who were still in the port city. The Haganah had driven out the majority of Arabs, but most Jews feared the consequences if the entire Arab community left the city. Aubrey Lippincott explained to the State Department why the Jews opposed the evacuation of the remaining Palestinians. He wrote that the Jewish leaders wanted the remaining Arabs to stay for 'political reasons in order to show democratic treatment,' and because, 'they will also need them for labour.'[27]

Despite their impressive military showing, the Jews of Palestine who had not yet established their own state were still highly sensitive about foreign opinion. They wanted support from the United States, the rapid departure of the British and the neutrality of the Arab states. Although they were anxious to rid themselves of the remaining Palestinians, the Jews feared the international reaction if the entire city was emptied of Arabs. Later, after the United States had recognized the Jewish state, the Arab nations had made their half-hearted military commitment, the British had departed and the United Nations had proven impotent, the Israelis would engage in a policy of unlimited expulsion of the Arab population, particularly in the Negev, Lydda–Ramle and, during Operation Hiram, in central Galilee. But in April they wanted some Arabs to remain in Haifa out of deference to world public opinion.

Besides, Lippincott was correct when he suggested that the

Jews still needed at least some Arab labour. After they took over the city, the Jewish Agency had an immediate need for enough Arab labourers to operate Haifa's oil refineries and port facilities that were essential to the Zionist war effort. During the crisis, Mr Richard Dix, the British director of the Consolidated Refineries in Haifa, was approached by several Jewish representatives who stressed the need to keep the refineries operating. Mr Dix told his Jewish visitors that he could keep the refineries operating, 'if an appreciable number of trained Arab operatives returned to work.'[28]

After the battle, Haganah Radio made a dramatic change in its propaganda line. Instead of urging the Palestinians to leave Haifa, the Jews now tried to persuade the remaining Arabs to stay in the city. On 23 April, the Jewish station announced, 'It is in the real interest of Haifa for its citizens to go on with their work.' Several days later a Haganah broadcast proclaimed, 'Jewish workers are replacing Arab workers until the latter return.' But the Jewish Agency was not happy about this since every man was needed for the army. On 25 April, Marriott reported that, 'whilst there still was an exodus of Arabs from Haifa,'[29] he was assured by Jewish leaders, 'with considerable influence over Arab labour that by the beginning of May, there will be more labour available here than there has been for several months.' In order to achieve this goal, the Jewish Agency used loudspeakers and radio announcements to discourage the Arabs from evacuating the city by boat or trucks under British protection.

Despite the Passover holiday, the rabbinical authorities gave permission for Jewish bakers to operate so that they could feed the hungry Arab population. On 26 April, the *Palestine Post* reported that in Haifa, 'peace and order began to return when two Jewish liaison offices were set up in the Arab section and Arabs were instructed by loudspeaker vans to report any cases of looting.' In the Jewish areas, the Haganah warned the population not to loot the deserted Arab businesses or homes, as this would frighten the remaining Palestinians. There continued to be a great deal of looting, however, particularly by the Irgun. But the Jewish Agency's efforts to convince the Arabs to remain was real, though hardly altruistic.

The tiny Palestine communist party also opposed the evacuation. The only political party open to both Jews and Arabs, the communists saw the evacuation under the protection of the British army as a plot between Jewish and Arab reactionaries acting in co-operation with the British imperialists. Tawfik Toubi, a young Arab communist stood in the centre of town distributing leaflets that proclaimed, 'Don't go away! Reaction and Imperialism want you to leave.'[30] He later recalled, 'I watched my friends and brothers leaving but I worked on the conviction that we should not leave our homeland.'

Despite the efforts of the Jewish Agency and the communists, about 6,000 Arab civilians were evacuated from Haifa by the British. On 25 April, the *New York Times* reported, 'The Arab population was being moved across the bay to Acre by British army landing craft and small boats, and plans were being made to move other thousands by British army trucks overland to Nazareth, neighbouring Lebanon and Nablus in the Arabs' so-called "triangle of strength" in central Palestine.' On the same day, according to the *Palestine Post*, 'the harbour area has been crowded with Arabs, men, women and children – poised for flight. They sleep beside their bundles and odd pieces of furniture that they manage to bring along by such transport as they could find.' While in the city, Arabs were 'hurrying about moving their belongings, staggering under the heavy loads of household goods.' Most of the Arabs were panic-stricken.

According to Abu Moussa, a police soldier in Haifa, the people, 'slept on the streets of the harbour for three days in the cold and rain. It was raining heavily for the first time in April in Haifa. People were sleeping in this rain without any cover.'[31] The sight of the refugees made an indelible impression on the young policeman. 'Some of them were barefoot and some of the women were without enough clothes to cover them. They left everything behind even their shoes. They were in a horrifying condition. Even now I feel a shudder in my body when I remember that scene.'

When asked why the people had left their homes, Moussa denied that they were following the orders of their leaders. He believed that they simply fled to save their lives. 'It makes no sense that someone leaves his money, his business, his house and his land without pressure and a serious threat against his life and the life of his family.'

According to General Stockwell, 'fear of the Jews had been building up for a considerable amount of time. The Arabs realized the strength of the Jews and they were of course worried that the Jews would overrun their houses and burn them and kill their children and wives. I think they just felt that this was the time to go and get to hell out of it as fast as they could.'[32]

General Stockwell had vivid memories of the panic of the Haifa Arabs. 'I was just standing in the port one day when a chap came in a magnificent motor car. He just jumped out of it and jumped into a little row boat and pushed off. I said, "What about your car?" He said, "I don't want it, it's yours."'

Not all of the refugees fled by boat. Some attempted to reach the Lebanese border by land since it was only about twenty miles away. Colonel John Waddy witnessed the stream of refugees heading north. 'They started out by private car and lorry and bus and one saw them loaded up with all sorts of their household belongings, carpets, mattresses, cooking material, all hanging on to the buses and trucks.'[33] The refugees who fled by land were just as panic-stricken as those who escaped by sea.

Major R. D. Wilson saw that the Arab population surging out of the town had good cause to be afraid. 'While they were in full flight they were engaged by the advance Jewish post which inflicted a number of casualties,' the British officer later recalled.[34] Royal marines, army units and British police tried to calm the terrorized Arab civilians but some of them were killed in the process. The Royal Marines 'had three officers wounded by Jewish fire as they sought to control the stream of refugees,' according to Wilson. Supervising the evacuation proved to be a difficult assignment for the British since they had to control the crowds of refugees, deal with Jewish snipers and whenever possible prevent looting. Among those wounded by Jewish snipers was the commander of the 1st Battalion of the Coldstream Guards.

It is not clear whether the snipers were acting under orders or were simply Jewish soldiers who could not resist firing at the refugees. Even after they left Haifa, the Palestinian civilians were not out of danger since as Wilson relates, they 'were open to attack by Jews on the way so whenever practicable their convoys were afforded military protection as far as the frontier.'

Those who reached Lebanon found that food, clothing and housing had been arranged in the port cities of Sidon and Tyre. Others who reached Jordan on the West Bank were less fortunate since few facilities were provided. But the vast majority of the refugees from Haifa had fled on their own to neighbouring towns where they once again found themselves in a war zone. In particular, the thousands who fled to Acre would soon experience another Haganah assault. By 25 April, the British reported to the United Nations Palestine Commission that in Haifa, 'the Arabs especially in the poorer quarters were continuing to evacuate but the general exodus had almost ceased.'[35] Only about 4,000 Arabs remained out of a community that once numbered 70,000.

At about the same time the British were reporting to the UN Palestine Commission, Golda Meir was visiting Haifa. She later briefed her fellow members of the Jewish Agency Executive about conditions in the city. Meir expressed considerable sympathy for the Arabs of Haifa, whom she compared to the Jews of Eastern Europe during the Second World War. She estimated that there were about '3–4,000' Arabs left in the city.

Meir gave a number of reasons for the exodus from Haifa. First she claimed that the Palestinians had been ordered by their leaders to leave but she offered no proof for this assertion. Closer to the truth is her report that many had fled because 'the Arabs were frightened by Deir Yassin and the shelling of Haifa.'[36] The Mapai leader blamed the Irgun for looting the area under their control. 'Not a thread was left in any of the houses, everything was sold on the spot.'

Meir was greatly concerned about the effects of the Palestinian exodus from Haifa on the economic life of this key industrial city. According to her, Arab labour was desperately needed in Haifa. 'There are no Arab workers at the port, oil refineries or the railroad station.' Labour was required in other areas as well. 'There is a serious problem with the services that must be maintained. People are needed at the port, telegraph, etc.' Meir was very annoyed by the attitude of the newly arrived

Jewish immigrants released from British detention camps on Cyprus because they refused to work in the reconstruction of the city 'unless they are paid 3.5 Palestinian pounds per day' despite the fact that 'We suffer from a lack of workers in the city.' Various categories of Jewish men not suited for front-line duty were being used to work in Haifa but they were not numerous enough. Meir noted, 'According to [the local Jewish leader] Abu Hushi, 2–3,000 Arab workers must be brought into the oil refineries otherwise production will cease.' Meir urged a policy of moderation toward the Arabs in Haifa to prevent a further exodus.

Largely for economic reasons, Golda Meir recommended that the remaining Arabs be allowed to stay in Haifa. But members of the newly formed left-wing Zionist Mapam party opposed the expulsion of the Palestinians because of their ideological commitment to a binational state in which Jews would share power with Arabs. There is reason to doubt the sincerity of the Mapam's opposition to the removal of the Palestinians. (Many of the Jewish commanders who expelled Arab civilians were members of Mapam. Also many left-wing kibbutzim were established on vacated Arab land, often within weeks of the expulsion.) However, Aharon Cohen, the Mapam expert on Arab Affairs, was genuinely concerned about the fate of the Palestinians in Haifa and on 28 April, he received a report from the city.

> The order by the Haganah to refrain from looting was issued when most of the looting was already over. Irgun people organized looting in Wadi–Nisnas which was only stopped by an ultimatum by the Haganah. Severe restrictions have been imposed on the Arab population with respect to freedom of the press, supply of electricity, etc. A lot of bitterness can be felt among the left-wing Arabs who in contrast to the Arab nationalists did not want to leave the city. They say that not enough was done by the Jewish authorities in order to convince the Arabs not to leave. The situation in which 150,000 of 350,000–400,000 Arabs in the Jewish state are now refugees may become a turning-point in the conflict. Palestinian Arabs who were not hostile may now become the main source of hostility.[37]

The last week in April was indeed to be a turning-point in the war as feared by the left-wing Zionists. As the conflict deepened, the policy of expelling Arabs would become more open and brutal. On 30 April Moshe Dayan told an American diplomat, 'the state must be homogenous, the less Arabs the better.'[38] During this period, however, Dayan was a low-ranking if somewhat indiscreet professional soldier. What counted was the attitude of Ben-Gurion who served as both Prime Minister and Minister of Defence. On 1 May, Ben-Gurion visited Haifa 'What a beautiful sight,'[39] he exclaimed as he saw some Arabs leaving the city. Soon after, the Zionist leader spoke to a group of Jewish notables in the city, telling them, 'It is not our duty to see to it that the Arabs return.' When Ben-Gurion asked to see Abu Hushi, the chief Mapai functionary in the city, he was told that he was busy trying to convince the remaining Arabs in Haifa to stay. The Prime Minister asked, 'Doesn't he have anything better to do?'[40] Everyone around Ben-Gurion understood his meaning. From then on, the short-lived Zionist effort to persuade the Arabs to stay in Haifa came to an end.

The following month on 6 June, Belchor Shitrit, the Minister of Minorities, visited Haifa. He had a meeting at the town hall with the Jewish leaders. Six weeks before they had asked the Arabs to stay but now the mood was quite different. Shitrit (who was far more liberal on the Arab question than his fellow ministers) spoke of the possible return of the Palestinians to the city. But the local Jewish leaders protested, 'There are no sentiments in war' making it clear, 'We have no interest in their returning.'[41] Even Shabtai Levy who had begged the Arabs to stay had a change of heart.

Much has been made of the Arab flight from Haifa by Zionist historians who maintain that it proves that there was an Arab plot to evacuate Palestine and a Jewish effort to prevent the exodus. The facts do not support either claim. For political and economic reasons the Jewish Agency tried to prevent the British-sponsored evacuation of a few thousand Arabs in Haifa after the overwhelming majority had already fled, many as a result of Zionist psychological warfare and terrorist tactics. Within a few months when the political and economic situation had changed, the new Jewish state would prevent the return of refugees to Haifa and would encourage those who had remained to leave.

The Haifa Arab Emergency Committee decided to reject the Jewish truce offer, primarily because of fears for the safety of their people. Commenting on the situation, the Israeli Josef Varshitz who was in Haifa at the time noted, 'There was a lot of shooting and as in any war a little looting. So although the Haganah was telling people not to go away, I can understand why they did.'

The British Consul Marriott reported to his government that General Stockwell's intervention, 'saved the Arabs from massacre.' The American Consul Lippincott spoke on 29 April, to Farid Sa'ad, a member of the committee that had negotiated with the Jews.

> Questioned about the Arab exodus, Sa'ad said that no order had been given to the Arab population telling them to leave. He said that those members of the National Committee who remained in Haifa were telling people to use their own judgement as to whether they should stay or leave. People were in a panic after the unexpectedly easy Jewish victory. Subsequent Jewish looting and attacks on refugees had simply added to the panic.[42]

The Arab leaders had every reason to fear for the safety of their people if they had decided to remain in the Jewish-dominated city. The Irgun was in the city excited after its 'victory' at Deir Yassin. They looted Arab areas but most Palestinians believed that they were capable of much worse. Throughout this period the AHC and the Arab governments urged that all Palestinians should remain in their homes, but in view of the deteriorating situation in Haifa, on 22 April the local leaders thought that it was necessary to provide an opportunity for those who remained to leave if they so desired.

The Arab defeat in Haifa set off a chain reaction of alarm throughout the Middle East. In Baghdad, the Iraqi Foreign Minister handed the British Ambassador a memorandum which called for the 'strongest condemnation'[43] of the Haifa affair because 'Arabs were exposed to massacre and dire suffering from which old men, women and children escaped but were compelled to fly in their thousands, turning their faces toward the Arab countries in their extremity of hunger and nakedness.'

The Iraqis questioned the procedure whereby the British evacuated Haifa first, although as the departure point of the British army leaving Palestine, one would have expected that Haifa would be the last town in Palestine to be evacuated. The Iraqi Foreign Minister believed that the withdrawal of the British army from Haifa had made possible 'these painful events there'.

The Syrians were also distressed. While the battle in Haifa was still raging, the British Ambassador in Damascus spoke to the Syrian President who showed 'considerable alarm and fear as to what may happen when news becomes public' of the Arab disaster.[44] The Syrian President's apprehensions were not without justification, for when the news of the fall of Haifa spread there was an outpouring of reaction by the general public in Damascus. There was a general strike in the Syrian capital as thousands of young people expressed, 'their determination to fight for the rescue of Palestine and condemnation for the savage crimes committed by the Jews.'[45]

In Amman on 25 April, King Abdullah met with the Iraqi Regent, the Lebanese Prime Minister and various Arab military leaders. Sir Alex Kirkbride, the British Ambassador to Trans-Jordan reported that, 'tremendous public pressure is being brought to bear on the King and the Regent to intervene with troops in Palestine immediately.'[46] The reason for this pressure was fear for the safety of Jerusalem and the fact that, 'Amman is crowded with Palestinian refugees.' Kirkbride noted that the royal leaders were, 'very apprehensive of embarking on a campaign against forces of unknown strength.'

Although the Arab masses were spoiling for a fight, their rulers, who were stunned by the speed and ease of the Jewish victory in Haifa, wished to avoid a military confrontation with the large and obviously efficient Haganah army. But it was becoming clear that no Arab government could stay in power if it ignored the public clamour for military intervention in Palestine. The British Ambassador sensed that against their better judgement the Iraqis, who had already sent several thousand volunteers as part of the ALA, would be forced to send their regular army into Palestine. But Kirkbride added that the Regent's main objective was to 'calm public opinion in Iraq rather than to save Arab Palestine.'[47] All over the Middle East the reluctance of the leaders to help their Arab brothers was overcome by public outcry.

In Beirut students declared that they would carry on civil disobedience and continuous fasting until Arab regular armies entered Palestine. On the evening of 23 April, Radio Beirut announced, 'the Arab armies will no longer be able to wait.' There was an appeal 'to everyone to let the Haifa battle be the stimulus for general sacrifices in money and blood.'

In Egypt there were demonstrations in Cairo and Alexandria. An American diplomat reported that the Egyptian government 'would be overthrown' if it did not intervene in Palestine.[48] In Baghdad the Prime Minister told the student protesters that his government would 'do its duty in Palestine.' The former chief of the Iraqi General Staff stated that 'any hesitation to help Palestine would do the greatest harm to the Arab cause.' The Iraqi general and the other Arab military leaders neglected to tell the Arab masses that their national armies were little more than palace guards which were too small and insufficiently trained to face the large battle-tested Jewish forces in Palestine.

Aubrey Lippincott who witnessed the battle did not rate the military potential of the Arabs very highly. He reported to Washington: 'Unless the Arabs get some organization and training, they will be a very minor obstacle to the Jews on the battlefield.'[49] Lippincott doubted that even if the regular Arab armies were sent to Palestine they could stand up to the Haganah any better than the ALA, Syrian and Iraqi volunteers. It seemed that in Haifa the Jews had had their way despite the presence of a large British Army.

The London government was not very happy about Jews taking over Haifa while it was still supposedly under British rule. On 22 April, when the British Foreign Secretary Ernest Bevin received the news about Haifa, he told Field Marshal Montgomery that the army had 'let him down' and caused great embarrassment for Britain's relations in the Arab states. Reports were circulating that thousands of Arabs had been killed in Haifa.

Bevin's anger with the army continued for some time.

Although he was not informed about Stockwell's decision to hand over key points in Haifa to the Haganah, the Foreign Secretary suspected that the British army had co-operated with the Zionist forces. At a meeting on 7 May, which was called to reconcile Bevin and Montgomery, the Foreign Secretary asserted: 'I still feel that we should not have lost control over the perimeter of Haifa and allowed so many Arabs to be driven out of the city.'[50] Bevin added, 'We had large forces there and in the neighbourhood and it was a blow to British prestige that it should have appeared for a time that the Jews were able to do as they liked.' Bevin realized that the complaints of the Arab governments that the British were responsible for the expulsion of so many Palestinian civilians from Haifa were at least partly justified.

Not everyone in London was upset by the news from Haifa. Dr Nahum Goldmann, an official of the Jewish Agency, told the American Ambassador that the pull-back of British forces from the residential area was a great help to the Jewish cause, as without General Stockwell's withdrawal, 'we would never have got Haifa.'[51]

Everywhere Jews were ecstatic about the great victory. In the Jewish section of Jerusalem, there was considerable excitement. The journalist Harry Levin recorded on 22 April in his diary, 'I must shake myself to believe the news from Haifa.'[52] When he met an old acquaintance, his friend expressed dismay at the speed of the victory. 'You don't have to believe it but it's true,' Levin told him. According to the journalist everyone in Jerusalem was asking, 'If it can happen in Haifa like that, why not in Jerusalem?'

Ben-Gurion was in the Jewish Agency building in Jerusalem when he received the news of the Haifa victory. As he was leaving his office, he was intercepted by Kenneth Bilby who asked him about the reports from Haifa. 'It's all true, we have it,'[53] Ben-Gurion replied. According to Bilby, 'It was one of the few moments that I saw the Jewish leader completely relaxed and the Haifa victory provided the stimulus.'

The Jewish leader had good reason to be pleased. Not only had the Haganah captured one of the largest cities in Palestine but the threat which Ben-Gurion had made in February that the war would 'change the composition of the population of the country'[54] was being carried out. With Haifa conquered, only Jaffa remained as an Arab thorn in the heartland of what would soon become the Jewish state.

CHAPTER V

The Fall of Jaffa

Jews are the mildest of men, passionately hostile to violence.

Jean-Paul Sartre

Shmuel Toledano, a young Jewish intelligence officer, had mixed feelings as he rode along with a column of Haganah armoured cars that was 'liberating' Jaffa, the largest Arab town in Palestine. For months there had been sporadic exchanges of gunfire between Jaffa and its Jewish neighbour, Tel Aviv. Many civilians had been killed so that the capture of Jaffa had become a major priority for both the Irgun and the Haganah. Toledano had done valuable intelligence work which contributed to the capture of Jaffa, including the setting-up of the well-known 'prostitute network', which had given the Haganah much information on the Iraqi and other Arab troops who were defending the city.

But now that Jaffa was in Jewish hands, Toledano walked through the nearly abandoned streets reflecting on the incredible misery which had been inflicted on so many innocent Arab civilians. When he entered the empty houses, the young Haganah officer could see the coffee cups that had been left on the kitchen tables by the civilians who had fled in terror. 'I just couldn't bear to see the tragedy,' he later recalled. 'I felt it in every building as we entered them one after another. I saw how families had left not knowing where to go.'[1]

For Toledano the conquest of Jaffa was devoid of the triumphant feeling that a soldier usually experiences after a victorious battle. He could not forget that tens of thousands of people were condemned to lead the lives of homeless refugees. 'Some went by boat to Gaza, others fled by land – but one saw the families were ruined,' he reflected.

THE FALL OF JAFFA

Not all of the Arabs had fled, however. Those that remained were rounded up by the Jewish soldiers. As an intelligence officer, Toledano was assigned the task of interrogating prisoners. The Haganah methods of dealing with captured Arabs were not particularly humane. According to Toledano, 'At the time there was no argument, you decided in a minute to kill somebody.' In Jaffa the Haganah command had given orders to kill captured enemy fighters. Of course, all the Arab prisoners claimed to be civilians. Toledano's job was to choose who among the prisoners had resisted the Jewish forces. Toledano suspected that one man who claimed to be a civilian was an enemy fighter. He was immediately shot. Decades later, Toledano remained affected by the crime. 'I still remember the face of that man and I can't get over it.'

The conflict between the populations of Jaffa and Tel Aviv was inevitable. Under the UN partition plan Jaffa would have been left as an Arab enclave surrounded by the territory of the Jewish state. It was clear that either forces from Jaffa would push out and conquer a corridor linking the city with Arab territory or Jaffa would be absorbed by the Jewish state.

As a consequence of the fighting with the inhabitants of Tel Aviv, the economy of Jaffa had largely deteriorated by early 1948. Factories had closed down, public transport came to a standstill and the famous Jaffa orange industry was wiped out, leaving most of the fruit rotting on the trees. The wealthier business class of Jaffa were among those who fled in the months following the partition resolution. The great majority of the population, however, remained in the city but they feared the worst. There were numerous incidents which aroused the concern of the people of Jaffa.

One Sunday in January a large truck loaded with oranges parked in the centre of Jaffa between Barclays bank and a government office building. The vehicle was driven by two Stern Gang terrorists. They had failed on a previous attempt to enter Jaffa, when Arab sentries guarding access to the city had become suspicious and opened fire on the truck. Now on their second try, they had penetrated into the heart of the city with a truck that contained more than just oranges.

Disguised as Arabs, the experienced terrorists walked away from the vehicle, stopping for coffee at a nearby restaurant before leaving Jaffa. Soon after, an explosion demolished many buildings in the centre of the city. According to a Jaffa resident, Basil Ennab, one of the buildings destroyed was 'sort of a feeding centre for children,'[2] many of whom were among the over 100 casualties.

The incident was a serious blow to the morale of the people of Jaffa. The local Arab committee greatly tightened security to prevent more Jewish terrorism. As part of their security plan, Basil Ennab recalls, 'the local committee took a decision to prevent anybody from leaving the town. In fact they put a roadblock on the only road out of Jaffa and that is why very few people left Jaffa.' Only people with business, medical or military reasons were allowed to leave the town.

The local committee in Jaffa, of course, was following the policy of the Arab League, the AHC and the ALA, all of which opposed the evacuation of Palestine. But whereas the Arab leaders all opposed the exodus of the Palestinians from their homeland, they were bitterly divided on just about every other issue.

Hassan Salame, appointed by the Grand Mufti as military commander of the Lydda–Ramle district, frequently clashed with Mayor Yusef Haikal who opposed his plan for aggressive action to link Jaffa with Lydda–Ramle. In early February when the Iraqi Major Abdul Wahab al-Shaykh Ali arrived in the city with eighty ALA soldiers, he was soon feuding with Salame who resented the presence of the ALA in an area which the Arab League had earlier declared to be under the Grand Mufti's military jurisdiction. Some weeks later Wahab was replaced by Iraqi Captain Abdel Najin al-Din, who arrived in Jaffa on 22 February with another company of ALA troops. Like his predecessor, Najin was soon trading insults with Salame.

Haganah Radio's Arabic-language broadcasts exploited the disputes among Jaffa's leaders in order to frighten the population. On 28 February, the Jewish station announced that, 'following the failure of last week's Arab attack against the Jews, and the terrific losses of the Arabs, the population started

THE FALL OF JAFFA

to criticize the new Iraqi commander as unable to cope with the situation.'³ Hassan Salame was also a frequent target of Haganah propaganda. It was claimed that the Mufti's commander was 'spreading terror in Jaffa among Arab notables.' On 25 March, Haganah Radio announced that supporters of Hassan Salame 'were so disgusted with his attitude toward the population that they had gone over to his opponents.' The Jewish broadcasts claimed that soon there would be open warfare in Jaffa between the various factions. The people of the city were informed that some of the notables of Jaffa had 'sent letters to Fawzi al-Kaukji and King Abdullah demanding their help and the dispatch of troops to save them from Salame and his men.'

Haganah Radio warned the people of Jaffa that they had also to be aware of the ALA volunteers who might loot the city at any moment. In addition, caution was urged since the ALA volunteers were said to be spreading disease. 'New smallpox cases have been discovered in Jaffa district,' the Jewish radio station announced.⁴ This epidemic was, 'due to a number of foreigners in town especially from Syria and Iraq. We are told that the Jaffa mayor sent a message to Syria asking that its people be vaccinated before being sent to Palestine.'

The inevitability of Arab defeat and the futility of their resistance was another recurring theme in Jewish propaganda. On 14 March, Haganah Radio boasted, 'fear filled the hearts of the Jaffa inhabitants as they stole into their houses and failed to open door or window.'⁵ The population of Jaffa was warned not to expect any help from the British. 'The police and British forces also rushed into their barracks and remained behind closed doors.'

After the fall of Haifa on 22 April, it was obvious that Jaffa would be the next major target of the Jewish forces. Haganah leaders were planning to implement Operation Chametz, which was aimed at surrounding and isolating Jaffa, thus avoiding a costly direct attack on the Arab positions. The Irgun, however, was anxious to win an impressive victory in sight of the people of Tel Aviv. The Irgun leaders decided to launch an assault before the Haganah. 'Our plan was to attack Jaffa at the narrow bottleneck linking the main town with the Manshieh Quarter which thrust northward like a peninsula into Jewish Tel Aviv,' noted Menachem Begin.[6] The Irgun aimed at breaking the neck of the bottle and reaching the sea, thus cutting the Manshieh district off from the rest of Jaffa. At 8 a.m. on 26 April, the Irgun mortars began shelling Jaffa, thus signalling the beginning of the assault.

Fighting those who were armed and prepared to resist was never the forte of the Irgun. Their offensive was soon bogged down. Begin was loath to credit the tenacity of Arab resistance. 'In the bottleneck of the Manshieh we learnt what all of the armies had learnt in the Second World War: there are few better defensive positions than a row of ruined buildings.' Indeed the intense mortar barrage destroyed the homes of numerous Jaffa inhabitants. But despite the intense destruction the Irgun broke off the attack after two days of combat.

On the evening of 28 April, the Irgun launched the second assault using explosives. Row by row, blocks of dwellings were blown up. This, in addition to the shelling, created panic among the Arab civilians. Within twenty-four hours, the Irgun fighters had reached the sea, thus realizing their principal objective, which was to cut the Manshieh district off from the rest of Jaffa.

About the same time that the Irgun was achieving its objectives in the Manshieh district, the Haganah launched Operation Chametz with a large-scale pincer movement from north and south. In the northern sector several undefended Arab villages were easily captured and their inhabitants expelled. To the south of Jaffa, the Haganah ran into Arab resistance, which was overcome with artillery.

The British were alarmed by the Jewish advance in Jaffa and they feared that the British army would once more be blamed for not preventing an Arab exodus. Indeed, as early as 10.30 a.m. on 26 April, the British military command at Jaffa noted in its situation report that 'roads at Jaffa congested by Arab lorries and buses carrying refugees.'[7] Foreign Secretary Ernest Bevin had advised the military that a Jewish victory at Jaffa should be prevented until the end of the British mandate on 15 May. The British commander at Jaffa, General Sir Horatius Murray later recalled that the Jews 'started to engage the other side without warning and quite ruthlessly.'[8] Since Jaffa was still under British control Murray regarded the Jewish

THE FALL OF JAFFA

attack as 'a blatant disregard of the occupying force which I simply wasn't prepared to accept.'

Murray sent for the Jewish liaison officer and told him that the Irgun and Haganah had to cease the bombardment of the city. The British officer addressed the Jewish officer bluntly: 'Unless you stop mortaring Jaffa, I shall shell Tel Aviv.' Since the British had not opposed the Zionist attack on Arab civilians at Haifa, the Jews thought that the British commander at Jaffa was bluffing. According to Murray, 'the liaison officer shrugged his shoulders and pushed off and the shelling didn't stop.' So Murray deployed a battery of artillery, a squadron of tanks and a battalion of infantry. Soon after, he gave the order to attack. There was also a warning attack by the Royal Air Force.

Meanwhile Sir Henry Gurney, the Chief Secretary of the Palestine government, sent a note to the Jewish Agency in which he warned, 'in the case of the present Jewish attacks on Jaffa and neighbouring villages, the Army and Royal Air Force will take full action in the areas of Tel Aviv and other places from which these attacks are launched if they do not cease immediately.'[9] Gurney added that the British attacks so far were on a 'minimum scale' but that 'considerably stronger measures will if necessary now be taken.' Soon after the Irgun stopped shelling Jaffa. 'When the mortaring stopped, we stopped', noted General Murray. Eventually a *de facto* cease-fire settled over Jaffa.

But the lull in the fighting did not bring tranquillity to the city. Within hours of the cease-fire, General Murray was asked by his staff to go up the road to see what was happening. 'I saw a scene which I never thought to see in my life. It was the sight of the whole population of Jaffa pouring out on to the road carrying in their hands whatever they could pick up.' Thousands of people were heading south, 'as fast as their legs could carry them. It was a case of sheer terror.' The exodus had started as soon as the Irgun attack had begun but the flow turned into a torrent after the cease-fire.

Basil Ennab makes clear that the local Arab National Committee opposed the evacuation but 'after the cease-fire they lost control.'[10] General Murray strongly denies that the Palestinians fled Jaffa 'because Arab leaders elsewhere ordered them to go.'

Murray believes that the population needed no encouragement to leave. 'These people had terror written on their faces and they couldn't get on the road to Gaza quick enough.'*

Haganah Radio's Arabic-language broadcast gave an accurate description of what was going on in the city. 'People are wandering about not knowing where to go and the general situation is chaotic.' Of course this and similar broadcasts were designed to exacerbate the hysteria that was being described. Among the first to leave were the Iraqi volunteers. Their new commander Michael al-Issa cabled ALA headquarters requesting instructions, but like Elias Koussa at Haifa, he received no reply. Thousands of civilians followed his men as they fled the city.

The Red Cross official, Jacques de Reynier, described the panic of the Arabs who were working with him: 'In the hospitals, the drivers of cars and ambulances took their vehicles, assembled their families and fled.'[13] They were not the only ones to leave in haste. 'Many of the ill, the nurses and even physicians departed the hospital wearing the clothes they had on and fled to the countryside. For all of them the obsession was to escape at any cost.'

General Murray's description of Jaffa after it had been evacuated by its civilian population closely resembles the observations of Shmuel Toledano and other eyewitnesses. 'It was as if a pied piper had been there. There wasn't a soul. Gas stoves were still burning in the houses, the shops were full of goods, the houses had obviously been left in a great hurry.'[14] Murray called Jaffa 'a city of the dead'.

What was the reason for the panic and flight of the Arab population from Jaffa? Most witnesses mention the terror

---

*During the fighting there were Arab broadcasts that reported but did not urge the evacuation of Jaffa. Damascus radio announced, 'reinforcements are arriving continuously in the town's defence from which women and children are being evacuated.'[11] Al-Inqaz Arab Radio referred to the evacuation of women and children from Jaffa as 'a temporary military measure'.[12] General Murray calls the Arab efforts to make it appear that there was an orderly evacuation 'a face-saving device' by the Arab authorities so that it would look as if they were directing an exodus over which they had lost control and which had been initiated against their orders.

caused by the presence in Jaffa of the Irgun and the constant bombardment of the civilian areas of the city as major reasons for the exodus. Some observers believe that the bombardment of civilians was done on purpose. Sir Henry Gurney wrote in his diary, 'The Irgun mortar attack was indiscriminately aimed at civilian targets and was designed to create panic among the population.'[15]

While not admitting that the aim of the Irgun was to terrorize the civilians in Jaffa, Menachem Begin is correct in his assertion that the reputation of the Irgun for brutality greatly contributed to the Arab exodus. He noted with pride, 'the information that the attack was being made by the Irgun had thrown the population into a state of abject fear. The second factor was the weight of our bombardment.'[16] Shmuel Toledano agrees with Begin on the principal causes of the Arab flight from Jaffa. He recalls that the Irgun had been shelling Jaffa for three weeks, which had the effect of 'making the Arabs very much afraid.'[17] Added to this were 'rumours based on the Irgun's reputation – many Arabs were under the impression that the minute the Jews entered the town, the inhabitants would be slaughtered. So the departure of the Iraqis was a signal for the exodus of the inhabitants.'

Kenneth Bilby, the American journalist, was told by Yusef Haikal, the Mayor of Jaffa, that many civilians had fled because hundreds of Arab men and women were slaughtered by the Irgun in the Manshieh district. 'I never found the slightest evidence to support this contention,' Bilby wrote, 'but the fact was that Haikal's story spread like sage fire among the Arabs of Jaffa and they needed no urging to get out.'

Because of the shelling of civilian areas, fear of the Irgun, and rumours of real and imagined atrocities, the Arab population fled Jaffa. Many of the refugees attempted to escape by sea. Any type of craft was used, including rowing boats, sailing boats, motor boats as well as larger vessels. The Shammout family were among the thousands who jammed the piers at Jaffa port. Iris Shammout, who was only twelve years old at the time, remembered how the defenceless civilians were fired on by the Jews. 'Those bullets went through the bodies of people standing by the seashore.'[18] This is similar to what happened at

Haifa and is confirmed by a British situation report from Jaffa that noted, 'Refugees fired on by Jewish snipers as they moved off.'[19]

According to Iris Shammout, 'Women and children were weeping and screaming' as they filed into small boats in an effort to reach a Greek steamship that they hoped would take them to safety. But many people were drowned because the tiny fishing vessels could not hold the multitude. Babies fell overboard as mothers had to choose which offspring to save. The Shammouts were luckier than most since all members of the family were able to get aboard the Greek vessel which eventually reached Beirut. But many of those who attempted to sail to Gaza or Beirut in small boats were lost at sea. Their bodies were washed up along the coast of Palestine.

There was also utter confusion on the roads leading out of Jaffa. As in many other crises, some people took the opportunity to exploit the misery of their brothers. Sir Henry Gurney noted, 'The evacuation is largely to Gaza and the cost to hire a lorry for the 40-mile trip is 150 pounds.'[20] Many had to spend their life's savings for the brief ride to safety for themselves and their family. Poor people found that even a simple barrow was worth more than all the valuables they carried.

Basil Ennab was reluctant to leave his home but, 'the bakeries were closed, groceries were closed and everybody was closed and nobody could fend for himself.'[21] With many of his neighbours gone, no way to buy food and the Irgun on the loose, Basil decided he had to flee. He hoped however, that 'by 15 May, which was the last day of the mandate, some solution would be found and then we would come back.'

Basil carefully closed down his house and locked the doors and a large iron gate which protected his property. He gave the key to his uncle, an old man who was among the few who decided to stay in Jaffa. Basil later recalled, 'I told him to come at least once a week to the house to open the outside gate and allow a nearby gardener to whom I paid money, to come and water my garden.'

Basil's uncle did as requested. For several weeks the old man attempted to maintain the property, since like most other people he expected that the refugees would return after an early political settlement. But one day he opened the outside gate to find Jewish soldiers in the house pointing Sten-guns at him.

There was a great deal of looting in Jaffa, particularly by the Irgun. At first the young 'freedom fighters' robbed Jaffa shops of dresses and ornaments for their girlfriends. Soon, however, everything that was movable was carried off from Jaffa: furniture, carpets, pictures, crockery and cutlery. Not content with looting, the Irgun fighters smashed or destroyed everything which they could not carry off, including pianos, lamps and window-panes. Ben-Gurion afterwards admitted that Jews of all classes poured into Jaffa from Tel Aviv in order to take part in what he called 'a shameful and distressing spectacle'.[22]

Another episode at Jaffa was the desecration of Christian churches by the Jewish soldiers. This was to recur all over Palestine throughout the war. Father Deleque, a Catholic cleric, protested that 'Jewish soldiers broke down the doors of my church and robbed many precious and sacred objects. Then they threw the statues of Christ down into a nearby garden.'[23] The Jewish soldiers laughed at the priest and ignored his protests. The cleric complained that the Jewish leaders gave reassurances about respect of religious buildings 'but their deeds do not correspond to their words.'

There was also some looting by the ALA troops. On 5 May, Sir Henry Gurney wrote in his diary, 'The remnants of the Arab Liberation Army are looting and robbing. This is what the Palestine Arabs get from the assistance provided by the Arab states. Perhaps our warnings against premature military action [by the Arab states] were not always strong enough.'[24] Throughout the war, the ALA was to prove a dubious asset to the Palestinians.

On the same day, Haganah Radio's Arabic service broadcast a report from Jaffa by one of its correspondents. He noted: 'In Jaffa there is no traffic except army vehicles. I drove through Jaffa streets and lanes for a long time with the hope of finding some Arabs or anything which might give a sign of life.'[25] According to the Haganah correspondent, 'Iraqi soldiers are stealing goods from shops and commercial stores.' More suspect however, was the Jewish reporter's claim that 'Arab gangs' were firing at each other in battles which resulted in 'an enormous number of casualties to such an extent that the British army was compelled to intervene.' There is no doubt that the ALA troops behaved badly in Jaffa but the reports of massive battles between various Arab factions was surely exaggerated if not invented and was designed to frighten the Palestinian population.

The British District Commissioner in Jaffa, W. V. Fuller, tried desperately to straighten out the chaos but he had little luck. Gurney noted, 'Fuller came from Jaffa and confirmed that of the original Arab population of 50,000 there are now only 15,000 left in town and more still going. The Mayor and remaining councillors have announced their intention of leaving before 15 May.'[26] But on 3 May, an Arab Emergency Committee was formed for the purpose of salvaging whatever was possible from the deteriorating situation. Fuller suggested that he act as intermediary between the Arab Emergency Committee and the Jewish authorities but the Haganah demanded direct negotiations with the Arabs.

On 13 May, an agreement was signed in Tel Aviv after the Arab Emergency Committee had discussed terms with King Abdullah and the Secretary-General of the Arab League. Under the agreement the Haganah pledged to abide by the Geneva convention. However, the agreement signed in Tel Aviv stipulated that anyone who had left Jaffa and wanted to return could only do so 'provided that Haganah command shall be satisfied that the applicant shall not constitute a danger to public security.'[27] This proviso was used as justification to keep thousands of Jaffa residents from returning to their homes. Indeed, thousands more residents of Jaffa fled soon after the Haganah took over the city on 14 May. Within a few weeks the total population of Jaffa was down to 3,000 out of an original Arab population of 70,000.

Much that has been written by Zionist historians about the Arab exodus from Jaffa is not supported by the evidence. They have suggested that the Arabs evacuated Jaffa 'under the protection of British tanks',[28] implying that the British encouraged the flight from the city. There is, however, no basis for such a charge since an examination of the British military records does not reveal any indication that General Murray's troops were ordered to aid the evacuation of Jaffa. Of course the cease-fire imposed by the British army created conditions that facilitated the Arab flight from the city. But the British had intervened in Jaffa in order to prevent an exodus of the civilian population, as had taken place at Haifa during the previous week. General Murray was surprised and disappointed that the Arabs fled in terror after he had halted the Irgun and Haganah bombardment.

It has also been claimed that when the soldiers of 'the Liberation army were let loose to add to the chaos and confusion,' the population of Jaffa decided to leave.[29] Certainly, there was some looting in Jaffa by the ALA. But this took place after the majority of the population had already fled. However, the looting by the Irgun had begun earlier when the Manshieh district was conquered, which was about the time the exodus started. Indeed, it was this looting by the Irgun rather than the later ALA misconduct that contributed to the panic of most Jaffa residents.

The Israeli historian Yehuda Bauer mentions Jaffa as one of the cities where 'the Jews offered the Arabs to stay.'[30] There is, however, no mention in Israeli document collections of an effort made by the Irgun or the Haganah to communicate an offer to the Arabs of Jaffa either before or during the mass exodus. And there is no indication that during the May negotiations the Jews showed any desire to keep the Arabs in Jaffa. There is in fact a great deal of evidence that reveals the true intention of the Jews.

The radio broadcasts beamed into Jaffa by the Haganah were clearly aimed at encouraging the population to flee. The fact that the bombardment of Jaffa residential areas was only halted after the active intervention of the British army and air force suggests that the Jews were determined to spread panic among the Jaffa residents. Had the Jews wanted the population of the city to remain, they surely would have used other tactics besides the bombardment of residential areas.

There is also no basis for the claim that the Arabs of Jaffa left under orders from their leaders. The testimonies of Israelis, British, Palestinians and neutral observers, all make clear that the flight from Jaffa was a spontaneous response motivated by the residents' fear that they would be slaughtered if they stayed in the city.

Most of the refugees who left Jaffa faced a bleak prospect. Those who fled to Gaza were placed in camps that soon would be crowded with people coming from various other regions of Palestine. Many other refugees from Jaffa settled in camps near Lydda. After the fall of that city they would end up in refugee camps on the West Bank where many people from Jaffa can still be found. The city of Jaffa was quickly settled by thousands of Jews and is now a suburb of Tel Aviv, which itself had originally been a suburb of Jaffa.

Menachem Begin called the conquest of Jaffa 'an event of first-rate importance in the struggle for Hebrew Independence.'[31] There can be no doubt that the capture of Jaffa was a major victory in the 1948 war. There was one prize, however, which overshadowed all others in Palestine. For both sides in the war, Jerusalem was to be the focus of their greatest effort.

CHAPTER VI

The City of Peace

> *Zionism meaning the reoccupation of Palestine has no attraction for me... The real Jerusalem is the spiritual Jerusalem. Thus the Jews can realize this Zionism in any part of the world.*
>
> Mahatma Gandhi

'We don't want to kill but for your own sake please move,'[1] blurted a Haganah loudspeaker in the early morning silence in an Arab section in Jerusalem. Fuad Bahnan, then a student for the Protestant ministry, was startled by the announcement, which was punctuated by heavy rifle fire. Within moments the residents were routed from their homes at gunpoint. According to Fuad, 'We were asked to pass through a line of armed young men carrying rifles. We were driven out.' Fuad noted that the civilians were not given any time to prepare. 'We were allowed to move out with the clothes we had on. One of our next-door neighbours, an elderly man of about sixty, I still remember him, had to move out of his house with his pyjamas on.'

Among those shot by the Zionists was Fuad's father who was gunned down in cold blood. Fuad took his father to a government hospital where he soon died. The young student had to bury the old man quickly since he wished to keep his father's death from his mother. Fuad's sister was graduating from college in Ramallah that afternoon. Leaving his mother in the care of his three brothers, Fuad drove to Ramallah to give a present to his sister on what should have been one of her happiest days. After the ceremony, Fuad drove back to Jerusalem to pick up his mother and brothers so that he could bring them to Nablus where the Bahnan family had a small house. Fuad then told his family that his father had been killed.

The scars of that day are still with Fuad. 'The shock of the situation and the impact of it broke me to pieces,' he later recalled. His feelings were 'torn between seeing my father dead, not breaking the news to my sister who was working so hard for so many years to graduate, and suddenly realizing that I was the responsible man in the family, a family already homeless.' But Fuad concedes that the Bahnans were luckier than most. 'We still had the small piece of land and a house in the village next to Nablus where we could find shelter.' (Many Palestinians who fled from Jerusalem were like the refugee Wadi Gumri, who left with nothing 'except my suitcase with two suits and two dresses for my mother which we carried on our back.')

Now a leading Protestant clergyman in the Middle East, Fuad Bahnan emphatically denies that the Arabs of Jerusalem were ordered by the AHC to flee. 'On the contrary, we were daily being urged by our leaders to stick it out and remain where we were.' There is abundant evidence to support his statement. As in other parts of the country, the Palestinians living in Jerusalem were urged, indeed coerced, by the AHC to stay in their homes. On 15 May, Jerusalem Arab Radio announced, 'Those who spread alarming rumours inciting the population to evacuate must be arrested.'[2] Even Haganah Radio admitted that 'the National Committee was refusing to give visas to anyone wishing to leave Jerusalem for Trans-Jordan.'[3]

In 1948, the Jerusalem region had a mixed population of 100,000 Jews and 105,000 Arabs. Under the United Nations partition plan the Jerusalem area would not be part of either the Arab or Jewish state but would be internationalized. Though the Jewish Agency publicly accepted the partition resolution, no Zionist could give up the claim to the city that contained the Wailing Wall and other important shrines of the Jewish religion. The city was also sacred to Christians and Muslims. Next to Mecca and Medina, Jerusalem was the most sacred city in Islam. But, as elsewhere, the defence of Jerusalem was hampered by the rivalry between the Grand Mufti and King Abdullah of Trans-Jordan who wished to annex the Holy City to his kingdom.

Despite occasional friction between the Haganah and the 'dissident organizations' the Jews of Jerusalem were united in their desire to drive as many Arabs out of the city as possible. In

THE CITY OF PEACE

particular the Jewish forces wished to push out those Arabs who lived in mixed neighbourhoods or in Arab enclaves in or near the Jewish section of the city that comprised the more modern western and southern areas of Jerusalem.

Loudspeaker vans were commonly used in Jerusalem to frighten the Arab population. Berta Vesta, a Christian missionary in Jerusalem, reported that the vans broadcast messages in Arabic such as: 'Unless you leave your homes the fate of Deir Yassin will be your fate!'[4] This is confirmed by the pro-Zionist author Harry Levin, who admits in his diary that the Jews employed loudspeakers to threaten the Arabs of the Holy City: 'The road to Jericho is open! Fly from Jerusalem before you are all killed.'[5]

Sheikh Badr,[6] an Arab enclave (which is now the site of the Israeli Knesset) was a particular target of Zionist intimidation. Several methods were used to frighten the residents. First, threatening posters were put up. Handbills advising, 'Leave for your own safety' were also distributed throughout Sheikh Badr. Arab leaders were threatened by phone. But the Zionists soon decided that the pressure had to be increased. Haganah raiding parties went into the area at night to cut telephone and electricity wires, throwing hand grenades on to the ground, firing into the air and in general trying to create an air of insecurity. Eventually the residents of Sheikh Badr were driven out.

As had happened elsewhere in the country, the Arab press in Jerusalem ceased publishing at an early stage of the war. On 28 April, Sharq al-Adna, the British-controlled radio, reported that, 'The non-appearance of the Arab press during the last few days has given rise to the rapid spreading of alarming rumours. The people now mainly depend on broadcasting stations for news of developments.'[7]

Some of the 'news' received by Jerusalem Arabs came from Haganah Radio's psychological warfare broadcasts in Arabic. On 24 April, the Jewish radio station reported, 'a state of alarm among Jerusalem's Arab population and a large number of Arabs are trying to evacuate the city.'[8] On 26 April, Haganah Radio claimed that the Arabs of the Holy City, 'felt the defenders' incapacity and started to evacuate Jerusalem for other districts either north or south of Palestine. Because of the great number of evacuees communications in the Arab quarter are difficult.'[9] This same broadcast noted ominously, 'among the evacuees are a great number of influential Arab personalities who hold key positions such as Dr Tanus. Evacuation by the leaders of their movement provoked the anger of the population. But the departure of the leaders of their districts for safer places has become quite a common occurrence.' The aim of these broadcasts was obviously to undermine the morale of the Arabs in Jerusalem.

The Katamon district in West Jerusalem was another area from which the local inhabitants were driven out by the Haganah. Populated by mainly Christian Arabs with some Muslim and British residents, Katamon took its name from an Orthodox monastery situated on a hill which dominated the district. According to Sami Haddawi, a long-time resident of Katamon, the section was regarded as a 'strategic area' which the Jewish forces needed if they were to secure their hold over West Jerusalem. On the night of 3–4 January, the Haganah made its move.

Their target was the Semiramis Hotel, one of the well-known landmarks of the district. The hotel was only two blocks away from Sami Haddawi's home so that he clearly recalls the huge explosion when the Semiramis was dynamited by the Zionists. A total of twenty-six people were killed, including a Spanish diplomat and numerous women and children. The Haganah claimed that the hotel had been 'used as a base for marauding Arab gangs and headquarters of the Arab military youth organization.' But the British administration, which still exercised at least nominal control, investigated the incident and found that the Jewish charge that the Semiramis was a military headquarters was 'entirely without foundation'. The British report called the bombing 'wholesale murder of innocent people'.[10]

According to Sami Haddawi, the bombing had a definite effect. 'The next morning the inhabitants of Katamon fled. Some returned to move their furniture away. Then a systematic blowing up of homes occurred until fourteen buildings were blown up around my home, but I stayed.'[11]

On 29 April, the virtually deserted Katamon was occupied by Jewish forces. Sami Haddawi was one of the few Arabs left in the district. But he was forced to leave. As he went he paused to look out from his verandah at one of the most picturesque views of the New City of Jerusalem. Haddawi thought back to happier days before the war had ravaged his community. 'I remember the pealing of the church bells to remind the Christian of his faith, the voice of the Muezzin high up in the minaret calling to Islam's sons to pray, the Jew wending his way at sunrise and sunset to the synagogue – all to offer to the Almighty prayers for his blessing and thanksgiving for the peace and beauty of the Holy City.'

Although so many of his neighbours had fled, Haddawi had remained because as a civil servant working for the mandate administration, he was reluctant to depart while the British still technically remained as rulers of Palestine. But in the early months of 1948 as the war intensified, it became increasingly difficult for an Arab to remain in Katamon. One day Haddawi went to visit a friend but he found that like so many others of his acquaintance he had been forced to flee by Zionist intimidation. While returning home, Haddawi saw a Jewish armoured truck parked at the top of a hill. He could hear a Zionist loudspeaker threatening in Arabic: 'The road to the Allenby Bridge is still open; flee before your fate will be the same as Deir Yassin!'

This incident made Haddawi realize that he could not hold out in Katamon much longer. So when the Zionists decided to occupy the area, the now jobless civil servant decided to flee. But as Haddawi lingered on his verandah he found it difficult to leave. However he did receive a little encouragement. 'As I stood there living over the past, I was suddenly awakened to reality by the sound of a bullet that hissed by almost taking my life in its stride.' Thus the last Arab residents of Katamon departed.

Soon after, the Zionists began their systematic looting of the area according to the Haganah Intelligence Chief in Jerusalem, Yitzhak Levi, Jewish soldiers and civilians 'broke into empty houses and took furniture, clothes and food. It was disgraceful!'[12]

On 10 May, in answer to an inquiry, the Jewish Agency

informed the British administration that in Katamon, 'the listing, collection and removal of the household goods is being done in an organized manner and under the immediate direction of a specially appointed senior officer of the Jewish Agency.' The British noted, however, that from areas near Katamon the former Arab residents saw 'Jewish trucks driving up, being loaded with property and brought out of the houses and being driven off to an unknown destination.'[13] The British requested the Zionists to allow some of the residents of Katamon to return since many people wished to reclaim their property, but the Jewish Agency refused saying: 'It is impossible at present to allow householders to return to the suburb because firstly the removal of goods whose ownership is in doubt has not been completed and because of the danger of mines.' Not long after, from their refugee camps in East Jerusalem, many of the former residents of Katamon could see Jewish immigrants moving into their homes.

The former residents of Katamon claimed that Arab civilians had been killed in the area by the Jewish forces. This was verified by a Red Cross doctor who visited the district after it was occupied by the Haganah. The Red Cross physician entered Katamon with two trucks in order to collect bodies. He asked a Haganah officer for assistance but he was told that the Jewish forces would not give any help in locating Arab corpses. As the doctor later noted, 'The only alternative was for me to act like a hound-dog and be guided by my sense of smell.'[14] His nose led him to a cave. The odour of decaying flesh was so bad that one of his orderlies was overcome. Once in the cave the sight was as bad as the smell. 'A group of bodies was piled in a heap, including soldiers, women and even a mule.' The Red Cross official once again asked the Haganah officer for help but he absolutely refused saying that all of his men were occupied. But the doctor noted: 'The fact was that a good number of them were hanging around doing nothing.'

The Red Cross official went back to the hospital and returned to the scene of the massacre with six people but they were not up to the job since 'they got sick in turn and were not able to help.' Eventually the doctor found an American volunteer who was able to assist in loading two trucks with the decaying bodies. News of the discovery of the bodies spread throughout the city.

A. L. Miller, a YMCA official, was in Jerusalem when the Zionist atrocities were revealed. He reported to his superiors that Arab morale was affected by the crimes committed by the Jews, which in his view 'really have been atrocities.'[15] Miller believed that the Jewish crimes greatly contributed to the Palestinian exodus. He noted: 'In my opinion the atrocities were committed with this in view.'

Some of the refugees from Katamon and other areas of West Jerusalem fled to the Arab-controlled portion of the Holy City. The Director of Refugee Affairs for East Jerusalem noted that 'most of these had to abandon their homes empty-handed except for the clothes they had on them at the time of their mass expulsion.'[16] By late 1948, there were 15,000 refugees in East Jerusalem, half of whom came from Jaffa, Haifa, and such surrounding villages as Deir Yassin, Kalonia and Castel. The other 7,500 came from West Jerusalem including 'Katamon, Upper and Lower Baka, Musrara, Sheikh Jarah, Nebi Daoud and El-Tor.'

Of the refugees in East Jerusalem '1,000 lived in the open, the rest were housed in mosques, convents, schools and Old City houses in ruinous conditions.' The health of the refugees in East Jerusalem was not good. 'They suffer from malnutrition and they show all the signs of weakness,' the Director of Refugee Affairs reported. Their daily ration was only 1,000 grammes of flour per person. As bad as the condition of the refugees in East Jerusalem may have been, it was better than the fate of other refugees who fled to the West Bank, Gaza or the surrounding Arab states.

One factor working in favour of the refugees in Jerusalem was the presence of many churches, convents and other Christian relief organizations in the Holy City. Frequently these institutions provided shelter and food for the destitute and bewildered Arab civilians. But often, however, as in Haifa, Jaffa and elsewhere the Christian institutions were themselves the targets of Zionist attacks. The Archbishop of York charged that in Jerusalem 'many convents, churches have been desecrated, their pictures and images destroyed and the figures of

Christ torn from crosses and defiled.'[17] Jewish forces shelled several churches killing three priests. Along with rape and looting, attacks on religious institutions were part of the usual operating procedure of the IDF in Palestine.

An important factor to consider when judging the conduct of the Zionist forces in 1948 is whether the Arabs acted with equal brutality during the conflict. There is of course a prejudice in all Western countries that assumes Third World people, especially if they are Muslim, are prone to brutality. But with the exception of the undisciplined irregulars, the Arab armies in 1948 often acted with great restraint. On 29 March, for example, Haganah Radio described what happened to some wounded Jewish soldiers who fell into Arab hands during one of the convoy battles. 'Arab doctors arrived in cars and promptly gave medical assistance to all Jewish wounded.'[18] The Zionist radio station added: 'We pay tribute to such a noble attitude which is not only humane but also respects international law.'

But after Deir Yassin the Palestinian irregulars were thirsty for revenge. On 13 April when the Palestinians learned that a convoy headed for Mount Scopus Medical Centre in Jerusalem was carrying Irgun terrorists wounded at Deir Yassin, the irregulars killed not only the terrorists but also scores of innocent Jewish medical personnel.

The only other major Arab atrocity in 1948 was also committed by Palestinian irregulars shortly after Deir Yassin, when the Kfar Etzion Kibbutz was overrun by Arab forces. As Yaacov Edelstein, a survivor of the massacre, recalls the irregulars had no officers or other restraining influence to organize an orderly surrender. Edelstein heard the Palestinians yelling 'Deir Yassin!'[19] as they slaughtered the Zionists who attempted to surrender. But Edelstein notes that the regular Arab troops obeyed their officers who ordered restraint. This was typical of the regular Arab armies in 1948 who generally treated Jewish prisoners of war and civilians with great chivalry.

This was most evident on 28 May, when the Jewish Quarter of Jerusalem fell into the hands of the Arab Legion forces commanded by Major Abdullah Tel. The proceedings were witnessed by Pablo Azcarate of the UN who noted that Tel acted 'with great affability and without a single word or gesture that could have humiliated or offended the defeated leaders in any way.'[20]

During the negotiations Azcarate saw some Arab soldiers beating a man so violently that he fell to the ground. The UN official was alarmed: 'Thinking that the victim was a Jew, my first reaction was one of indignation and protest.' But Azcarate soon realized that the man being beaten was 'an Arab irregular whom the soldiers of the Legion had surprised in the act of looting.' Since he was only a boy, the Legion soldiers agreed to let the looter go at Azcarate's insistence. The UN official wrote in his memoirs that Tel's men treated several other potential looters 'with the greatest vigour and severity.'

But the Arab troops were humane in their handling of the captured Jewish civilians. Among those taken prisoner were Rabbi Mordechai Weingarten and his daughter Rivka. They had some apprehension because of what Azcarate calls, 'Jewish propaganda against the Arab Legion.' But as Rivka later remembered: 'I must say that the Jordanian soldiers behaved wonderfully well. I will never forget what my own eyes saw.'[21] According to the Jewish woman, 'The first thing the soldiers did was to give us all cold water to drink. They gave out bananas to the children and cigarettes to the soldiers. I also saw them carrying old men and women in their arms to help reach Zion Gate.'

Some of the Israeli wounded were brought to the military hospital in the Jewish Quarter. An official of the hospital expressed great apprehension to Azcarate since he believed that the Arabs 'would leave not a wounded man alive during the night.' But that evening when a fire developed, Azcarate noted that the Jordanian troops displayed great chivalry. The Jewish wounded were rescued by 'those same soldiers of the Legion who had remained to guard and protect the hospital and who according to the assistant director were not going to leave a single man alive.'

Most of the Jewish women and children were sent at their request to the Israeli-occupied portion of Jerusalem. The captured men were taken to Trans-Jordan as prisoners-of-war. Leo Wissman remembers how he and the other Jewish captives were treated. 'A Legion sergeant asked us if the soldiers had stolen anything from us. Yes – our watches. So most of the men got their watches back.'

At several points the Jewish prisoners were surrounded by angry Arab civilians shouting 'Deir Yassin! Deir Yassin!' According to Rivka Weingarten, many of the threatening Palestinians were 'Arabs from villages taken by the Israeli army.' These people had been routed from their homes by the Zionists. Because they had been so violently expelled from their homes, the Palestinian refugees had no sympathy for the Israeli prisoners-of-war. But the Arab soldiers kept order and discipline. There is no evidence that any harm came to any of the 1,500 Jewish soldiers or civilians captured in the Old City.

The resistance of the Trans-Jordanian Arab Legion prevented the Zionists from overrunning all of Jerusalem. But in a large part of Galilee, the local population had no protection against the invading Zionists except for the unreliable ALA force. Like the city dwellers of Haifa, Jaffa and West Jerusalem, the inhabitants of dozens of small villages would be forced into a cruel exile.

CHAPTER VII

The Road to Safed*

The day might come when one no longer hears of the wandering Jew but only of wandering Arabs.

Camille Chamoun, Lebanese Minister of Interior, 7 May, 1948

Amina Musa, a Palestinian peasant woman, was understandably nervous as she watched her husband prepare for his morning prayers. For years she had observed him perform the familiar ritual, but they had always been in their home in Kabri, a small village in Galilee. Now they were fugitives, forced to flee their home when the area was invaded by Israeli troops. The day after their departure, on 21 May, Kabri was occupied by units of the Carmeli Brigade. The hamlet was an important prize for the Israelis since it was near a Jewish settlement and the men of Kabri had successfully blocked several attempts to supply the Israeli outpost.[1]

After they had fled their home, Amina and her husband took refuge in an orchard where they spent the night. While her husband was still saying his morning prayers, Amina spotted a friend running down the road toward her. He did not stop, however, but while hurrying past, he urged the couple to follow him since they were in great danger. It soon became apparent that he was right.

Not long after, the couple were captured by Israeli soldiers who were headed toward Kabri. The soldiers stole Amina's jewellery, including her gold earrings, a necklace and four bracelets. One of the Israelis who spoke some Arabic kept

---

*An important source for this chapter is Nafez Nazzal, *The Palestinian Exodus in Galilee*, a doctoral dissertation containing interviews with several hundred refugees from Galilee. I have verified many of their stories using Israeli, United Nations and other non-Arab sources, as indicated in the notes.

taunting his captives saying: 'I will give this necklace to my girlfriend.' Amina was too terrified to respond. She expected no mercy and the soldiers were in no mood to show leniency to any Arab. When the Israelis spotted smoke coming from Kabri, they danced with delight.

Amina and her husband, as well as half a dozen other Arabs, were driven in an armoured car back to their home village. Amina gasped as an Israeli officer put a gun to her husband's head, insisting: 'You are from Kabri!' Realizing that the Israelis hated the men of Kabri, all of the Arab captives including Amina's husband claimed that they were from another village. However, an Arab traitor working for the Israelis identified the men as residents of Kabri. The Israelis took away Amina's husband and five other men.

The women waited, hoping to find out what had become of their loved ones. After a while a Jewish officer came to Amina, telling her not to cry. 'I will bring your husband back,' he told her, adding off-handedly, 'Of course he is dead.' The officer showed Amina a picture of Faris Sirhan, a well-known supporter of the Grand Mufti in Kabri. 'Tell Faris,' he said, 'we will occupy Palestine and then we will go after him in Lebanon.'[1]

Amina slept in the field that night, not knowing if the Israeli officer had told her the truth about her husband. The next morning, she and several friends returned to the village. There they met a woman in tears who told Amina, 'You had better go see your dead husband.' She found him with a bullet in the back of his head. With the help of several other women she dragged the corpse a considerable distance to the village cemetery, where they dug a grave. With great difficulty, they turned the body sideways hoping that it was facing Mecca as required by Islamic law. After six days of mourning, Amina fled to Syria with an elderly relative.

Amina Musa was one of the tens of thousands of Palestinian Arabs who were forced to flee from their homes in Galilee by an invading Israeli army in the spring of 1948. It was common practice for the Israelis to murder captured Arab men who they believed had offered resistance (see pages 82–3, 114–15). Women and children were often terrorized and robbed before being forced to flee. After the population was expelled at gunpoint, the towns were usually destroyed except for those homes that were considered suitable for occupancy by Jews.

The march of the Israeli army through Galilee began in Tiberias, on the shores of the sea of Galilee. The announcement of the partition resolution in November 1947 was the signal for sporadic fighting in Tiberias. Since the Jewish community in the city was large (6,000 out of 11,000) and because most of the Jews lived on a hillside overlooking the old town, the Arabs who lived there were at a disadvantage. In order to weaken their opponents, the Jews of Tiberias distributed a great amount of printed material in Arabic that warned the population not to hinder the partition resolution or co-operate with 'militant outsiders'.

There were in fact thirty ALA foreign volunteers who led the defence of the Tiberias Arab community. For some time their presence gave the Arabs apparent superiority over the local Jewish forces. But when it was learned that the British were about to evacuate Tiberias, a company of élite Palmach troops were sent to reinforce the town's Jewish militia. On the night of 17–18 April, a co-ordinated drive was made to cut the Arab section of town in two. Barrel-bombs, loudspeakers and 'horror sounds' were used to frighten the civilian population. The terrified Arabs appealed to the British to protect them. Although they were leaving, the British army agreed to extend their protection for a few more days to the Arab population of Tiberias. Responding to a request for assistance, King Abdullah of Trans-Jordan sent thirty trucks to evacuate women and children, since he feared a massacre like the one that had taken place at Deir Yassin only a few days previously.

After some reluctance, the men of Tiberias agreed to leave with the women and children. They were encouraged by the British who did not wish to get involved in any further fighting. A severe shortage of space developed, and as a result many household belongings had to be left behind. Even so, there was not enough room in the trucks so that wagons and barrows were used to carry the panic-stricken Arabs. Despite the inconvenience, most Tiberias residents considered themselves lucky. As Abdullah Sayigh recalled, 'We were able to leave the city unharmed and without another Deir Yassin.' On the evening of 18 April, the British army commanders in Tiberias reported that all of the Arabs had gone, 'leaving the town completely in Jewish hands at 1900 hours.'[2]

The Arabs claimed that during and after the battle the town was looted by the Jewish residents and soldiers. Later the UN sent an investigator, Captain F. Marchal, who verified the Arab claims. In particular the Belgian officer noted that Zionist troops had sacked and desecrated Christian religious establishments in the town including the 'Holy Place' convent. Marchal commented:

> In spite of the guarantee given several times by the Jewish authorities to respect churches, convents, schools and other buildings belonging to the religious community, those places have been submitted to depredations committed at Tiberias undoubtedly by the Jews, although these places were private property. They have been occupied by troops without any notice and sometimes without any necessity.[3]

It is unlikely that the desecration of Christian and Muslim religious establishments was ordered by high-level Jewish officials. In all probability they were actions taken by junior officers and enlisted men who were expressing their contempt for the Arabs by defiling their religion. The Jews realized that in Palestine where religion was taken very seriously, the desecration of churches, mosques and other religious buildings and monuments would serve to terrorize the population and convince them of the necessity to flee.

Tiberias was the only town in Palestine where an Arab government assisted the inhabitants to leave. King Abdullah had responded to a request that he send trucks to rescue Arab civilians from a massacre. Soon after, however, he would encourage all Palestinians to stay in their homes and urge those who had left to return.

After the occupation of Tiberias, the Palmach forces moved up the road that leads to Safed, the unofficial capital of Arab Galilee. During Operation Matateh (broom), the Jewish soldiers cleared the numerous villages that were clustered along the Tiberias–Safed highway. Ghuweir was a village not far from

THE ROAD TO SAFED

Tiberias. When the people of this hamlet heard of the fall of Tiberias, they were not unduly alarmed, since the loss of a city with such a large Jewish population was not unexpected. They hoped, however, that their village, which was completely Arab, would be able to resist the Jewish forces. As a precaution, the people of Ghuweir sent a delegation to see Abed Shishakli, the commander of the Arab League volunteers in Galilee, to ask him for arms.

At the meeting, Mukhtar Fayiz Khamis of Ghuweir told the ALA commander that with arms the people of his village were willing to stay and fight the Palmach forces. 'I have no orders to supply villagers with arms,' Shishakli replied. He suggested that the delegation go to Damascus and present their case to the Arab League Military Committee, which might give the order to distribute arms to the villagers. Fayiz Khamis was infuriated by Commander Shishakli's attitude. He argued with the ALA officer who refused again and again to give the peasants rifles: 'You have no orders to arm the villagers.' 'Do you have orders to surrender them to the Jews?' Mukhtar Khamis asked.

When Mukhtar Khamis returned to Ghuweir empty-handed, many of the women and children fled al-Rama which was far away from the advancing Palmach army. Only about forty-eight poorly armed men with a few dozen rounds of ammunition each, decided to remain in the otherwise deserted village. On 22 April, a group of Jews from a neighbouring settlement requested a meeting with Mukhtar Khamis. The Jews who came to Ghuweir were well known to the villagers. They told the Mukhtar apologetically that a Jewish army planned to take over the road to Safed and all the villagers along the route must flee or fight the Palmach which would inflict heavy casualties on the Arabs. Mukhtar Khamis did not reveal to his Jewish visitors that the village was already largely deserted. He told them that the villagers did not plan to attack the Palmach but that they did plan to defend their homes.

Several days later, when the Palmach forces occupied Ghuweir, the armed men fled to al-Rama, where their families had already moved. When the Jewish army captured al-Rama, the Palmach commander ordered the Arab civilians to assemble at the centre of the village. A Jewish soldier stood on top of a rise and shouted, 'All Druse* may return to their homes.' After they left he addressed the other Arabs. 'You must leave for Lebanon. Anyone who dares to take any belongings will be shot.' Many young men were not allowed to leave with their families but were taken as prisoners-of-war by the Palmach. Al-Rama, a Christian village, had a parish priest who later testified, 'The Jews kidnapped forty men.'

The expulsion from al-Rama took place after the completion of Operation Matateh, when there were UN observers in the area. An American UN observer spotted the villagers on the road after they had been forced out of their homes by the Jews. Dr Abdullah Sherban, a local doctor, told the UN investigators, 'I have been expelled from my village with all of the Christian inhabitants. I would like the UN to take action so that such a shame be stopped.' After a thorough investigation at al-Rama, Commandant Perrossier of France, a senior UN observer, stated in his report: *'The Jews have terrorized the Christian Arabs to force them to emigrate to Lebanon so that the Jews can get their land.'*[4] He also noted, 'The acts of looting in the village are similar to those in all of the villages evacuated by the inhabitants.' Some villagers, however, suffered a worse fate than the people of Ghuweir and al-Rama.

As they prepared for the attack, a chance for revenge seemed within reach of the men of the 3rd Battalion of the Yiftach Brigade. The target of the élite Palmach unit was Ein Zeitun, a village known for the atrocities its inhabitants had committed against Jews over the past decade. During the night, weapons and supplies had laboriously been hauled into place so that by the early morning of 2 May, the Palmach soldiers were in a position for the long-awaited attack on the strategically placed hamlet.

Ein Zeitun lay about a mile north of Safed. Home of some 820 Arab farmers, Ein Zeitun takes its name from a mountain

---

*The Druse are an Arabic-speaking religious minority who have long had a strong animosity towards Muslims. When the dispute developed between Jews and Arabs in Palestine, most of the Druse favoured the Jewish side. To this day, the Druse enjoy rights in Israel which are denied to Muslim and Christian Arabs especially membership in the armed forces.

stream which runs through the village. Despite its scenic beauty its location is unfortunate, since any invader who wishes to control Safed and the surrounding valley will need to occupy Ein Zeitun. Within a few weeks after the fall of Tiberias, the Israelis were planning an attack on Ein Zeitun as a prelude to an assault on Safed.

The battle took place in the early morning. The Palmach soldiers threw hand grenades and used one of their commonest terror weapons, a primitive Davidka 'drainpipe' mortar which made a huge sound designed to frighten the Arab villagers. Although there were many armed men in Ein Zietun, they were no match for the well-trained Palmach soldiers. Gradually the armed men began to retreat, allowing the Jewish forces to gain control of the village.

The inhabitants of Ein Zeitun had agreed that if they were attacked, the armed men would retreat while the old people, teenagers and women with small children would remain in their homes. Foolishly, the people of Ein Zeitun left themselves at the mercy of their revenge-seeking enemies. Soon after entering the village, the men of the Yiftach Brigade herded the villagers into a large courtyard where they were threatened with mass execution. Yusuf Ahmad Hajjar suddenly stood up and exclaimed, 'Our village has been captured. We have surrendered and we expect to be treated humanely.' Obviously possessing more courage than wisdom, he warned the soldiers that if they harmed the people of Ein Zeitun, the culprits would be punished by the Arab armies when they occupied Galilee. The Palmach soldiers were infuriated. One of the officers slapped Hajjar and ordered his soldiers to choose thirty-seven teenage boys at random while the rest of the villagers were forced into the storage rooms of the village mosque.

After being taken away, the young men were never heard of again. According to a pro-Israeli writer, 'the fate of the hated men of Ein Zeitun who happened to fall into Jewish hands is unclear.' Some of the surviving relatives still hold out hope that the young men are alive, but most have few illusions. When asked about the fate of her brother, Munira Hamid Shaibi replied, 'I do not think my brother is alive. I think the Jews have killed him.'[5]

The women and children of Ein Zeitun were escorted by Palmach soldiers to the western edge of the village. The men of the Yiftach Brigade fired over their heads, forcing them to run in terror. As was the usual procedure in such cases, the civilians were stripped of all their belongings before being sent to neighbouring villages, where their presence could be expected to spread panic and fear. In the days that followed the attack on Ein Zeitun, the Yiftach Brigade continued Operation Matateh.

The Arab High Command was greatly alarmed at this time by the large number of Palestinian Arabs who were fleeing in terror from their villages. On 5 May, the headquarters of the Arab Liberation Forces issued a threat carried by Radio Damascus that if any Palestinian Arab 'deserts his village, his house will be destroyed and his crops set on fire'[6] by the Arab armies. Equally concerned was King Abdullah of Trans-Jordan who was playing host to thousands of unwelcome refugees from Galilee and other parts of Palestine. The Trans-Jordanian monarch admonished the Palestinians: 'Let those who left their dear homes return.'[7] The King praised the courage, heroism and endurance of those who remained in Palestine despite the 'despotism imposed on the population' by the Zionists, whom he accused of murder and other atrocities in Deir Yassin, Tiberias and Haifa.

The Egyptians also desired a halt to the Palestinian exodus. According to Radio Cairo on 5 May, the Egyptian government had decided 'not to allow Palestinian men age eighteen to fifty to take refuge on Egyptian territory.'[8] In view of the extremely strong tendency for Arab families to stay together, an order barring men from entering Egypt would also help stem the flow of women, children and old people as well. Similar appeals were made in radio broadcasts from Damascus and Beirut.

Arab broadcasts tended to portray an optimistic picture of the military situation in an effort to persuade the Palestinians to stay in their homes or return to them if they had already left. Radio Damascus asked all Palestine Arabs 'to return to their native land in order to participate in our holy crusade, especially as victory is obviously on the side of the Arab armies and the majority of Arab villages are perfectly secure.' But this was not true since the Israelis continued their relentless advance.

THE ROAD TO SAFED

The next goal of the Palmach forces was the capture of Safed. This appeared to be a very difficult task since, on paper at least, the Arabs had several key advantages. Safed was populated by 9,500 Arabs and about 2,400 Jews. Most of the Jewish population was of the ultra-orthodox type who were not enthusiastic about political Zionism. Many of these religious people saw no reason why they should take up arms in order to create a Jewish state.

The British, believing that the Arabs were sure of holding the city, favoured them, just as they favoured the Jews in Haifa and Tiberias. As Faujz Qadurah, a member of the Safed militia recalled: 'Upon the British evacuation of 16 April, we occupied all the city's strategic points.' These included the central police station, the Government House and the citadel from which the Arabs should have been able easily to dominate the whole city. According to Qadurah, confidence ran high among the Arabs of Safed: 'We were the majority and the feeling among us was that we could defeat the Jews with sticks and rocks.'

But the defenders of Safed soon realized that their position was not as secure as they had first believed. This was especially true as they began to hear about the Palmach occupation of the surrounding villages. The loss of Ein Zeitun was a heavy blow. 'The fall of this village left the city besieged from the south and north,' noted Issa Abed al-Khadra, a local merchant.

On 10 May, Allon ordered his main attack against Safed. The Palmach troops attacked the Arab-held strongpoints using a considerable number of mortars. In 1957, when the Israeli journalist Uri Avneri interviewed Allon, the Palmach commander revealed, 'While planning the capture of the Arab part of Safed, it was not our intention to prevent the flight of the Arab population.'[9] This was certainly an understatement. The most insidious weapons against the civilian population were loudspeakers which announced that the population had best leave the town since the Jews were about to use the atom bomb. The pro-Zionist writer Arthur Koestler saw many of the prisoners captured in Safed and he noted that they, 'seemed convinced that the Jews had a secret weapon called the "adum" which makes fire spout out of the earth and houses cave in without visible cause.'[10]

The Palmach's efforts to terrorize the Palestinians were greatly facilitated by the conduct of the foreign volunteers who constituted most of the city's defence force of 750. Sari Fanish, the commander of the Trans-Jordanian troops, left Safed on the eve of the Palmach attack on orders from King Abdullah, who preferred to see the Jews in Safed rather than his rival, the Grand Mufti. The Trans-Jordanian monarch wished to thwart Mufti Haj Amin's plan to set up a Palestinian government in Safed. Several of the ALA commanders including Abed Shishakli, the leader of the Arab volunteers in the area, were also not in Safed when the Palmach attack was launched. According to a member of the local militia, Usama al-Naqib, when 'rumours spread that the ALA had begun to withdraw,' the news had such a depressing effect that 'the people began to flee in panic.'

The Arabs of Safed had a reputation of having committed many atrocities against the Jews, particularly during the Arab Revolt of the 1930s. Because of the past animosity, the Palmach forces did not try to treat the population of the town in a benevolent manner. The British feared 'a massacre threatened by Safed Jews' against the Arab civilians.[11]

There was in fact no massacre of Arab civilians at Safed but prisoners captured during the fighting were treated by the Zionists with brutality. Netiva Ben Yehuda has written honestly about the slaughter of several groups of Arab POWs during and after the battle for Safed.

In one case she saw an intelligence officer torture about ten Arab prisoners with a hoe until they bled to death. 'He beat these wounded men, burnt men who had not slept for days with their lips swollen from lack of water.'[12] The intelligence officer refused to allow the accumulated bodies to be carried out of the interrogation room since he wished to frighten the other Arabs who were brought in. Ben Yehuda was overwhelmed by the experience. Many of her fellow Palmachniks were also disgusted by the sight of blood and splattered brains. But the intelligence officer had only contempt for their humane sentiments.

He mumbled as he murdered the helpless prisoners: 'These Palmachniks! Weaklings, what do they think? They escaped!

Did they think we can maintain a state without such things? And is this the first time? So where are we to get men with guts to do things for us? Maybe we should hire people? Or hire some British? Free some Nazis!'

Ben Yehuda was so enraged that she took the intelligence officer's stick and broke it in two. But this did not end the horror. The intelligence officer got a new stick and continued. His principal aim was to discover the identity of the Arab commander.

When the last prisoner was brought in, he saw the heap of bodies and began to laugh. Bending over with laughter, he pointed to the bodies saying: 'This world is shit! See this.' He kneeled down and turned over one of the bodies which had teeth and brains knocked about but was better dressed than the others. It soon became clear that he was identifying the sought-after Arab commander whom the Jewish intelligence officer had just beaten to death.

The Jewish victory in Safed was a shock to the Arabs who remained in Upper Galilee. With Safed gone, there wasn't much to stop the Palmach's advance. Allon admits that he was quite anxious to drive the remaining Arabs out of the region. He later wrote that his aim was 'to cleanse the Upper Galilee and create a continuous strip of Israeli territory in the region.' He wished to do this before 15 May, when the proclamation of a Jewish state was expected to lead to the intervention of the Arab League armies. Allon noted that the Palmach had sustained considerable losses, so that he looked for ways 'which did not require us to employ force in order to cause the tens of thousands of sulky Arabs who remained in Galilee to flee.' He decided to use a whispering campaign:

> I gathered all of the Jewish Mayors who had contact with the Arabs in different villages and asked them to whisper in the ears of some Arabs that great Jewish reinforcements had arrived in Galilee and that they were going to burn all of the villages in the Hula valley. They should suggest to these Arabs as their friends that it was best for them to escape while there was still time. Thus the rumour spread in all parts of the Hula valley that it was time to flee. There was a massive exodus.[13]

While the Palmach forces were pushing the Arabs out of the Hula valley, the Golani Brigade was assigned to Operation Gideon, which consisted of mopping-up operations in the Beisan valley, south of Tiberias. Joseph Weitz, who was in charge of acquiring land for Jewish settlement, coveted the Beisan valley for future colonization. On 26 March, he wrote in his diary: 'Our action should aim at the evacuation of the entire Beisan valley except for Beisan town.'[14] But after most of the valley was 'purified of Arabs', on 5 May the Golani Brigade began a siege of Beisan town.

The first to flee Beisan were the wealthy families in the town. Most of the other people understood their desire to leave. As Muhammad Ahmad Shuraidi, a fisherman in Beisan explained, the rich people had been politically active and had contributed money to buy arms. Since they were strong supporters of the resistance to Zionism, everyone understood that the wealthy people would be the first to suffer reprisals under a Jewish occupation.

On 11 May, the Golani Brigade shelled the town. Soon after, they captured high ground near Beisan, from which they dominated the approaches to the town. This advance greatly affected the morale of the people of Beisan. The Jews telephoned from a police station outside the town asking for the surrender of Beisan. Ma'mun Darwics Ahmad remembered, 'They gave us ten hours to surrender, offering safe passage to those who wished to leave.' Although the town did not surrender, many people left to avoid further shelling.

Among those who left were Issam Tahtamuni and his family. As he relates, 'Two of the men who worked for us came to the house at dawn and suggested that we leave the city while there was still a chance.' Issam loaded two donkeys with a few of the family's personal belongings and left for the Jordan valley. The road was full of people anxious to cross over the river into Trans-Jordan. The next day, 12 May, the Mayor and local priest surrendered the town. They drove around with the Jewish commander to see to the surrender of arms.

Many people remained in the town for about a month under Israeli rule. In mid-June the Jews ordered that they leave. The Arab population were loaded into trucks and driven to the river

THE ROAD TO SAFED

where they were forced to cross over into Trans-Jordan.

With the end of the British mandate on 15 May, the leaders of the Jewish community in Palestine proclaimed the birth of *Medinat Yisrael* (State of Israel). It was perhaps more than accidental that Ben-Gurion and his associates did not use the name *Eretz Yisrael* (land of Israel) which was the biblical name for the original Jewish kingdom. *Eretz Yisrael* was considered inappropriate since the state proclaimed on 14 May was only part of the area which had long been claimed by the Zionists. It would take another war with the Arabs almost two decades later before the Zionists could fulfil their aspirations (as well as confirm the fears of the Arabs) and overrun all of Palestine.

The official Israeli Proclamation of Independence included a call to the 'sons of the Arab people dwelling in Israel to keep the peace and play their part in the development of the state with full and equal citizenship.' This assertion seemed more than a little hollow in view of the expulsions that had already taken place. At about the same time, a Voice of Israel radio broadcast in Arabic informed its listeners about their rights under the Jewish state but warned ominously: 'Every one of you is held responsible for your behaviour.'

Immediately after the proclamation of Israeli independence the Arab states sent their under-sized regular armies into Palestine for the first time in order, in the words of King Abdullah, 'to protect unarmed Arabs against massacres similar to Deir Yassin.' The reasons for the intervention of the Arab League members were more complex than King Abdullah suggested, but a desire to protect Palestinian civilians from expulsion and massacre was a major factor in the decision of Syria, Iraq, Lebanon, Egypt and Trans-Jordan to intervene in Palestine.

In all of these countries, the will of the people as expressed in street demonstrations was a force which could not be ignored. No Arab government could long stay in office if it did not placate the demand of its own people that something be done to save the Palestinian Arabs. The true facts of Deir Yassin and the expulsion of the Arabs from so many towns and villages were bad enough. But reports (some originating with the Western press) printed in newspapers in Cairo, Amman,

Baghdad, Beirut and Damascus greatly exaggerated the atrocities committed by the Jews so that many people in these capitals believed that not only were tens of thousands of Arab civilians being expelled from their homes but that tens of thousands more women and children were being butchered.

Most people in the Arab world did not doubt Camille Chamoun, the Lebanese Minister of Interior when he stated: 'The establishment of a Jewish state in Palestine is merely the prelude to the establishment of a Jewish state in Syria, Lebanon and Trans-Jordan.'[15] The Arab world recognized that Zionism was different from the usual type of colonialism practised by the Western powers. 'The imperialists were anxious to occupy countries for economic or military reasons,' according to Chamoun, 'but they did not usurp the very homes of the people as the Zionists did.' The expulsion of their Palestinian brothers convinced many people in the Arab world that Zionism was far more dangerous than British or French colonialism, which essentially interfered little in the everyday life of the people under their rule. Egypt, Syria, Lebanon, Jordan and Iraq had been under colonial influence but their colonial rulers had never expelled the population in order to settle hundreds of thousands of Europeans. If the Zionists succeeded in Palestine, how long would it be before they invaded other Arab countries?

There was considerable hesitation by the Arab states to intervene in Palestine in view of their military weakness. On 12 May, the United States Secretary of State, George C. Marshall, gave an assessment of the Middle East situation. As a former United States Army Chief of Staff, Marshall was well qualified to judge the military strength of the Arab states. According to Marshall, 'Lebanon has no real army' and Syria 'has neither arms or an army worthy of the name.'[16] He noted that because of 'political and economic disorders,' Iraq 'cannot afford to move more than a handful of troops' to Palestine while Egypt, which suffered from 'strikes and disorders', was also militarily weak. The only military force of any consequence in the Arab world was the Arab Legion of Trans-Jordan, but its 5,000 men could never hope to match the army of 70,000 which Israel was eventually able to put in the field.

At the same time the Palmach was advancing through

THE ROAD TO SAFED

western Galilee, Jewish forces were attacking Acre, the ancient fortress city. Unlike Safed and Tiberias, Acre was supposed to be in the Arab state under the UN partition plan. Its Arab population of 25,000 was doubled by refugees from areas already overrun by Jewish forces, especially Haifa. Most of these people had already been through a great ordeal, having fled by land or sea under harrowing circumstances. Acre suffered from a shortage of food, sanitary facilities and medical supplies. These problems were greatly exacerbated during the Israeli siege which began on 28 April.

The Carmeli Brigade subjected Acre to a heavy mortar barrage which wreaked havoc among the refugees. Several days later, British observers in the area reported, 'The Jews have cut the aqueduct supplying Acre with water and almost simultaneously there was an outbreak of typhoid there.'[17] The water cut-off probably did not cause the epidemic but the two events had a significant psychological impact which greatly facilitated the exodus from the town. The Carmeli Brigade also used sound-trucks and other methods of psychological warfare to encourage the Arab flight. Indeed, when they captured Acre on 18 May, they found that most of the nearly 50,000 residents and refugees were gone. The 4,000 Arabs who remained in Acre were subjected to a reign of terror.

Several months after the Israeli capture of Acre, Lieutenant Petite, a United Nations observer from France, visited Acre to investigate Arab charges that those Palestinians who remained under Israeli rule were being mistreated. Petite reported that looting was being conducted in a systematic manner by the Israeli army which was carrying off furniture, clothes, and any other property that could be used by new Jewish immigrants who were being settled into the city. The UN observer reported that the looting was part of 'a Jewish plan to prevent the return of refugees,'[18] similar to what was being done in other parts of the new Jewish state.

Lieutenant Petite noted that the Jews had murdered at least 100 Arab civilians in Acre. In particular the Israelis killed many residents of the new city who refused to move into the portion of the old city that was being used as an Arab ghetto. The Israelis considered the new city totally off-limits to Arabs.

The case of Mohammed Fayez Soufi was typical. He was forced to leave his home in the new part of town and was relocated in the portion of the old city of Acre that had not been demolished. When Mohammed and four of his friends went back to their former homes in the new city to get food, they were stopped by a gang of Israeli soldiers who put a pistol to each of their heads and forced them to drink cyanide. Mohammed faked swallowing the poison but his friends were not so lucky. After half an hour, three of the Arabs died and were tossed in the sea by the Israelis. Several days later, their bodies were washed up on the shore.

Lieutenant Petite suspected that the murders of Arab civilians in Acre were the work of Israeli soldiers who were acting without orders from their superiors. But there can be no doubt that the atrocities reflected the contemptuous attitude toward Arab civilians which prevailed in the Israeli army. The Israeli High Command certainly did nothing to punish those who committed the atrocities reported by the UN officials in all parts of the Jewish state.

The UN observers came to Palestine as part of a team headed by the mediator, Count Folke Bernadotte of Sweden, after a cease-fire came into effect on 11 June. This first truce lasted only four weeks, until 9 July, when fighting broke out again. During the truce the IDF Intelligence branch wrote a report on 'The Emigration of the Arabs of Palestine 1 December 1947–1 June 1948.'[19] In a recent article[20] the Israeli historian Benny Morris attaches great significance to this document, which he believes gives an accurate analysis of the causes of the first half of the Palestinian exodus.

Some of the information in the report is undoubtedly correct, including the estimate of 391,000 refugees up to 1 June. It is also significant that the IDF Intelligence branch dismisses any 'socio-economic' causes of the exodus. The report notes that during the early months of the war 'the Arab economy so long as the inhabitants stayed in their places was not damaged in a manner which destroyed the population's capacity to subsist.'

Equally important is the absence in the report of any indication that there was a general appeal by the Arab leadership ordering the Palestinians to flee their homes. There is the

THE ROAD TO SAFED

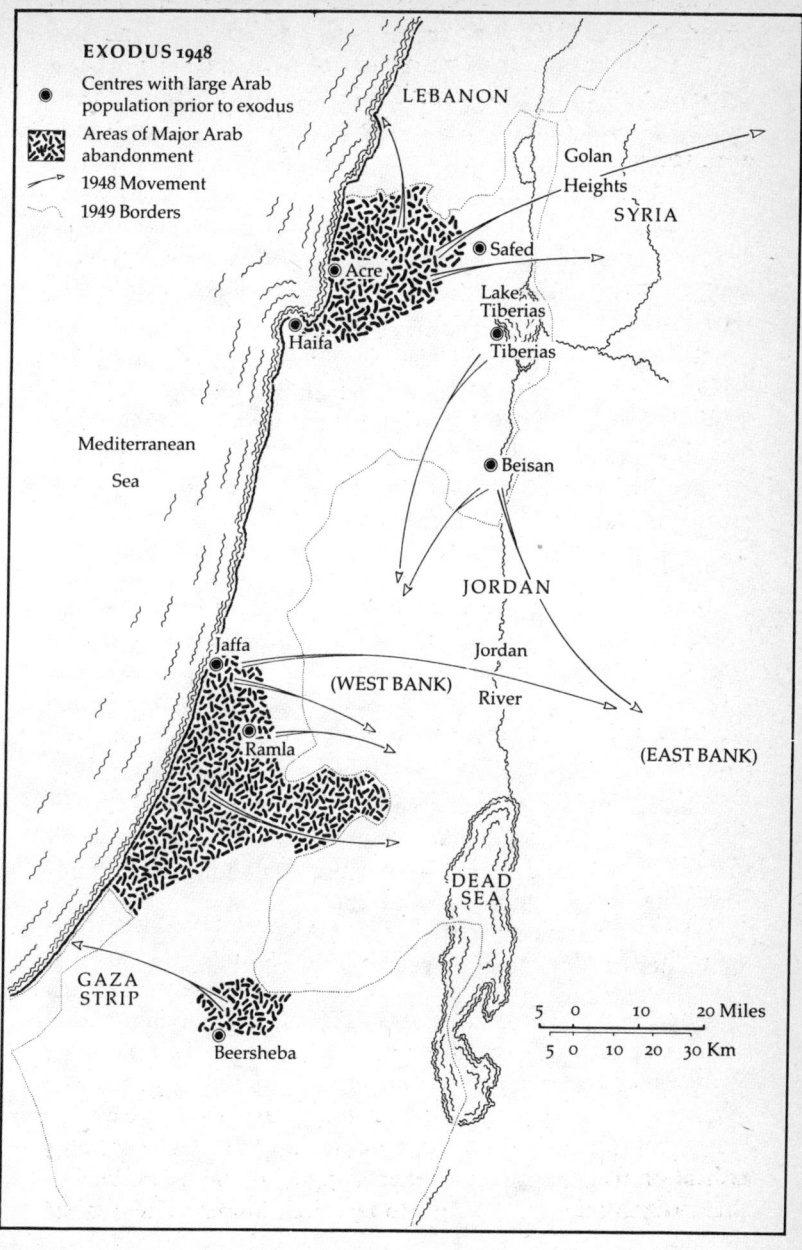

claim that about 5 per cent of the pre-June refugees left as a result of evacuation orders by the Arab leadership for certain villages where the population belonged to ethnic groups that collaborated with the Zionists or because 'there was no possibility of defending the villages.' This is probably correct since Druse or Circassian villages that collaborated with the Zionists were sometimes attacked by Arab forces. A few towns were also evacuated by Arab forces in order to spare the population from Zionist terrorism.

The report notes that 2 per cent of the pre-June refugees left as a result of a Jewish whispering campaign in the Hula valley and along the coastal plain which was aimed at frightening away the Arabs. There was in fact a whispering campaign in many parts of Galilee and the coastal plain (see pages 141–2) by Jews who attempted to intimidate their Arab neighbours into fleeing. The number of Arabs involved, however, was far larger than 2 per cent of the pre-June refugees.

According to the Intelligence branch, about 70 per cent of the refugees left because of 'direct hostile Jewish operations' including the activities of the Irgun and Stern Gang. Of the refugees supposedly only 2 per cent were the victims of 'expulsion orders'. However, the report does not make it clear how Jewish military action caused the exodus of the remaining 68 per cent of the refugees. This of course greatly limits the value of the document. As we have seen, most of the refugees succumbed to various degrees of coercion ranging from threatening radio and sound-truck broadcasts, leaflets and frightening noises, desecration of churches and mosques, bombardment of civilian areas and the blowing up of homes, execution of hostages, looting and rape. Certainly, far more than 2 per cent of the early refugees were expelled from their homes at gunpoint. There is, in fact, evidence of a Jewish policy to drive out Arabs even in the early part of the war.

At about the same time during the June truce that the IDF report was being composed, Yaacov Shimoni, deputy director of the Middle East division of the Foreign Office, wrote to his superior, Elias Sasson. Shimoni said that he had directed that if the war was renewed, in the fighting zone, the army should 'strongly advise the population to evacuate.'[21]

The issuing of such orders, which surely had to have the approval of Ben-Gurion, clearly indicates that even in the early months of the war the IDF was 'strongly advising' Palestinians to leave, as part of its usual method of operation. Though later the Israelis would become more direct and brutal in expelling Arabs, even in the early phase of the war there was a policy to get rid of Palestinian civilians whenever possible. In fact as we have seen, Plan D, which was drawn up before the war started, provided for the intentional expulsion of many civilians.

When the conflict was renewed on 9 July, the policy of intimidation mentioned by Shimoni was put into effect during the 'Ten Day War' between the First and Second Truce. In central Galilee most of the towns occupied in July by the IDF were forced to evacuate, with one notable exception.

When the people of Nazareth heard that many of the surrounding towns had fallen, they were ready to flee. But according to Elias Sruiji, a local doctor, Arab soldiers 'stopped us and forced all the people to return to the city.' This turned out to be lucky for them, since the Israelis had orders to exercise restraint in the home town of Jesus. Chaim Laskov, the Israeli commander, recalled, 'We had specific instructions not to harm anything, which meant that we had to take Nazareth by stratagem.' Indeed Ben-Gurion ordered that when the town was taken unauthorized soldiers should not be allowed into Nazareth and that the army should avoid 'any possibility of looting and desecration of churches and monasteries.'[22] He even decreed that 'if there is any attempt at robbing by our soldiers, a machine gun should be used without mercy.'

Druse living near Nazareth supplied the Jews with considerable intelligence so that on 16 July, the town fell into Israeli hands before any resistance could be organized. Only one Israeli was killed and one wounded in the attack. A delegation of Christian clerics came out to meet the conquerors. Their request that the civilian population should not be forced to evacuate was granted. When Abraham Yaffe, an Israeli officer, entered Nazareth, he met a man whom he had driven out of another town in Galilee. 'Have you come to turn us away again?' the Arab inquired. 'No, not in Nazareth,' Yaffe answered. 'Nazareth is a holy place, a holy town. The world is watching us. You are not going to be a victim here.' The IDF was careful not to allow too many troops to enter Nazareth, most of whom were stationed at a police fortress outside the town.

Ben Dunkelman was appointed as military governor of Nazareth and the surrounding region. Despite the initial orders for the troops to show restraint, the Israeli High Command was not sure what to do with the population of Nazareth. Several days after the capture of the town, Chaim Laskov came to Dunkelman with orders from the High Command that he evacuate the population. Dunkelman recorded his reaction to the evacuation order that was brought to him by Laskov. 'I told him I would do nothing of the sort – in view of the promises to safeguard the city's people, such a move would be superfluous and harmful.' Dunkelman reminded Laskov that only a few days before, 'he and I as representatives of the Israeli army, had signed the surrender document in which we solemnly pledged to do nothing to harm the city or its population.'[23]

Later that day, Abraham Yaffe told Dunkelman that on orders from the High Command he was replacing him as military governor. Dunkelman wrote, 'I complied with the order but only after Abraham had given me his word of honour that he would do nothing to harm or displace the Arab population.' Dunkelman believes that his stand did some good. 'It seems to have given the High Command time for second thoughts, which led them to the conclusion that it would, indeed, be wrong to expel the inhabitants of Nazareth. To the best of my knowledge, there was never any more talk of the evacuation plan and the city's Arab citizens have lived there ever since.'

The Israelis were wise to restrain their conduct in Nazareth. They realized that the expulsion of Christian Arabs in one of the holiest Christian locations would produce unfavourable headlines all over the Western world. Mansour Kardosh, a local businessman, observed that, 'Nazareth was always considered to be a pro-Catholic town and any conqueror would have to think twice before causing a mass expulsion which would invoke the wrath of Rome.'[24] And so the 14,000 people of the town were allowed to remain. Nazareth was the exception that proved the rule. Most towns where the population was not expelled by force were spared by the Israelis for a definite reason.

At the same time during the 'Ten Day War' that Nazareth was overrun, the Israelis were also launching an offensive on another front where the inhabitants would not be as fortunate.

CHAPTER VIII

The Lydda Death March

And when the blast shall sound
Upon the day when man shall flee his brother...

Koran LXXX, 33–34

Civilians ran for cover as an armoured unit of the Israeli 89th Commando Battalion fired its way into Lydda, an Arab town not far from Tel Aviv. At the head of the column in an armoured car he called 'The Terrible Tiger' rode Major Moshe Dayan, a relatively obscure professional soldier who had personally recruited the men of his battalion including a contingent of Stern Gang terrorists. Dayan was eager to prove that his method of lightning warfare would win quick results against the Arabs. For forty-seven minutes on the evening of 11 July 1948, Dayan and his armoured forces terrorized both the defenders of Lydda and the neighbouring town Ramle, as well as their Arab civilian population.

Keith Wheller, a reporter for the *Chicago Sun Times*, witnessed the attack. In an article titled 'Blitz Tactics Won Lydda', he wrote that as the Israeli vehicles surged through the town, 'practically everything in their way died. Riddled corpses lay by the roadside.'[1] Not all of the casualties were members of the Arab Legion that was defending the town. Kenneth Bilby of the *New York Herald Tribune* who entered Lydda in the company of an Israeli intelligence officer noticed 'the corpses of Arab men, women and even children strewn about in the wake of the ruthlessly brilliant charge.'[2]

The Israelis were not keen to take prisoners. Netiva Ben Yehuda, a young female member of the Palmach, recalled that a soldier 'went through the streets of Lydda with loudspeakers

THE LYDDA DEATH MARCH

and promised everybody who would go inside a certain mosque that they would be safe.' Hundreds of Arabs entered the Dahmash Mosque believing that nothing would happen to them if they sat quietly with their hands on their head. But according to Ben Yehuda 'something did happen.'[3] In retaliation for a grenade attack after the surrender which killed several Israeli soldiers, over eighty Arab prisoners were machine-gunned to death. The bodies lay decomposing for ten days in the July heat. The Dahmash Mosque massacre terrorized the people of Lydda.

The Israelis were equally violent in Ramle. On the evening of 11 July, the Voice of Israel Radio announced 'the inhabitants of the two towns were panic-stricken and both civilians and soldiers attempted on several occasions to flee.'[4]

Yigal Allon, commander of the central front, praised Dayan because he had 'charged with great daring into Lydda.' Prime Minister Ben-Gurion wrote that he had 'become acquainted with Moshe Dayan from Lydda–Ramle which was the greatest of our conquests.' But Israeli propaganda broadcasts which claimed that the Arab civilian population had fled were not accurate. The day after the attack while Israeli forces were still conducting 'mopping-up operations' in the Lydda–Ramle region, Allon and Ben-Gurion met with Brigade Commander Yitzak Rabin to consider what should be done with the large civilian population which was falling into the hands of the Israelis.

At a Cabinet meeting several weeks earlier, Ben-Gurion had declared 'war is war'[5] adding that the Arabs 'will have to bear the consequences after they have been defeated.' But during his conference with Allon and Rabin, the Prime Minister maintained a stoic silence as the two young commanders outlined the problem. Rabin later recalled that he and Allon believed that they could not leave a large civilian population 'in our rear where it could endanger the supply routes.' Finally as the conference ended, the two young commanders walked outside with Ben-Gurion. Allon repeated his question, 'What is to be done with the population?' Ben-Gurion waved his hand in a gesture which clearly meant 'Drive them out.' After the Prime Minister left, Allon and Rabin consulted on the matter and agreed to follow his directive to expel the Arab population from the Lydda–Ramle region.*

Because of the war, Fouzi al-Asmar found himself in a peculiar situation for a ten year old. Most boys of his age dislike school but Fouzi sincerely regretted that the local grammar school in Lydda had been closed and his studies interrupted for many months. Fouzi was the youngest son of a middle-class Christian-Arab family which traced its ancestry in Palestine back for at least eighteen generations. With the outbreak of hostilities between Arabs and Jews much had changed for Fouzi besides the closing of the school. When the lad had inquired as to reasons for the war he was told: 'The Jews want to expel us in order to bring in Jews from far away countries.'[6]

One afternoon in July as Fouzi was playing football on the sports field of his deserted grammar school, he saw masses of people running in his direction. The expressions of fear on their faces told him that something was seriously wrong. The boy headed home where he found out that Lydda as well as Ramle had been captured by an Israeli army. There was much speculation in his home about what all this meant, but no one would dare go outside to find out what was really happening. Intrigued by what he was hearing the boy asked, 'Mother, what does a Jew look like?' His mother asked Fouzi if he remembered 'Uncle Ahroni', who always seemed to have a sweet for Fouzi and the other children. But his mother's response only added to Fouzi's confusion since he could not see the connection between the kindly Jewish railroad official and the Israeli soldiers who were trying to drive the Arabs from their homeland.

Several days later soldiers arrived in Fouzi's neighbourhood and began searching for arms. They announced that the residents of the district must walk over to the football field and

---

*Rabin described his participation in the Lydda–Ramle campaign in a portion of his memoirs which was censored by the Israeli government but was released to the press by his translator. *New York Times*, 29 October 1979, *Newsweek*, 9 November 1979.

leave their homes open. On the football field the Arab civilians were divided into three groups. Because there was a train depot nearby many of the people in the area were railroad employees. They and their families were put into the first group. The Israelis wanted the railroad to begin operating as soon as possible, thus the railroad employees and their families were allowed to remain. Most men between sixteen and forty-five who were not railroad employees were taken away as prisoners-of-war because the Israelis charged that they had resisted after the surrender. The third group consisted of the families of those who had been taken captive. They were told to go home and prepare themselves, 'because the Red Cross would come next morning to take them to King Abdullah', a reference to the ruler of Trans-Jordan.

However, the following morning the women, old men and children were not met by the Red Cross but by Israeli soldiers who shouted 'Go to King Abdullah' and 'You go to Abdullah' as they ejected the people from the town.

A blind teenager Raja'i Buseilah (now an English professor at an American University) remembers being huddled with the other frightened people of Lydda. 'The streets were full of sound and bustle, more of relief than of loss, of disaster, of the misery lying in wait on the road.' Raja'i's keen ears heard the Israeli loudspeakers broadcasting from trucks, warning the people that they had better leave quickly or they would suffer a similar fate as those massacred in the Dahmash Mosque. The hordes of civilians were marched eastward, each step taking them closer to their new life as refugees.

As the *London Economist* reported, 'The Arab refugees were systematically stripped of all their belongings before they were sent on their trek to the frontier. Household belongings, stores, clothing, all had to be left behind.'[7] Though blind and defenceless, Raja'i recalls, 'I was searched twice and lost a watch.' According to Saba A. Saba, another Palestinian youth, some were treated even more brutally. 'Two of my friends were killed in cold blood. One was carrying a box presumed to have money and the other a pillow which was believed to contain valuables.' Sayid Nasrallah had a similar experience. 'A friend of mine resisted and was killed in front of me. He had 400

Palestinian pounds in his pocket.' Most of the people, however, turned over their valuables without a struggle.

Young Fouzi witnessed how his friends and neighbours were treated as they were being forced out of town. Standing there, he shook his head saying, 'Mother, I don't believe these Jews are at all like Uncle Ahroni.'

After robbing them the Israelis forced the people toward the area where the Arab Legion had taken up position because they wished to burden the Jordanians with the care of thousands of destitute civilians. According to Yitzhak Rabin, 'There was no way of avoiding the use of force and warning shots in order to make the inhabitants march ten to fifteen miles to the point where they met up with the Legion.'

Some of the shots fired by the Israelis found their mark since several of Fouzi's neighbours and family members were shot down in cold blood along the road. Years later, Fouzi's aunt who was among those expelled, recalled the death march. 'It was a ten-hour walk and we did not have food or water. Many died on the way. Abandoned children were seen wandering around crying. There were some who urinated and drank their own urine.' Without food or water, many of the people soon collapsed in the stifling 100° midsummer heat. A few of the Arab men lunged at nursing mothers and pinned them to the ground, but not to rape them. In their frenzied thirst, the men wished to suck a few drops of moisture from their lactating breasts.

As he marched, Raja'i's blindness was a blessing since it spared him the sight of much of the surrounding misery. But his ears betrayed him. 'I was made aware, slowly by piecemeal, through exclamations or incoherent phrases, that some of those who lay dead had their tongues sticking out, covered with dust and down.' In order to retain his sanity he recited from the Koran. Although he had memorized the entire holy text, he could now recall only a few lines of Sura 80, in which Allah rebukes the Prophet for having spurned the wisdom of a blind man.

> And when the blast shall sound
> Upon the day when man shall flee his brother . . .

Also among the expelled was a twenty-two-year-old medical student who had returned from the American University in Beirut so he could be with his family in Lydda during the turmoil in Palestine. George had come home just in time to be with his relatives and neighbours as they were turned out of their homes by the Zionists. The sight of the dying children, sick and old people marching in the heat of the sun, made an indelible impression on him – it became the turning-point of his life. It took every ounce of his strength and courage to survive the ordeal. Like so many others he was forced to drink his own urine to prevent death by dehydration. George vowed that some day he would seek vengeance for the atrocities inflicted on his people. This was an oath he was to keep before the entire world.

The Arab civilians marched like a column of ants down the dirt road through wild hill country. Overhead they were buzzed by small low-flying Israeli aircraft whose principal mission was to urge the expelled Arabs along as they trudged uphill through country which was covered with thorn bushes. Most of the marchers believed that the day would never end. The sun refused to move from its position above as the women and old men prayed for evening or the sight of King Abdullah's Arab Legion.

The mood of these tragic events would later be captured by Ismail Shammout, an eighteen-year-old survivor of the death march who would eventually become a recognized artist. Ismail was expelled from Lydda along with his parents and eight brothers and sisters. While marching in the blazing heat, he spotted some water. He rushed to fill a pot he was carrying. He later recalled, 'At that moment a jeep pulled up with three people. One of them, a Zionist officer, got out. He pulled a gun and put it to my head and ordered me to put the water down.'[8] The Arab teenager had no choice but to obey.

Ismail would never forget the thirst of the thousands of people who trudged on, not knowing where they were going. He saw people chewing grass in the hope of obtaining a bit of moisture. Others drank their children's urine. By the roadside pregnant women were prematurely delivering babies, their labour brought on by the strain of their ordeal. None of these infants survived. Since no one had any opportunity to bury the dead, they were covered with grass and abandoned.

Eventually Ismail managed to get some water out of sight of the Israeli soldiers. Although the water was dirty and obviously polluted he drank some while soaking his clothes in the reddish liquid. As Ismail attempted to return to his family, people followed him hoping to get a few drops of the precious fluid. One woman sucked at his moist shirt.

Many of those on the death march came from Ramle. Abu Hassan was a prominent member of the community who represented Ramle on the government tax assessment committees. When the Zionists invaded Ramle, five Israeli soldiers broke into his home and ordered him and his family to leave, saying 'This is our country and these are our homes; get out!'[9]

But according to Abu Hassan not all the members of his family left willingly. 'My first-born aged sixteen years tried to protect his mother and grandmother from the rough handling of the intruders only to be shot dead.' The rest of the family were dumbfounded by the murder as they were pushed out of their home with rifle butts. They were not allowed to take anything and indeed Abu Hassan was robbed of the few coins in his pocket. But this was not the worst part of the tragedy. 'We were not allowed to attend our dead son. How and where he is buried I shall never know.'

Although brutality was common in Ramle, some Israelis showed compassion. When Zionist troops broke into another home, the officer in charge offered the Arab women to his men. One young woman was taken to a bedroom by an Israeli soldier who spoke unaccented Arabic, saying to the girl: 'Don't be afraid, I am an Arab Jew and I intend to treat you as my sister!'[10] The young woman was overjoyed and she kissed the soldier's hand. The Oriental Jew let the girl out a side door and she was able eventually to rejoin her family.

But not all of the women of Ramle were so lucky. A woman who calls herself 'Hanan' reported what happened when Zionist troops broke into her Ramle home. Her father begged the troops to leave his family alone. But the officer in charge threatened to avenge Arab insults against Jews. After robbing the house the Zionist officer pointed to 'Hanan' and told his men 'She is yours, take her.' Her father was shot when he tried to stop the soldiers.

'Hanan' was taken to a bedroom where she was attacked by three Israeli soldiers. 'They threw me on the bed and helped each other to undress me and before I was attacked, I fainted. I came to, bleeding and in pain and realized that the three soldiers had raped me in turn.'* The young woman was taken back to join her family where she found her father dead on the floor with her mother bending over him weeping. Soon after the Israeli soldiers shoved 'Hanan' and her mother toward the door and warned them that if they wished to remain alive they should join the crowd in the street. The residents of Ramle were loaded into trucks and driven part of the way to Ramallah but had to walk the last few miles.

'Hanan' saw that all her neighbours had suffered the same fate as her family. Sari Nasir recalls that his family was routed out of his home in Ramle by a Jewish soldier who came to the door and told Sari's father that everyone must leave. 'Otherwise you know what will happen. What happened at Deir Yassin will happen to you.'[13] The reference by the Zionist to the massacre at Deir Yassin where 250 Arab civilians had been butchered a few months earlier was enough to make the Nasir family and thousands of others flee Ramle.

Sari's account of the exodus from his home is just as gruesome as the ordeal suffered by the people from Lydda. He recalls a day of terror. 'Small children carrying smaller children in their arms. Women on the way sitting, crying and waiting for their husbands, waiting for their children, sending children back for someone who was missing.' According to Abdul Mukrahim the people of Ramle were especially terrified since, 'the Jews fired over their heads' to keep them moving along the steep uphill climb.[14]

---

*There is Israeli evidence of rape and looting in Ramle. On 21 July Agriculture Minister Aharon Cizling stated at a Cabinet meeting 'It has been said that there were cases of rape in Ramle. I can forgive acts of rape but I won't forgive other deeds which appear to me graver.'[11] Ben-Gurion noted in his diary on 15 July about Lydda and Ramle, 'The bitter question has arisen regarding acts of robbery and rape in the conquered towns.'[12]

'Hanan' has a similar memory of the death march. 'Israeli soldiers moved among the crowds striking them with the butts of their rifles or firing a few shots into the air to speed them on their way.' 'Hanan' also recalled 'the wailing of the women, the crying of the children and the chanting of prayers by the men seeking God's intervention.' As with the people from Lydda, many old people from Ramle died. Since there were no tools to bury the dead, 'Hanan' saw stones being placed over the bodies after a few prayers were recited by the family. Each time she saw such a sight it reminded her of her own father who had been shot down and she began to weep.

Abu Hassan from Ramle had lost his sixteen-year-old son but his ordeal was not over. He has bitter memories of the death march. 'With machine-gun fire speeding us on our way, many fell by the wayside. My aged mother passed away from sheer exhaustion.' Like so many others he could not give her a proper burial so he heaped stones over her to protect the body from wild animals and birds of prey.

Not all of the Israeli soldiers approved of the way Arab civilians were being treated. 'There were some fellows who refused to take part in the eviction action,' recalls Rabin. Many of the Israeli soldiers were graduates of youth movements where they had been taught 'values such as international brotherhood and humanitarianism' – values which they now were being ordered to violate. The Israeli High Command found it necessary to indoctrinate the men with 'prolonged propaganda' in order to justify what Rabin called 'a harsh and cruel action'.

Eventually most of the 60,000 Arab civilians from Lydda–Ramle came to refugee camps near Ramallah in territory controlled by the Jordanian Arab Legion. On 2 August, the refugees were visited by Count Folke Bernadotte, a United Nations mediator sent to resolve the Arab–Israeli dispute. Bernadotte had done valuable humanitarian work at the end of the Second World War, helping to assist Jewish and other European refugees who survived Nazi concentration camps. But he was not prepared for what he saw as thousands of Arab civilians stormed his car. 'I have made the acquaintance of a great many refugee camps,' Bernadotte wrote, 'but never have

I seen a more ghastly sight than that which met my eyes here at Ramallah.'[15] The refugees shouted that they wanted to return to their homes. They had obviously been through an extraordinary ordeal. Bernadotte noted: 'There were plenty of frightening faces in that sea of suffering humanity.'

Later the Swedish mediator told an American diplomat that the condition of the Arab refugees from all parts of Palestine who were 'without food, clothing and shelter was appalling.'[16] As for the property of the Arab refugees, Bernadotte said that 'Apparently most had been seized for use by Jews.' Indeed on a visit to Lydda–Ramle he had seen Israeli soldiers 'Organizing and supervising the removal of the contents from Arab houses.'

After visiting the refugee camps at Ramallah, Bernadotte had lunch with Arif al-Arif, the Administrative Governor of the Ramallah area. Arif told Bernadotte the story of the exodus from Lydda–Ramle. People had been shot, others died from thirst and sunstroke while all had been robbed of their possessions by the Israeli army. Prophetically, Arif warned that if the Palestinian Arabs did not receive justice, 'they will educate their children for generations to carry on war against the Jews.'

As the whole world knows, the Palestinians have not received justice and Arif al-Arif's prediction plagues us even to this day. Many of the survivors of the death march from Lydda–Ramle have sought vengeance against their tormentors. George the young medical student from Lydda completed his studies but later repaid in kind the terrorism suffered by his people. Dr George Habash planned some of the most famous PLO operations including the hijacking of many airliners.

News of what happened at Lydda–Ramle spread soon after the expulsion. A Red Cross team visited the area and made a detailed report that was obtained by interested governments. The Americans learned from the Red Cross that 'the Jews on capturing Ramle forced all the Arab inhabitants to evacuate the town except Christian Arabs whom they permitted to remain.'[17] (Israelis were sometimes but not always more lenient towards Christian Arabs.)

Some members of the Israeli government objected to the expulsion of so many civilians from the Lydda–Ramle area but most agreed with the policy of removing Arabs from newly conquered territory. Ezra Dannin, an Israeli government adviser on Arab affairs, probably reflected the feelings of most government officials when he wrote on 16 August:

> If the High Command believes that by destruction, killing and human suffering its aims will be achieved faster then I would not stand in its way. If we don't hurry up our enemies will do the same thing to us. If the inhabitants of Lydda–Ramle were allowed to remain and we had to care for them in a humane way then the Arab Legion could have captured Tel Aviv.
>
> It is good for both peoples that there will be a complete separation. I will therefore do everything possible in order to reduce the number of this [Arab] minority.[18]

Dannin was often consulted by Ben-Gurion on Arab affairs. His letter makes clear that he and his colleagues knew and acquiesced in the methods used to expel Arabs by the IDF at Lydda–Ramle and elsewhere. There is no evidence that Ben-Gurion ordered the killings, rape or looting of civilians; indeed he was concerned about such activities since they undermined morale and discipline. But the Prime Minister and most of his Cabinet believed that the army should do whatever was necessary to make sure that the Arabs were pushed out of and stayed out of Israeli territory.

Another article by the Israeli journalist Benny Morris deals with Lydda–Ramle. Morris relies on Israeli military records, but there are indications that these files are unreliable with regard to the expulsion of Arab civilians from Lydda–Ramle and other areas.* Morris states that the population of Lydda–Ramle 'were perhaps as eager to leave the area of Israeli jurisdiction as the Israelis to see them leave'.[19]

In view of the brutal conduct of the Zionists from the first moment they entered Lydda, it is not surprising that many

---

*For example several months after the expulsion from Lydda-Ramle the IDF sent the Israeli Foreign Office Hebrew translations of several leaflets that had been passed out to the civilian population of the two towns. The Foreign Office had obtained the original Arabic language version of the leaflets and complained to the Chief of Staff that the translations submitted to the diplomats were 'inaccurate'.[20] Apparently the army did not want accurate versions of the

THE LYDDA DEATH MARCH

Palestinians were terrified at the prospect of remaining under Israeli rule. But Rabin makes it clear that 'the population of Lydda did not leave willingly.' Had the IDF treated the people of Lydda humanely most of them probably would have preferred to remain in their homes, but Israeli policy aimed at a 'complete separation'.

Morris states that the Arab estimates of 335 civilian deaths during the exodus from Lydda–Ramle is 'certainly an exaggeration'. In fact 335 is a very conservative figure since tens of thousands of infants, sick and the elderly were forced to march all day in midsummer heat, with 'warning shots' being fired by their Israeli tormentors.

Rabin's testimony about Israeli brutality during the death march is supported by Ezra Dannin who makes it clear that there was 'destruction, killing and human suffering' at Lydda–Ramle. Certainly many were killed when the infamous 89th Commando Battalion (later to become the butchers of Dawayma) blasted their way into Lydda. Morris admits that hundreds of unarmed civilians were killed in Lydda during an 'uprising' after the surrender. He also notes that 'in the confusion' detainees in the mosque and church were shot. The Arab estimate of 400 civilians butchered during the occupation of the city would appear to be accurate.

Many hundreds more died in the refugee camps in Ramallah shortly after the exodus. An American report notes that the death-rate in the camp was 'undoubtedly high among infants due to malnutrition and diarrhoea.'[21] In all, probably about 1,000 Arab civilians died during and immediately after the expulsion from Lydda–Ramle. They would be followed by many more fatalities in other areas of Palestine during the later part of the war.

The expulsion from Lydda–Ramle took place during the 'Ten

---

pamphlets in government files since they contained brutal threats against the Arab civilians. The Foreign Office informed the Chief of Staff that in the future they desired more accurate reports but that if this was not possible they would send Ezra Dannin to IDF headquarters to be briefed orally about the treatment of Arab civilians in any towns that were occupied. Since the Israeli Foreign Office did not trust the accuracy of IDF written reports on the treatment of Arab civilians there is no reason why anyone else should.

Day War' between the First and Second Truce. But the imposition of a truce did little to ease the suffering of the Arab civilians who continued to be expelled from their homes in the tens of thousands while the diplomats discussed the future of their country.

CHAPTER IX

The Troubled Truce

Blessed are the peacemakers, for they shall be called sons of God
                                                        Matthew 5:7

On the evening of 17 July, a stranger arrived with a letter addressed to the notables of Jaba, an Arab village not far from Haifa. When the messenger told the people of Jaba that the note he carried came from Mahmud Almadi, they were noticeably apprehensive. Almadi was a lawyer and farm owner from the area who frequently acted as an intermediary with the Jews. Many of the villagers did not trust him. However, most people in Jaba believed that it was useful to negotiate with the Jews, particularly in time of war. But the villagers soon learned that the Israelis had no interest in discussion. In the note they demanded that the notables of Jaba as well as those from the neighbouring hamlets, Ghazal and Izzam, meet with Israeli officials at 9 a.m. on 19 July, to arrange the surrender of the three villages before the second nationwide truce came into effect later that day.

Since the beginning of the war, the population of the three villages had been increased by a large flow of refugees, particularly from Haifa. There were now over 8,000 Arabs living in the area, which was well inside Jewish-controlled territory. The Israelis had no intention of allowing so many Arabs to remain in such a strategic location, so close to the vital Haifa–Tel Aviv highway. During the 'Ten Day War', the villagers had fought with Israeli convoys and had destroyed some of the trucks which carried valuable supplies from the port of Haifa to the Jewish capital.

In the early morning hours, the elders of the three villages made their decision. 'We will defend our villages until the truce comes into effect today at 5 p.m.,' they answered the Israelis. They agreed to a meeting at 4 p.m., one hour before the country-wide truce, instead of 9 a.m. as demanded by their enemies. But the Israelis were in no mood for compromise; they would accept nothing less than total surrender, regardless of any truce agreement.

At 9 a.m. the Israelis launched an attack against the three villages. Although tanks and aircraft were used, the villagers put up a stiff resistance. The Israelis stepped up their assault, completely ignoring the 5 p.m. cease-fire. They attacked the villages every day for almost a week. Particularly devastating were the air attacks, against which the Arab villagers had no defence. Several types of bombs were used and the villages were strafed after each bombing run. Yusuf Abu Mahmoud of Ghazal later recalled, 'The airplane attacks killed about thirty and wounded thirty-five more from our village.' There were many casualties in the other towns. But for several days, the Arabs refused to surrender or flee their homes.

On the afternoon of 21 July, the people of Jaba received another message from Mahmud Almadi who claimed that he had 'received a letter from the Red Cross which stated that at 12 noon the next day, the Red Cross with the Jews would like to come to pick up bodies after a meeting at Wadi Armahara.' The village elders agreed to a meeting and said that they would carry a white flag to Wadi Armahara. It soon became apparent, however, that the request for a meeting was only a ploy to catch the villagers off guard. That night the three villages were bombed, after which there was a ground attack by Israeli tanks and infantry. Sound-trucks circled Jaba warning the citizens, 'yield or we will destroy the whole village.'

By Saturday, 24 July, the villagers could no longer resist the Israeli attack. The civilians began fleeing the three villages. Hajid-Had Saleh, an elder of Izzam, was horrified that 'during the evacuation women and children were attacked with machine-gun fire from enemy aircraft.' Other survivors reported that the Israelis machine-gunned the fleeing civilians while not neglecting to steal livestock, money and valuables whenever possible. After forcing the villagers out, most of their homes were destroyed so that they could never return.

Since the assault on the three villages took place after the Second Truce came into effect, the United Nations Truce Supervising Board investigated the Arab charges with regard to the Israeli attacks. The Tel Aviv government admitted assaulting the villages but claimed that it was not a violation of the Truce since it constituted a 'police action' within Israeli territory against bandits in an area which had long since been evacuated by Arab civilians.

In their report the United Nations Truce observers dismissed the Israeli explanation on every count. Their investigation revealed that the Israelis had attacked the three villages 'despite the attempts made by the inhabitants to negotiate with the Israeli army at the commencement of the Second Truce.' In all, over 8,000 civilians 'were forced to evacuate' their villages by the Israeli army, which 'systematically destroyed Ein Ghazal and Jaba'. The UN could find no justification for the attack, since the Arabs had not violated the Truce. Clearly the only reason for the assault was to push 8,000 Arabs from Israeli territory. Count Bernadotte, the United Nations mediator, requested that the Tel Aviv government allow the civilian population of the three villages to return, but his appeal was ignored.[1]

There were many other villages along the highway between Haifa and Tel Aviv where the population had been pushed out earlier in spring 1948. Not all of these towns had resisted as fiercely as Ghazal, Jaba and Izzam. Josef Argaman who lived in the area on Kibbutz Sedot Yam recalls how the Arabs near the highway were forced to evacuate. He denies official Israeli government claims that there were Iraqi and other Arab League forces operating in the area. To him the struggle was between the Jews and Palestinians for control of the land.

In Caesarea according to Argaman many Arabs left on their own out of fear when they heard from fleeing refugees that Haifa had fallen. But Argaman notes that several hundred Arabs who remained in the town were the target of Haganaḥ intimidation. In order to frighten these people Argaman and his fellow kibbutzniks shot into the village at night. They destroyed among other things the crescent at the top of the village mosque. 'The Arabs took this as a bad omen and some more left the village but a few stubbornly refused to go.'[2]

As further intimidation Argaman and his fellow home guard volunteers entered the village and sat in the coffee house. They openly displayed their weapons, but true to Middle Eastern hospitality the Arabs served them coffee 'on the house'. Some of the Palestinians engaged the Jews in conversation reminding them of several Israelis who had been killed in recent fighting. 'For every one Jew who is killed we will kill 1,000 Arabs' the kibbutzniks boasted. The people of Caesarea got the message and the remaining Palestinians fled.

In another village Argaman remembers that 'the people left after Haganah came into the town and started to tear the tiles off the houses.' Gradually most of the villages along the Haifa–Tel Aviv highway were emptied. Transportation was provided to make the flight of the refugees easier. Argaman notes: 'With my own eyes I saw how Red Cross and Red Crescent people organized the evacuation of the inhabitants of the region who were concentrated at the village Faradis. This was an orderly evacuation done apparently in co-operation with Haganah Headquarters.'[3]

There is Red Cross documentation for Argaman's story of an evacuation of Palestine civilians from the coastal area. On 14 June 1948, during the First Truce, Arab authorities on the West Bank informed the Red Cross that a large group of the elderly, women and children from the coastal plain were being 'detained by the Israeli military authorities.'[4] (As we shall see, it was common practice at this stage of the war for the Israelis to seize all able-bodied Palestinian men even if they were unarmed and send them away to concentration camps or use them for slave labour.) The Arab authorities on the West Bank asked the Red Cross to intercede to have the Palestinian women, children and elderly released. Soon after, the Israelis told the Red Cross that they would release 1,000 women, children and old people on 18 June 1948.

There was considerable confusion among the West Bank leaders over where to put the new refugees since every town was already swamped. Nablus, for example, already had 30,000 refugees who lacked food, water and housing. It was soon decided to divide the 1,000 new refugees among several West Bank towns.

The transfer began at 10 a.m. on 18 June. About forty buses and thirty-five wagons left the West Bank to pick up the released civilians. The convoy crossed no man's land where it was met by Israeli officials and Dr Goury of the Red Cross. The experience made a deep impression on the Red Cross personnel. The official report notes that as the people crossed no man's land, 'It was a moving scene with women carrying enormous bundles on their heads while in their arms were two or three small children.' It was not easy to load the terrified people into the buses. The Red Cross personnel were forced to act like police officers. But when the convoy reached Tulkarm on the West Bank, they received a great ovation.

Efforts were again made to expel Palestinians during the Second Truce which began on 19 July after the 'Ten Days War'. In many parts of the country non-resisting Arabs were treated brutally. On 17 August Dr Paul Mohn, a representative of Count Bernadotte, spoke with Israeli Foreign Minister Sharett about the problem. Dr Mohn pointed out to Sharett that the Israeli military authorities were 'destroying Arab villages occupied by them,' and that furthermore, 'on certain occasions Israeli armoured cars had encircled Arab villages in which the population was living peacefully and after herding the male inhabitants together had taken those of military age to concentration camps.'[5] Dr Mohn warned Sharett that such actions 'would make a very bad impression on public opinion if it were known that their intention was to make the return of the Arab inhabitants more difficult.'

The return of the Arab refugees was one of the chief preoccupations of Count Bernadotte and his UN team. But in his effort to get the Palestinians back to their homes, the Swedish diplomat ran into the firm opposition of the Israeli leadership. As early as 4 April, Ben-Gurion told a delegation from his Mapai party, 'We shall enter the vacated villages and settle in them.'[6]

One of the staunchest advocates for the expulsion of the Palestinians was Joseph Weitz, the director of the Lands Department of the Jewish National Fund. On 18 May, Weitz spoke to Moshe Shertok (Sharett) about the Arab refugees. He asked the Foreign Minister, 'Should we do something so as to transform the exodus of the Arabs from the country into a fact so that they return no more?'[7] Weitz noted in his diary that Sharett 'blessed any initiative in this matter. His opinion is also that we must act in such a way so as to transform the exodus of the Arabs into an established fact.' Over the next few months a series of actions were taken by the Israelis to make sure that the Arabs who fled or were expelled would never return.

On 1 June, a group of Israeli Cabinet ministers which included Ben-Gurion had the first of a series of meetings to decide what to do about the Arab refugees. Ben-Gurion made it clear that the military would be used to prevent Palestinians returning to their homes, business or land. 'Commanders are to be issued orders in this matter' he decreed.[8]

At about this time Weitz, along with Ezra Dannin, an adviser to Ben-Gurion on Arab affairs and Elias Sasson, director of the Middle East division of the Foreign Office, formed on their own initiative a Transfer Committee, similar in intent to the one on which Weitz had served in 1938. On 6 June, the self-appointed panel submitted to Ben-Gurion a three-page memorandum outlining how to promote the exodus of Palestinian Arabs and how best to prevent their return. Among their suggestions was the 'destruction of villages'[9] as well as 'the settlement of Jews in some villages and towns so that a vacuum would not be created.' By and large their suggestions were already being implemented. Many emptied villages were being settled with Jewish immigrants while other former Arab towns with inferior housing and a poor location were being destroyed. The Committee's suggestion for 'propaganda against a return' was also being put into effect.

On 10 June, a Voice of Israel radio broadcast noted that a group of Arabs had asked to return to their homes in Israel but were told by the Tel Aviv government 'we can never reconsider the return of refugees as long as a state of war still exists.'[10] Similar Jewish radio broadcasts in Arabic made it clear to refugees that they were not welcome to return. Those who did not get the message from radio broadcasts would be convinced that they were not wanted by land mines, barbed wire, booby traps and police dogs. Many would be killed in the attempt to return home.

The attitude of the Zionist leaders toward the refugees was best expressed by Moshe Sharett who wrote in a letter on 15 June that 'The most spectacular event in the contemporary history of Palestine – more spectacular in a sense than the creation of the Jewish state – is the wholesale evacuation of its Arab population.'[11] Sharett believed that a massive return of Arab refugees was out of the question. 'The reversion to status quo ante is unthinkable. The opportunities which the present position opens up for a lasting and radical solution of the most vexing problem of the Jewish state are so far reaching as to take one's breath away.'

On the following day (16 June) at a Cabinet meeting, Ben-Gurion spoke out against a return of Arab refugees. Sharett agreed: 'They will not return. This is our policy, they shall not return.'[12] A complication, however, was the attitude of the left-wing Mapam party, a coalition partner of Ben-Gurion's Mapai. The left-wing party had just issued a document on 'Our Policy Towards Arabs During the War' which 'opposed the tendency to drive the Arabs out of the territory of the Jewish state'[13] and 'opposed the destruction of Arab settled areas which is not dictated by immediate military necessity.' (Mapam would later note 'the shameful cases of looting, improper treatment of Arab civilians and destruction of villages which cannot be justified by military necessity and which constitute a moral failure.') Out of deference to Mapam and perhaps to avoid American disapproval the Israeli government refrained from any public declaration that the Palestinians would not be allowed to return.

Thus when Sharett met Count Bernadotte on 17 June, the Israeli Foreign Minister was evasive with regard to the return of the refugees. Bernadotte asked: 'What would be the policy of the Israeli government with regard to the 300,000 Arabs who had left the Jewish areas; would they be allowed to return after the war and would their property rights be respected?'[14] Sharett answered that 'The question could not be discussed while the war was going on.' He added that 'property rights would be respected', despite the fact that Sharett had encouraged the Israeli policy of destroying Arab homes and businesses.

Bernadotte was dissatisfied with the attitude of the Israelis on the refugee issue. So were the Americans. According to the American Consul-General in Israel, James B. McDonald, 'while the Arab refugee problem attracted little public attention in Israel, the government was aware of its far reaching implications.' On 27 June, McDonald reported that Foreign Minister Sharett had indicated in a recent speech that there could not be a return of the refugees until there was a 'general political settlement'.[15] Sharett had also stated that the 'Arabs could not return except as full citizens of the Jewish state acknowledging its authority and sovereignty.' It would soon become clear, however, that the Israelis were not prepared to accept the return of Arab refugees under any circumstances.

The American chargé d'affaires in Egypt was concerned about the repercussions if Israel refused to allow any refugees to return. He warned that it would 'confirm the current Arab view that no peace or security exists for Arabs if a Jewish state is permitted and that statements by Zionists that they seek Arab friendships have no basis in fact.'[16] He was also concerned that if Israel kept the refugees out it would convince the Arabs that the 'real intention of the Jews is to confiscate refugee property and enterprises in Israel in order to provide space and economic opportunities for Jewish immigrants.' Such sentiments were shared by both the leaders and public opinion in all the Arab states.

The Arabs had correctly evaluated the Israeli attitude. The refugees had left behind a considerable amount of property. Before the war 50 per cent of the citrus orchards in Israeli territory had been Arab-owned as well as 90 per cent of the olive oil groves and 10,000 shops, stores, and other businesses. The Zionist plans to bring huge numbers of Jewish immigrants to Israel were almost impossible without the homes, the land, and the businesses of the Palestinian Arabs. But more important, the expulsion of the Palestinians solved the problem presented by an Arab minority which comprised about half the population of the Jewish state provided under the UN partition resolution. It was clear that the viability of the Jewish state was questionable as long as it had such a large Arab population. The war created an opportunity for the Israelis to solve this problem by expelling the Arabs. Having done so, there was never any likelihood that they would take back the refugees at a time when they were still in the process of 'evacuating' those that remained in Israel.

But the Arab states wanted the return of the refugees. On accepting the Second Truce, Pasha Azzam, the Secretary-General of the Arab League, had demanded the repatriation of the Palestinians to their homes. On 24 July, when Azzam met with Bernadotte, he renewed his request for repatriation, warning that the Palestinians would become radicalized if they were allowed to remain in the refugee camps. Azzam asked Bernadotte to undertake humanitarian relief on behalf of the refugees and that he make it possible for them to return to their homes, especially those who had fled from Jaffa and Haifa. Bernadotte agreed to help, and for the remainder of his life he devoted himself to this task.

On 26 July, Bernadotte met with Sharett in Tel Aviv. The United Nations mediator asked the Israeli Foreign Minister if his government would consider the readmission of Palestinian Arabs. Sharett gave a firm reply: 'The Jewish government could under the present conditions, in no circumstances permit the return of Arabs who had fled or been driven from their homes.'[17] Despite Sharett's negative answer, after the meeting Bernadotte sent the Israeli Foreign Minister a formal request that 'a limited number, to be determined in consultation with the mediator, especially from those living in Jaffa and Haifa, be permitted to return to their homes as from 15 August.'[18] Bernadotte assured the Israelis that 'the danger to Jewish security is slight' since 'a differentiation may be made between men of military age and all others.'

Bernadotte's approach was to try to persuade the Israelis to accept a limited number of Arabs back in the hope that if these people were successfully resettled, the remainder might eventually follow. The exclusion of young men blunted the Israeli argument over security concerns. Besides, once the women and children were repatriated a strong humanitarian case could be made for the return of the men of military age. During his discussion with Sharett in Tel Aviv, the Israeli Foreign Minister had expressed a slight softening of attitude with regard to the return of the Haifa Arabs, so that in his letter Bernadotte utilized Azzam's suggestion for the repatriation of the Haifa and Jaffa Arabs as a first step.

The United States government was also anxious to confirm the true intention of the Israelis with regard to the repatriation issue. After the American legation in Tel Aviv made inquiries, they received a memorandum from the Israeli Foreign Ministry on the subject. This document constitutes one of the earliest indications of the official Israeli explanation of the causes of the Arab exodus.

> The charge that these Arabs were forcibly driven out by Israel authorities is wholly false; on the contrary, everything possible was done to prevent an exodus which was a direct result of the folly of the Arab states in organizing and launching a war of aggression against Israel. The impulse of the Arab civilian population to migrate from the war areas, in order to avoid being involved in the hostilities, was deliberately fostered by Arab leaders for political motives. They did not wish the Arab population to continue to lead a peaceful existence in Jewish areas, and they wished to exploit the exodus as a propaganda weapon in surrounding Arab countries and in the outside world.[19]

The Israelis did not explain how the Arab states 'deliberately fostered' the exodus, nor was any evidence presented to show that the Israelis had done 'everything possible' to prevent the flight of the Palestinians. In their memorandum to the Americans, the Israelis expressed concern for the Jewish communities in the Arab countries. There were in fact hundreds of thousands of Jews in the Arab world, the largest communities being in Iraq, Morocco, Yemen and Egypt. Obviously the fate of these people would be affected by how well the Israelis treated the Palestinians.

On 1 August, when Sharett answered Bernadotte's request for the admission of a limited number of Palestinian Arabs, the Israeli Foreign Minister also referred to the 'fate of the Jewish communities in the Arab countries.'[20] But Sharett did not acknowledge the fact that fair treatment of the Palestinians was the best way to avoid reprisals by the Arab states against their Jewish minorities.

The main reason for Sharett's letter to Bernadotte was to refuse the UN mediator's request to allow small groups of Arab refugees to return to Haifa and Jaffa. The Israeli Foreign Minister's carefully worded reply represented the official view of Ben-Gurion and his Cabinet. This rejection of Palestinian repatriation was to remain Israeli policy for many decades. Sharett claimed that 'the reintegration of the returning Arabs into normal life, and even their maintenance, would present insolvable problems. The difficulties of accommodation, employment and ordinary livelihood would be insuperable.' But Israel would soon absorb even larger numbers of Jewish immigrants. In their case the problems of 'accommodation, employment and ordinary livelihood' were solved mainly at the expense of the Arab refugees.

In his letter to Bernadotte, Sharett expressed sympathy for the Arab refugees since 'our people has suffered too much from similar tribulations for us to be indifferent to their hardship.' But in a private letter to Weizmann later that month Sharett expressed the determination 'to explore all possibilities of getting rid, once and for all, of the huge Arab minority which originally threatened us.'[21] Sharett's contemptuous attitude toward the Palestinians was reflected in the Israeli treatment of those Arabs who remained in the new Jewish state.

Fouzi al-Asmar, the ten-year-old boy from Lydda, and his immediate family had been spared the death march which followed the expulsion of most Arabs from the Lydda–Ramle region. But their life under Israeli occupation did not make them feel that they had been fortunate. A Jewish family lived on their property and they and most other Arabs who were allowed to remain on the outskirts of Lydda were forbidden into those parts of the town that were reserved for Jews. Indeed, an Israeli report notes that many of the Arabs who were not expelled from Lydda were 'roaming about without food in the fields and are afraid to enter the city.'[22]

The Christian Arabs were treated somewhat better than the Muslims.* On Sunday the Christians were even permitted to

---

*Belchor Shitrit, the Israeli Minister of Minorities, gave the reason why the Christians in Lydda were treated better. 'The Christians had suffered at the hands of the Muslims. They did not participate in the fighting. . . They did pay taxes and contributions which were forced on them by the Muslim fighters.'[23]

ride on the passenger train to attend church. At first Fouzi could not understand why they were being allowed such a great luxury. He was disturbed when Muslims called his family 'Christian traitors'.[24] His mother explained to him that the aim of the Jews was to turn the Palestinians against each other. She emphasized, however, that the Christian Arabs must not allow Israelis to divide the Palestinians. When the boy mentioned the problem to his father, their conversation was overheard by an Israeli officer who called his father aside and gave him a warning.

Fouzi was an obedient child but he and his friends could not overcome their curiosity to find out what was going on in Lydda. Against his father's orders, he and some friends went where no Arabs were permitted. Lydda had been a prosperous town. Many of the homes had originally been built by Christian German colonists who later sold their property to prosperous Arabs. The homes in Lydda were well furnished and the stores stocked with expensive merchandise. When he sneaked into town Fouzi saw Israeli soldiers loading trucks with merchandise which was being taken out of the shops and many of the homes. Fouzi was 'shocked on the visit by the sight of this large city completely deserted, the houses open, the shops broken into and the remaining merchandise rotting.'* The youngster and his friends were wise enough not to touch anything or to reveal their presence. Those Arabs who remained on Israeli territory were under military rule. They could be imprisoned or expelled by Israeli soldiers for the slightest infraction of any regulation including the 6 p.m. to 6 a.m. curfew.

Soon after the looting of Lydda, Jewish families moved into the better homes. They would simply choose a house they liked and occupy it. No thought was given to the previous Arab owner who had either been expelled or was living in the Arab ghetto outside town. Even after Lydda was resettled with Jews, no Arab was allowed into town without a pass. An Arab who was once a prosperous businessman or railroad official and who now worked at a menial job might be allowed back in the city

---

*Shitrit noted in a report on Lydda: 'The occupation army has taken or destroyed all that is found in the city.'[25]

only as part of a work detail. He might pass the fine home where he and his family had lived but where he was not permitted to enter since it was now occupied by a family who only a few months before had lived thousands of miles away.

Although only ten years old, Fouzi considered himself lucky when he got a job picking fruit and vegetables on land that had once been Arab-owned but which the Jewish owner paid Arab children pennies a week to work. For a time Fouzi attended school but the shame of being forced to salute the Israeli flag and singing Hatikva every day was too much to bear. He preferred to work in the fields.

In Haifa during this period, the condition of the Arabs who remained under Jewish rule was equally bad. Within a few months of their conquest of the city, the Israelis were able to operate all the essential industries. There was no longer any need for Arab labour. The American Consul Aubrey Lippincott reported: 'All Arabs who remained in Haifa are being screened by Jewish authorities and required to obtain identity cards and must swear allegiance to the Israeli state.'[26] The condition of those who attempted to come back to the city from the surrounding countryside was even worse. 'Arabs who returned to Haifa are considered illegals,' Lippincott reported. The Israelis were 'permitting only those to remain whom they consider satisfactory after thorough investigation.'

On 11 December 1948 the Israelis launched one of their 'security checks' in the Wadi Nisnas section of Haifa. It was a house to house search by police and Ministry of Minorities personnel who were looking for Arabs who had 'infiltrated' back into their homes. According to an Israeli report 'about 300 people were arrested' in the raid.[27] 'Some were deported across the borders of the State of Israel' while 'others were detained for further investigation.' The goal was to make sure that 'the Arab population in Haifa should not be allowed to grow.' The people of Haifa lived in constant fear of these raids.

The Arabs of Haifa were also constantly being uprooted so that their homes could be used for Jewish settlement. In late December 1948, a Jewish official requested that the Minister of Minorities halt the transfer of all Arabs to 'special neighbourhoods' since 'concentration of Arab citizens in a ghetto is an undesirable thing in itself.'[28] The official added 'It will cause much physical suffering to families of peaceful Arabs and their condition of living will worsen due to the shortage of living quarters.' His appeal was not granted since most of the Arabs in Haifa were moved from their homes into the ghetto.

In view of the Israeli treatment of Arabs under their control, the AHC had serious reservations about the repatriation of the Arab refugees to Israeli territory. On 12 August, Bernadotte received a cable from one of his aides: 'Arab Higher Committee addressed report to Arab League opposing repatriation to Palestine.'[29] The reasons given were that 'repatriation would include recognition of Haganah and the Jewish state' and 'refugees would be used as hostages and no economic possibilities given to them by the Jews.' The American Minister in Syria received a copy of the AHC memorandum to the Arab League. He reported to Washington that repatriation was also opposed by the Palestinian AHC because it would 'permit the Jews to exploit refugees in a political sense, possibly winning their votes in a likely plebiscite.'[30] Many Palestinian leaders still believed that there would be an election in Palestine in which both Arabs and Jews would vote on the form of government for their country. They feared that the returning refugees might be coerced by the Israelis into voting for the recognition of the Jewish state.

Several days after he received the cable from Damascus, Bernadotte was contacted by Elias Koussa, an Arab lawyer living in Haifa who also opposed the repatriation of the refugees. Koussa had been a member of the Arab committee that had negotiated the evacuation of Haifa. He had decided, however, to remain under Israeli occupation, one of the few Arab leaders to do so. Koussa wrote to the UN mediator about 'the condition existing in the Jewish state relating to Arab affairs.'[31] He could not understand why the UN mediator and the Arab governments were so anxious for repatriation. The Haifa lawyer was not opposed to repatriation in principle, but he saw no way that the returning refugees could expect fair treatment from the Jews, particularly in view of the way they were treating those Arabs who had remained under Israeli control. According to Koussa, the returning Arabs would inevitably 'fall into pauperism' because 'the Jewish authorities will not provide work and employment for them.'

It was clear to Koussa that the Israelis did not wish to have the refugees back since 'in Haifa a considerable part of the Arab businesses and residential quarter is being demolished by the Jewish authorities.' It was the same all over Israel. As for the rural Arab population, Koussa stressed, 'to cause them to return to their villages before their animals, cattle and other belongings are restored would serve no useful purpose.'

But the Israelis were not only stealing the animals, but the land itself. To an agrarian people whose very identity was associated with ownership of land, this theft of their farms was a crime they would never forgive. On 30 June, the Israelis issued their first 'Abandoned Areas Ordinance'. Within a few weeks a thin veneer of legality was given to the seizure of thousands of Arab homes and businesses. Not only were the lands of Arab refugees considered abandoned but even Arabs who fled a few miles from their homes within Israeli territory found that they had no right under Israeli law to reclaim their property when they returned several weeks later. What economic and political rights could the Israelis be expected to grant to Arab refugees who had fled to hostile Arab countries? It was obvious to the Palestinian AHC that if the refugees were allowed to return to Israel they would end up in refugee camps under the control of the Zionists who would not return them to their homes but who might keep them as wards, or even worse, as hostages.

The Arab governments that were playing host to the refugees took a different view from the Palestinian AHC since these countries wished to be relieved of the burden of caring for so many unwanted guests. The Arab governments individually and collectively through the Arab League, constantly made it clear that they desired a return of the refugees to their homes in Israeli territory. It soon became apparent, however, that regardless of the attitude of the Palestinians or any Arab government, the Israelis had no intention of allowing repatriation. For half a century, the Zionists had awaited an opportunity to get rid of the Arabs. Having done so, no argument from friend, foe or neutral observer would convince them to accept the Arabs back. Bernadotte was disappointed at his failure to secure the return of the refugees but he was able to improve the conditions in the camps that had been set up on the West Bank and in Lebanon, Syria and Jordan.

At the outset conditions in these camps were atrocious. A large number of the refugees on the West Bank and in Lebanon were camping on the ground under trees or in caves. Water supplies were often polluted, while sanitary facilities were usually non-existent. There was great danger of typhoid and other epidemics. The refugees were supposed to receive 500 grammes of bread plus some vegetables but the distribution of these supplies was irregular. About 85 per cent of the refugee population consisted of children, nursing mothers, the old and the sick. Considering the huge number of dependent people, the medical facilities available to them amounted to only a small fraction of what was required.

Those who fled to the West Bank were not well received by the native inhabitants, who although they were fellow Palestinians looked down on the refugees as a landless rabble. 'You sold your land to the Jews and now you come to squat on our land,'[32] the refugees were told by the local people. As the refugees had not received any payment for their land, such remarks were particularly offensive. 'If they had only been able, they would have denied us even a glass of water,' one refugee later recalled. Those who had been expelled from their homes in Israel learned the meaning of the Palestinian saying, 'the landless is despised'. They had fought the Jews to protect their land and now even their fellow Palestinians regarded them as traitors who had disobeyed the orders of the Arab League that they remain in their homes.

The journalist Kenneth Bilby visited one of the early refugee settlements on the West Bank. The tent camp in the Jordan valley on the approach to Jericho had perhaps 20,000 inhabitants. These destitute people collected wild brush, which they used for their mattresses. What scraps of food they could collect frequently made up their only nourishment. While Bilby was in the camp, everyone was discussing one of their fellow refugees, a businessman from Haifa. Days before, he had taken his two sons behind a tent and shot them through the head before turning the gun on himself. The Israelis had taken his home and his business and refused to allow him to return, nor would they compensate him for his property. Once a prosperous man, he was now penniless and he could not bear to see his children starve.

Bilby next visited a tent camp at Ramallah, which was even worse. He saw a widow whose only garment was a flour sack. The American reporter would never forget the monotonous wail made by the woman's five hungry children. Agonized she asked Bilby what had happened to her home. 'I could have told her it was probably occupied by a family from Bulgaria or Poland but I stalled with a don't-know answer.'[33]

The Ramallah district, which had received almost all of the people expelled from Lydda–Ramle as well as numerous other towns, was swamped with 125,000 refugees. The Red Cross made an effort to help the destitute civilians but the situation was desperate. A Red Cross report notes, 'At Birjeit, which had a population of 1,200, today has between 14,000 and 15,000 people living there; at Jifna the population has gone from 500 to 10,000.'[34]

Most of the refugees were 'very miserable' since they received only a meagre ration of flour and had no health care. The refugees at Jifna were in a particularly bad condition. At one point the Red Cross team was approached by a mother carrying an infant. The woman demanded help for her child. But when she showed her infant to the Red Cross doctor he saw it was a lifeless skeleton.

The authorities on the West Bank were clearly overwhelmed. There was a need for every type of food and medicine as well as DDT and water purification tablets to prevent an epidemic. The Red Cross team reported that 'A problem of this magnitude cannot be solved by the Palestinians themselves.' The report urged massive international aid to solve the short-term problem but the only real solution was the peaceful return of the expelled Palestinians to their homes.

The Zionist leaders were determined that the Palestinians would never return to what had become the Jewish state. Foreign Minister Sharett asked Yaakov Shimoni and Ezra Dannin to present a memorandum outlining a plan to prevent the repatriation of the Palestinians. The memorandum which was submitted on 5 August, suggested 'pulling down Arab houses', a propaganda campaign to get the Zionist view of events to 'local and possibly foreign journalists' and the drawing up of a plan for 'the settlement of the refugees in Arab lands'.[35] Sharett immediately approved this programme including the plan to permanently relocate the refugees in neighbouring Arab countries.

On 10 August, Bernadotte met Sharett in Jerusalem and once again the UN mediator pressed the Israeli Foreign Minister about the return of the refugees. Sharett would not agree to any repatriation but stressed the desirability of relocation in Syria and Iraq, which he claimed could easily absorb the refugees. If the Palestinians were to return Sharett warned that it would create a problem and a perpetual source of friction between the Jewish state and its Arab neighbours. Sharett made it clear that it was 'in the interest of all concerned' that the Arab minority in Israel be small.

About a week after this meeting, there was a conference on 18 August in Tel Aviv at which Ben-Gurion discussed the Arab refugee situation with many of the experts on Arab affairs. None of the members of the left-wing Mapam party were invited. (Shimoni referred to Mapam's 'departure from reality and their ideological hallucinations' on the Arab question as the reason why they were not invited to the meeting.)[36] According to Shimoni there was unanimous agreement at the meeting that 'everything should be done to prevent the return of the refugees.'

One of the participants at the meeting, D. Horowitz of the Finance Ministry, complained that while the Israeli leadership was agreed that no Arab should return, in the field there was no uniform policy. He noted:

> There is a difference between policy and reality. In a village near Nazareth a group of children who escaped and hid in caves were not allowed to return to their village. Each area commander thinks the Arab question is in his hands alone. The official policy should be communicated to the military authorities – since up to now the practice has been wholly arbitrary.[37]

The next day orders were issued to army commanders making it clear that under no circumstances would any Arab be allowed back into Israeli territory.

The question of Arab property was also discussed at the 18 August meeting. David Ha'Cohen, an IDF intelligence officer, suggested that as part of a peace treaty in order to encourage the Arabs not to return, the refugees could be compensated for the property they were forced to leave behind. He had no doubt where the money to compensate the Arabs would come from. 'American Jews will be able to buy Arab property in this country,' he told the conference since 'American Jewry's yearly income is 11 billion dollars.'[38] Besides the property of the refugees, the Israeli leaders also coveted the property of the Israeli Arabs. Another participant at the meeting noted that those Arabs still in Israel 'will be forced to prove their right to their own property.'[39] Ben-Gurion was anxious to get rid of the Israeli Arabs. He asked the conference, 'Would it not be possible to exchange Arabs for Jews?' Minorities Minister Belchor Shitrit liked the idea. He believed that 'One should make an effort to exchange Arab Jews for Israeli Arabs.'

The conference reaffirmed the plan to set up a Transfer Committee to study ways of permanently resettling the Palestinian refugees in Arab countries. Efforts were made to persuade foreign journalists to support the Israeli transfer scheme. (In a private letter Shimoni notes 'articles in the world press' that reflected support for the resettlement of the Palestinians in Arab countries.)[40]

The 18 August meeting made it clear that the Israelis were prepared to stop at nothing to prevent a return of the refugees. They were willing to spend billions of (American Jewish) dollars to make sure that their new state would be *goyim rein*.

Although Bernadotte could do nothing to repatriate the Palestinian Arabs, he did have some success in relieving some of their misery in the refugee camps. The Arab League had appealed to the International Refugee Organization for aid but to no avail. At Bernadotte's request the UN Secretary-General sent Sir Raphael Cliento of Australia to survey the status of the refugees. He reported that their health and living conditions were in a precarious state.

In August Bernadotte appealed to the United Nations International Children's Emergency Fund (UNICEF) and to the member states of the UN for assistance. The UN mediator secured agreements with several of the Arab states so that aid for the refugees could be facilitated. Sir Raphael Cliento from his office in Beirut attempted to co-ordinate the relief effort for all the Palestinian refugees scattered in five countries. Aid was eventually received from thirty-three countries, including considerable assistance from the United States. Israel's only contribution was to carry out more expulsions, which would eventually increase the number of refugees to 750,000. Bernadotte hoped, however, that the refugees might return as part of a comprehensive peace plan.

Bernadotte's most important effort to solve the Arab–Israeli dispute was embodied in a ninety-page report which he submitted to the United Nations Security Council on 16 September. The mediator proposed that Jerusalem would be internationalized while the Negev and Lydda–Ramle would be part of an Arab state that would include Jordan and the West Bank. The entire area of Galilee including portions still in Arab hands would be given to Israel. In his earlier plan, the UN mediator had envisaged a union between the Jewish and Arab states in Palestine as well as a *de facto* limitation of Jewish immigration to Israel. But he now noted that Israel was 'a living, solidly entrenched and vigorous reality' which must be recognized as a sovereign and independent state with no outside interference in any internal matter including immigration.

At the very outset of the report Bernadotte made it clear that 'no settlement can be just and complete if recognition is not accorded to the Arab refugee to return to his home.'[41] With regard to the origin of the exodus Bernadotte wrote, 'as a result of the conflict in Palestine almost the whole of the Arab population fled or was expelled from the area under Jewish occupation.' It is significant that the UN mediator did not mention any evacuation orders by Arab leaders to the Palestinians.

Bernadotte noted 'numerous reports from reliable sources of large-scale looting, pillage and plundering and destruction of villages without apparent military necessity' in Israeli-controlled territory. Bernadotte vigorously affirmed Israeli liability, 'to restore private property to its Arab owners and to indemnify those owners of property wantonly destroyed.' Through his staff, the UN mediator was aware that all over their territory the Israelis were stealing Arab property and land while destroying those homes that were not suitable for use by Jews.

Bernadotte was also aware of the mass immigration of Jews into Israel, while Arabs were being denied the right to return. 'It would be an offence against elemental justice,' Bernadotte wrote, 'if these innocent victims of the conflict were denied the right of return to their homes while Jewish immigrants flow into Palestine and indeed, offer the threat of permanent replacement of the Arab refugees who have been rooted in the land for centuries.'

Although Bernadotte's efforts to bring peace to Palestine were undoubtedly sincere, if at times naïve, he was never popular with the Israelis, many of whom suspected him of strong pro-British inclinations. Some Israelis had a far worse opinion; as early as 16 June, the Stern Gang's radio station referred to the UN mediator as 'a tool of Anglo-Saxon imperialism'. As it became clear that the Swedish count wanted Israel to make concessions including the internationalization of Jerusalem, acceptance of UN observers and the repatriation of the Palestinian refugees, the Stern Gang leaders became convinced that action would have to be taken.

On Friday, 17 September, the day after he submitted his peace plan, Bernadotte arrived at Kalandia, a small Arab airfield just north of Jerusalem. Travelling with the count was General Agee Lundstrom, his chief of staff. They were met at the airport by a party of officials which included the senior UN observer in Jerusalem, Colonel Serot of France. Count Bernadotte had received a warning that there was a plot against him but it was his custom to ignore all threats to his person. He also disregarded Lundstrom's advice that they did not pass directly from the Arab into the Jewish zones since the Israelis frequently fired on any vehicle that crossed into their lines. Bernadotte rebuffed his chief of staff's warning. 'I have to take the same risks as my observers and moreover, I think no one has the right to refuse me permission to pass through the lines.'

Bernadotte and his three-car motorcade were able to pass

from the Arab to the Jewish section without incident. After lunch with Dov Joseph, the Governor of Jerusalem, the UN party proceeded to inspect various UN and Red Cross facilities in the Jewish sector. Bernadotte rode in a brown Chrysler which flew the UN and white flags. He was seated in the rear of the vehicle with General Lundstrom and Colonel Serot.

In the Katamon quarter of Jewish Jerusalem, the three UN vehicles were stopped by an Israeli jeep occupied by several men wearing the dark khaki uniforms typical of the Israeli army. One of the men put a machine gun through the left rear window and sprayed bullets point-blank at Bernadotte. Colonel Serot lunged forward in a vain attempt to save the mediator – a gesture which cost him his life. General Lundstrom was momentarily pinned down by Serot's body which shielded him as the assailant continued to shoot. The UN vehicle rushed to Hadassah Hospital but it was too late. Bernadotte had been hit by several bullets any one of which would have been fatal.[42]

In the days immediately after the assassination, the Israeli government displayed remarkable insensitivity.* Colonel Moshe Dayan who was military commander of the Jewish forces in Jerusalem promised 'diligent and unrelenting pursuit' of the responsible parties. But the actions of the Israeli government fell far short of this goal. Although the Stern Gang sent several faked messages to indicate that the murders had been committed by a fictitious terrorist group, few doubted who was responsible. To assuage foreign public opinion, Ben-Gurion ordered a round-up of the usual suspects, including several hundred Stern Gang members. But those who had planned and carried out the assassination were never really punished. Several later admitted their involvement, a fact which did not hurt their careers in Israeli public life. Indeed one of those primarily responsible in planning the murders, Yitzhak Ysenitsky, using the name Yitzhak Shamir, was to serve as Israeli Foreign Minister under his fellow terrorist Menachem Begin, whom he succeeded as Prime Minister. This cavalier attitude of the

---

*The Israelis presented the UN with a bill for 150 Israeli pounds to cover the cost of post-mortem examination and embalming of the peace mediator who had been killed in Israel by Israeli citizens.

THE TROUBLED TRUCE

Israeli government toward the assassination went practically unnoticed by most Western countries, including the United States. The Arabs pointed out that had *they* been responsible for the brutal murder of the peace envoy, economic, diplomatic and possible military action would have been taken against them by the West.

After Bernadotte's assassination, the peace plan embodied in his report was regarded by many as his last testament and as such deserved serious consideration. British Foreign Secretary Ernest Bevin announced in parliament that 'the recommendations of Count Bernadotte have the whole-hearted and unqualified support of the government.' On 21 September, four days after the mediator's death, American Secretary of State Marshall told the United Nations General Assembly that 'the United States considers that the conclusions contained in the final report of Count Bernadotte offer a generally fair basis for the settlement of the Palestine question.'

President Truman, however, had not approved Marshall's statement. In the midst of the Presidential campaign, Truman feared that American support of the Bernadotte plan would be perceived by the American Jewish community as an effort to force Israel to make concessions. The Republican nominee Thomas Dewey announced his disapproval of the late mediator's proposals, hoping to win New York's critical electoral votes. Truman was forced to suggest publicly in a speech in New York that 'no matter what you read in the papers', his administration would never force Israel to make concessions.

Despite Truman's assurances, Tel Aviv feared that Bernadotte's plan had the support of both the British and American governments. There were some provisions of the mediator's report which met with Israeli approval. Bernadotte's inclusion of Jaffa and the whole of Galilee in the new Jewish state was obviously welcomed. The suggestion in the report that the Palestinian refugees receive financial compensation could eventually be used as a wedge by the Israelis to substitute monetary compensation in place of repatriations. But Bernadotte's unequivocal affirmation that the Palestinians had the right to demand nothing less than the return of their land and property in Israel, made it impossible for Tel Aviv to accept the late mediator's proposals. Besides, the Israelis had no intention of accepting the internationalization of Jerusalem or the return of Lydda–Ramle and those portions of the Negev they had already conquered.

At the United Nations, Sharett asserted that Israel did not consider that the report of 16 September even provided a basis for discussion. Secretly the Israelis planned new military operations in Galilee and the Negev which would make it clear that with an army of 70,000 the new Jewish state was willing and able to take the disputed territory by force of arms.

CHAPTER X

Operation Hiram

Destroy all of that land; beat down their pillars and break their statues and waste all of their high places, cleansing the land and dwelling in it. For I have given it to you for a possession.

Numbers 34: 52, 53

The fighting had ended several days before but US Air Force Captain E. J. Zeuty continued his daily patrols of central Galilee. This was an important part of his duties as a UN observer in the region. From his base at Safed, Zeuty rode his jeep up and down the roads in the area. He frequently met Arab refugees who were fleeing the fighting, which had started on 29 October, when the Israelis had launched Operation Hiram. This offensive was designed to complete the conquest of Galilee that had begun during the spring. Many of the refugees told Captain Zeuty horror stories. He was not prepared, however, for what he saw on the morning of 3 November.

In the first light of day, Zeuty noticed a column of women and children heading down the road. They seemed particularly ragged, and he later learned that they had been marching for days from Elabun, their village many miles away. In his report, the American officer wrote that the refugees were with 'Jewish civil police who were guarding them.' When he questioned the Israelis about the destination of their prisoners 'they could give no answer.' The absence of young men among the prisoners was conspicuous and ominous. The women tearfully told the story of how most of their men had been murdered or kidnapped. Gradually, after intense investigation by several teams of UN observers the tragedy of Elabun unfolded.[1]

For some time the area around Elabun had been occupied by Fawzi al-Kaukji's ALA forces. When the Israelis attacked on 29 October, the Arab volunteers fled, as they had done on so many other occasions. At 5 a.m. on 30 October, Israeli forces entered the village. The people of Elabun, all 750 of whom were Christian, had taken refuge in the two local churches. A yellow flag of submission flew from the Orthodox church and a white banner from the Greek Catholic church.

The leaders of the community were Father Hanna Daoud, an eighty-five-year-old vicar of the local Greek Catholic church and his son Markos, also a Greek Catholic priest. For two centuries, the Daoud family had been Greek Catholic clergymen in Elabun. When the town was occupied, Father Markos approached the Jews saying, 'I put my village under the protection of the State of Israel.' But the Israelis refused to be placated. Their commander held the Arab civilians responsible for the mutilation of the bodies of two Jewish soldiers who had fallen during the fighting. Father Markos pleaded that the villagers were not responsible for what obviously was the work of the retreating ALA volunteers. 'Assemble all of your people in the village square' was the curt reply.

On the square in front of Father Markos' house, the Jewish commander yelled, 'You want to make war, here you have it!' as his men mowed down four young men with machine guns. Three other youths including a boy of seventeen were taken to a nearby field where they were killed in a similar manner. In all, thirteen young men were murdered in the early morning hours.

The remaining villagers were evicted from their homes. As was the usual Israeli practice, the surviving young men were seized as prisoners-of-war even though there was no evidence that they had resisted the invaders. In groups the women and children were marched off to the Lebanese border. It is not known how many perished during the exodus, but considering the conditions and the attitude of the Israelis, the casualties may have been considerable.

The looting of the Christian town included the desecration of the churches and the destruction of numerous sacred icons. Furniture, livestock and all other movable property was carried off by the Israelis. There was little effort made by the Zionist soldiers to camouflage their crimes, so the UN observers had no difficulty evaluating what had happened. The American officer, Captain Zeuty reported, 'There is no doubt in this observer's

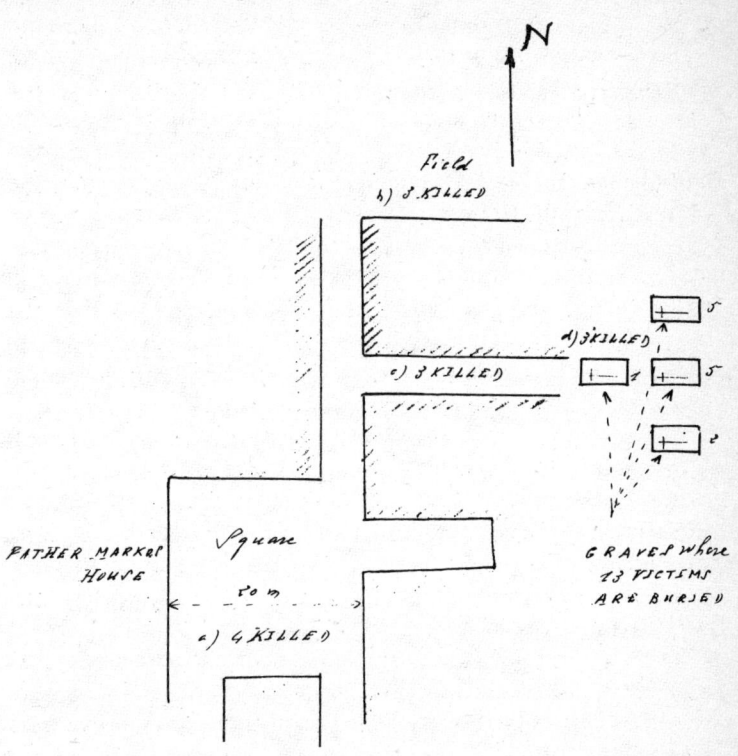

Captain Zeuty's sketch of the El Labun Massacre

mind that the Jews committed murder and plunder.' Much evidence was given by Father Markos who pointed out to the UN observers many important facts, including the locations where the murders had taken place and the burial sites of the victims. Commandant Perrossier, a French UN observer, was uncomfortable that Father Markos had given much of his evidence in the presence of an Israeli liaison officer. Perrossier noted: 'Having seen how the Jews behaved in Upper Galilee, I fear that this priest will suffer retaliation.'

The behaviour of the Jews in Upper Galilee in October was even worse than their conduct during the spring offensive in Galilee. Scores of villages were occupied by the Israelis and as indicated in the reports of the UN observers, there was a disturbing pattern of murder and looting followed by the mass expulsion of civilians. During the earlier campaign in Galilee murders had generally only been committed in villages which had resisted or which had a reputation of committing atrocities against the Jews. But during Operation Hiram some of the worst Israeli crimes took place in towns that peacefully offered to surrender.

There were several reasons why the Israelis were noticeably more brutal during their October offensive. Although there were many UN observers in Galilee during Operation Hiram, in general the Israelis were less concerned about foreign public opinion than during earlier campaigns. As the war went through its various stages, the Jews became increasingly bolder as the power of their military forces grew. By October, the Israelis realized that no one could stop them from creating a sizeable Jewish state that would be largely free of Arabs. Adverse publicity in the American and European press about Zionist war crimes or the forcible expulsion of the Arabs was not as great a concern as it had been a few months previously.

Besides, it was becoming more difficult to expel the Arabs necessitating more brutal methods. In the May offensive in Galilee, it had been sufficient for Allon to send Jewish notables to Arab villages in order to frighten off the Arab civilians of some towns before the Palmach army had even arrived. In other villages a short bombardment or firing over the heads of the Arab civilians had been enough to get the message across. Many of the people of Galilee fled in the spring believing that they would return to their homes in the van of the Arab armies.

By October the people of northern Galilee realized that if they left their homes, they probably would never return. According to Mansour Kardosh during the later stage of the war, 'people had already learned some lessons.'[2] Many refugees from Acre, Safed and other towns conquered in the spring fled to the unoccupied portions of Upper Galilee. They made it clear to the people who lived there that those who left their homes would become permanent refugees. Rumours were also circulating about the condition of the refugees in the Arab countries and on the West Bank. Since they knew what was at stake, most of the people who lay in the path of Operation Hiram were determined to remain in their homes. The Arab civilians would find, however, that the Israelis would stop at nothing in order to drive them out.

Many of the towns where atrocities had been committed were visited by teams of UN observers who came from France, Belgium and the United States. Although they could hardly be accused of a pro-Arab bias, their reports unanimously portray the brutal methods employed by the Jews, who resorted to murder in order to encourage the population to flee during the October offensive.

In Operation Hiram the Israelis used four brigades and a considerable number of tanks in their effort to eliminate the bulge of Arab-controlled territory in central Galilee. As the Jews had conquered a large part of both western and eastern Upper Galilee already, the territory controlled by the ALA in north central Galilee was attacked from three sides.

Safsaf was a small village which lay directly in the path of one of the Israeli columns. On the night of 29 October, many of the villagers were killed in an Israeli air attack. At sunrise the next day, Jewish forces entered the town. The villagers became apprehensive when the Israeli soldiers ordered them to gather in the central square. Um Shaladah al-Salih has vivid recollections of that tragic morning. As they lined up the civilians, the soldiers ordered four girls to accompany them to the well to fetch water for the villagers. But the young women never got to the well. 'Instead, they took them to our empty houses and raped them,' Um Shaladah recalled.

Worse was in store for the young men of Safsaf. Um Shaladah watched in horror. 'About seventy of our young men were blindfolded and shot to death, one after the other, in front of us.'[3] The Israelis then threw the bodies into a nearby stream. After such a massacre it was unnecessary for the Israelis to evict the survivors, most of whom left on their own. In most villages, however, the UN observers found a pattern of murder and looting followed by the kidnapping of the young men and the forcible expulsion of women, children and old people.

Two kilometres north of the main Acre–Safed highway lay al-Bi'na and Deir al-Assad, two Arab villages whose people earned their living from cattle raising and olive tree cultivation. Before the Israeli offensive about 500 ALA soldiers operated in the area but, as usual they retreated when Operation Hiram was launched on 29 October. The following day the Mukhtars of the two villages along with fifty peasants went to Birwa to implement their surrender. On Sunday, 31 October at 10 a.m., the Israeli forces entered al-Bi'na and Deir al-Assad.

The Jews gathered the entire population in a field between the two towns and demanded that they turn over their weapons. About 100 rifles were given to the Israelis. By afternoon the children and elderly became exhausted and were in need of water. Some of the Arab men asked if they could get water from a nearby well. Everyone thought that the young men would bring back water for their family and friends but the Israelis had other plans: 'They killed them with automatic fire near the well', testified Hassan Muhidun Askbar. After investigating his charges, UN observers described the murders as 'wanton slaying without provocation'.[4]

The villagers who were now panic-stricken were robbed of all their valuables. Most of the young men were separated from their families and herded into trucks which were driven off to an unknown location. The Mukhtar asked the Israelis that the remaining civilians be allowed to stay overnight in their homes but promised that they would leave the next day. He feared for the safety of the women, children and older people if they were forced to travel at night. But according to Kamal Sulaiman Abdulmuti, 'The Jews rejected the Mukhtar's request and gave us half an hour to leave.'[5]

After the thirty minutes were up, the Israelis began firing. Most of the bullets went over the heads of the civilians but Abdulmuti's nine-year-old son was wounded in the knee. There was a scene of utter confusion as the mob ran for their lives in the direction of the Lebanese border. Abdulmuti was lucky because he and his family were able to find shelter in an orchard. Later they were able to get food at Beit Jann, a village of Druse who were not forced to evacuate.

The young men from Bi'na and Deir al-Assad were held for several days in concentration camps along with men from many other villages in Upper Galilee. They were not fed but were frequently beaten and interrogated. Any belongings which had not already been stolen were taken from them. They were then released near the Arab lines on the West Bank. At Lajjun shots were fired over their heads to frighten them and force them towards the Arab positions. US Air Force Colonel Charles N. Staton confronted Jewish officers with the evidence regarding their treatment of the Arab men who had been expelled from their homes and forced to evacuate Israeli territory. The Jewish commander at Lajjun denied that any Arab civilians had been forced over the lines. 'Had it taken place I would have known about it,' he told the American colonel. But in his report Staton wrote, 'Regardless of the denial I believe it did happen.'

Indeed, in all of their reports the American, French and Belgian observers who were in Galilee soon after Operation Hiram came to conclusions similar to Colonel Staton. The chief observer F. P. Henderson informed UN headquarters that with regard to Israeli atrocities, *'There is no doubt in the minds of observers that Jewish troops did murder civilians in these villages.'* Besides Bi'na and Deir al-Assad, the observers visited numerous other villages including Kafr An'an and Ahtat al-Batouf. Significantly the UN observers concluded, 'There is no evidence indicating that the citizens of any of the above villages resisted by force the Israeli occupation.' The UN observers noted that Israeli conduct during Operation Hiram was *'certainly in keeping with the known policy of some factions of the*

Israeli forces in uprooting Arabs from their native villages in Palestine by force or threat.'[6]

The Middle East section of the Foreign Office had considerable influence in determining Israeli government policy toward the Palestinians. But Operation Hiram had been planned rather hastily and the Middle East Department had not been consulted. On 12 November, after the offensive, Shimoni of the Middle East Department wrote to his Chief Elias Sasson who was in Paris:

> Our suggestions and instructions did not reach the army and were not carried out in the way we asked. So it happened that the treatment given to refugees who lived in the Galilee was different from one place to another – in one place people were expelled while in another they were allowed to stay. In one place a surrender was accepted – and with this the obligation to let the inhabitants stay and defend them – while in another a surrender was rejected. In some places better treatment was given to Christians while in other places no distinction was made between Christians and Muslims . . . we asked that no Arab inhabitants remain in the Galilee even more so concerning refugees who came there from other places but nobody asked our opinion or informed us that the conquest of the Galilee was about to take place.[7]

We see that the conclusion drawn by the UN observers that there was an Israeli policy of 'uprooting Arabs from their native villages in Palestine by force or threat' was in fact accurate. However, much depended on the whim of the local commanders, not all of whom gave the expulsion of civilians top priority. In some cases Israeli units were too busy fighting the enemy to divert strength to clear out the local population. In quite a few villages people were expelled but risked their lives to get back to their homes. Thus thousands in the Galilee escaped expulsion to the annoyance of many Israeli leaders.

There was some discussion at the UN Security Council about the methods used by the Zionist forces during Operation Hiram. The Arab states charged that the Jewish troops had murdered many innocent civilians in their effort to drive out the indigenous population in central Galilee. The Israeli representative Abba Eban denied these charges and asserted that the local Arabs had fled on their own or had been encouraged to leave by their leaders. Ralph Bunche, who had replaced Count Bernadotte as the UN mediator in Palestine, told the Security Council, 'United Nations observers reported extensive looting of villages and carrying away of goats, sheep and mules by Israeli forces. The looting appeared to the observers to be systematic, army trucks being used.'[8]

Some of the looting was of a more personal nature. In the village of Jish in the Safed district, the thievery was particularly vicious.[9] Two days after the village was captured, Israeli soldiers stole money, jewellery, and other valuables from several homes. An Arab member of the Knesset later noted: 'When the people who were robbed insisted on being given receipts, they were take to a remote place and shot dead.' The village complained to the local commander who had the bodies brought back to the village. 'The finger of one of the dead had been cut off to remove a ring.' In a conversation with Ben-Gurion one of the Prime Minister's most trusted military advisers Fred Grunich revealed that among the atrocities he had observed was 'the horror of the seizure of the Arab village Jish including the massacre of civilians.'

Most of the Israeli atrocities in Upper Galilee were motivated by a desire to terrorize the population into fleeing. Some murders were committed for vengeance or to cover up looting. A few Zionist outrages appear to be almost senseless brutality. The American diplomat William Burdett reported to Washington that 'after the surrender in three Arab villages in the Galilee area, the Jews ordered the villagers to turn in all of their arms in twenty-five minutes. When unable to meet the deadline, five men from one village and two each from another were selected at random and shot. Killings confirmed by UN investigation.'[10]

UN observers frequently found however that the Israelis attempted to cover up their crimes and to impede the investigators. This was certainly true in Majd al-Kurum. A total of nine people, including two women, were murdered by Israelis in the village. Several UN teams visited the village attempting to obtain information. On 11 November, a team including A. Pallemans, a Belgian Warrant-Officer, came to Majd al-Kurum. Pallemans was a persistent and intelligent investigator. He spoke fluent Arabic but he pretended to a Jewish liaison officer that he did not know the language. The Israeli officer agreed to act as interpreter but as Pallemans suspected, he changed the testimony of the villagers they interviewed. In response to one question the Jewish officer claimed that an Arab villager had said that the people of Majd al-Kurum were well fed and content. But according to Pallemans the Arab had really said, 'We have no food whatever and are not allowed to till our fields.'

Despite the attitude of the Jewish army officers, Pallemans was able to collect a great deal of information. Earlier in the day, the Israelis had refused to allow another UN observer to take a photograph of houses that had been blown up but Pallemans insisted on his right to take pictures. The Jews reluctantly granted his request that a body of one of the Arab victims be dug up. When this was done Pallemans noted that the Israeli liaison officer 'was far from being pleased and if he had been in a position to stop the inquest, he would certainly have done so.' In his final report on Majd al-Kurum, the Belgian officer noted, 'there is no doubt about these murders.'[11]

Many of the Arabs who had returned to Majd al-Kurum testified that the Israeli reign of terror had not stopped. They were fired at when they attempted to go into their fields and they were frequently robbed and beaten by the Jewish soldiers. On one occasion, an Arab called Pallemans to one side and said that the people of the village had been warned by the Zionists that they not give testimony about present or past atrocities.

Although a Jewish officer publicly told a gathering of the villagers that there would be no reprisals against those who gave information, the UN observers were not satisfied that the villagers were safe. Indeed Pallemans and several other observers who visited Majd al-Kurum sent a letter to UN headquarters which stated that after examining the physical and oral evidence, they were convinced that the Arab villagers had

OPERATION HIRAM

suffered cruelly under Jewish occupation. They made it clear that they were 'concerned about the safety of the remaining inhabitants.' Their principal fear was that 'the Jews may commit further acts of violence in retaliation for the information given to the observers.' The letter was signed by two American, two French and one Belgian UN observer.

The Red Cross was also active in the Galilee after Operation Hiram. In early November Dr Emil Moeri of the Red Cross visited several towns which had recently fallen under Israeli rule. He reported, 'The Arab towns and villages occupied by the Jewish forces are in a critical situation. All of the able-bodied men have been arrested and taken to work camps as if they were prisoners-of-war.'[12]* The women and children were left in a pathetic state. Unable to harvest the crops, the remaining civilians were ravaged by disease.

About 60 per cent of the people examined by Dr Moeri had malaria. He also found many cases of typhoid, rickets, diphtheria and scurvy (in a country where citrus fruit was a principal crop). In almost every village, there was a total lack of medical services. Dr Moeri was frequently surrounded by women who begged him to treat their sick children. Because of the high Arab birth-rate and the absence of men, the Red Cross physician found that children under three comprised about one-fifth of the total population in all of the towns and villages he visited. Dr Moeri reported a critical need for a wide variety of medical supplies and personnel. It was obvious that the Israelis were making life as miserable as possible for those Arabs who remained in Galilee so as to encourage them to leave.

In the period immediately after the war, in all areas of their new state, the Israelis used brutal methods to encourage the remaining Arab population to flee. On the southern front in the Negev, most of the Arab population had been expelled during the conflict. In the armistice agreement that ended the war, the Israelis promised to treat those who remained in a benevolent

---

*A British report notes the Zionist policy of using Palestinian civilians as forced labourers. 'The Jews have shown themselves apt imitators of their Nazi oppressors since this is the kind of tactics the Nazis would have employed.'[13]

manner. But like so many other agreements made by the Zionists their pledge not to molest the Arabs left in the Negev would not be honoured.

CHAPTER XI

There Could Have Been Peace

A time for war and a time for peace.

Ecclesiastes 3:8

On 22 December, the Israelis launched the last offensive of the war against Egypt. Arab disunity, particularly the rivalry between King Abdullah of Trans-Jordan and King Farouk, convinced the Israelis that none of the Arab states would assist Egypt. In a letter to General Riley, the Chief UN supervisor, Walter Eytan of the Tel Aviv Foreign Office, indicated that Israel had launched the attack, 'to defend its territory and hasten the conclusion of peace.' Within a short time, the only Egyptian-held territory in Palestine was a twenty-five-mile square strip around Gaza and the town Faluja behind the Israeli lines, which was occupied by the Egyptian 4th Brigade. Angered at her failure to receive aid from the other Arab states, Egypt decided to heed the UN Security Council's call which required that she enter into armistice negotiations with Israel. On 22 February, the Egyptians and Israelis concluded an agreement.

Under the terms of the armistice, the Egyptian 4th Brigade was allowed to evacuate Faluja, which was deep inside Israeli territory. On 26 February, the first convoy from Gaza arrived at Faluja, the scene of some of the heaviest fighting on the southern front. The convoy's mission was to evacuate the Egyptian garrison as well as any Arab civilians who might wish to leave Israeli territory. Travelling with the convoy were Ray Hartsough and Delbert Roplogle, members of the American Friends Service Committee (AFSC), who planned to administer to the needs of the Palestinian civilians remaining in Faluja and the neighbouring towns. The first order of business for the

Quaker volunteers was to arrange for the distribution of food to the Palestinians whose lives had been disrupted by the war.

Roplogle and Hartsough decided to advise the civilians to stay in their homes, particularly in view of the conditions in the Gaza refugee camps. They had received the personal assurance of Foreign Minister Moshe Sharett that those who remained would not be molested by the Israeli army. The Quaker volunteers accepted the Israeli assurances.

The Palestinians were not so certain that they would be treated humanely. When they arrived at Faluja, Roplogle and Hartsough were surrounded by Arab civilians who asked, 'Shall we go to Gaza or shall we stay in Faluja?' In particular, the Palestinians wanted to know, 'If we stay, will the Jews hurt us?' The Quaker volunteers told the Arabs that they had received assurances in writing and the personal guarantee of Sharett that the civilians in the Faluja area would not be molested. After the Quakers made this point, the Arabs asked, 'We have one more question to ask. If we stay will the Jews hurt us?' Hartsough recalled that he answered in the negative, 'and then someone in the group would ask the question again and again. So it would continue as long as we stayed there.'

Despite their apprehensions, 500 people in Faluja and 1,500 in the neighbouring town, Iraq el Menskiya agreed to remain under Israeli rule. Some inhabitants of Iraq el Menskiya came to the Quaker volunteers and said, 'Most of the people who are leaving are from Faluja but most of the people from our town are staying.' Hartsough replied, 'You are wise people. It may be hard at first but you will have your homes and later you will be allowed to work on your lands.' By encouraging these people to stay, the Quakers had assumed a grave responsibility.

On Monday, 29 February, Major Oren of the Israeli army arrived with a contingent of Jewish military police. When the Quaker volunteers asked him if they could distribute food to the Arab civilians, the Israeli officer replied, 'It will be all right for you to distribute food but you cannot do it tomorrow for we are to begin a sixty-hour curfew during which time the people will not be allowed out of their homes.' However, Major Oren gave permission for Hartsough and a Quaker nurse who spoke fluent Arabic to visit the homes of Arab civilians.

The next day the Quaker team visited Iraq el Menskiya and spoke with the Mukhtar. In an excited voice the village leader reported, 'The people have been molested by frequent shooting, by being told that they would be killed if they did not go to Hebron in Arab territory and by the Jews breaking into their homes and stealing things.'[1]

The Quakers soon began treating the victims of Israeli terrorism. Some of the Palestinians had been beaten badly. One man had two bloody eyes, a torn ear and a badly bruised face. Most of the injured were Arab men who had attempted to stop Israeli soldiers from raping their women. When the Jews broke into the homes looking for loot and women, the Palestinian men usually put up a fight but they were no match for the armed soldiers.

Soon Hartsough's courtyard was full of civilians who were shouting at him in Arabic. When he asked his interpreter what they were saying, he answered, 'They want you to let them bring things from their homes and come stay here near you because they are afraid of the Jews.' The civilians demanded to be taken to Hebron in Jordanian-controlled territory.

When a UN official asked an Israeli officer why the Arab civilians were being treated so badly, he replied, 'It happened in Germany, China and everywhere that soldiers get out of control at times like this. It is all part of war.' But the UN observers would not accept this explanation. Colonel Williams, the chief UN official in the area, sent a message to Tel Aviv: 'Continual shooting by the Israeli forces during the sixty-hour curfew, soldiers beating up the men, reported attempted rapes and much breaking into houses and stealing. Such conduct is a disgrace to the Israeli army and a definite breach of the evacuation agreement.'[2]

The next day Hartsough spoke with Captain Gerah who was assigned as Israeli liaison officer to deal with Arab civilians. Gerah told Hartsough, 'I have an order for you. You and your Quaker team must leave Faluja.' Hartsough told him that he had received permission to remain from many Israeli officials but Captain Gerah insisted that the Quakers leave. The Jewish officer finally allowed the Quakers to remain, pending instructions from Tel Aviv. But it was clear that the Israelis did not want the Quakers to see any more.

Captain Gerah agreed to speak with some of the people who had been molested by Israeli soldiers. At first he insisted that their stories were false but he gradually began to concede that their charges were well founded. At one point, an old woman with dirty bandages on her feet was brought in. When the Quaker nurse took off the bandages, she found in each foot a bullet hole which the old woman had received from Israeli soldiers who had broken into her home.

That night the Mukhtar of Faluja told his people that those who wished to leave for Hebron could do so if they had their things packed and on the road ready to leave by 7 a.m. the next morning. As Hartsough wrote, 'How many want to go! All of them.' At Iraq el Menskiya, the entire population of 1,500 also wished to leave but Trans-Jordan which already had its share of refugees would accept only the 500 from Faluja.

Hartsough tried to persuade the Israeli authorities to tell the Arab civilians that they were still welcome to stay in their homes and that they would not be molested. Although some Israeli officials privately assured Hartsough that the civilians were free to stay, they refused to make any statement to the Palestinians. Somewhat later, Hartsough told Dr Paul Mohn and Captain Zahl of the UN staff of his conversations with the Israelis while expressing his hope that the Arab civilians would be well treated. The UN officials did not share Hartsough's confidence in Israeli assurances. 'I don't believe them,' Captain Zahl told the Quaker volunteer. Dr Mohn explained, 'Mr Hartsough is a Friend [Quaker] and always believes the best possibilities in people.'

Hartsough's hope that the Israelis would not mistreat the Arab civilians was largely based on his belief that he would be allowed to remain in Israeli-controlled territory. The next day, however, he was told that the Quaker team could not stay with the people of Iraq el Menskiya. Hartsough returned to Gaza where he became depressed because he could not be with the civilians, 'who had planned to stay and then after four days of Jewish rule in their village, all planned to leave.' In a report on his relief mission, the Quaker volunteer wrote about the refugees: 'The last time I saw them, they were sitting at the roadside with all of their belongings waiting for trucks which will never come.'

Israeli Foreign Minister Moshe Sharett received several protests from the UN and the American Friends Service Committee over Israeli mistreatment of the population of Faluja and Iraq el Menskiya. Under the armistice agreement with Egypt, the Israelis had promised that with regard to the people of the Faluja area, 'All of those civilians shall be fully secured in their persons, abodes, property and personal effects.' On 6 March, Sharett wrote to Colonel Yaacov Dori of the Israeli General Staff urging him to call off the campaign of terror against the Arab civilians who remained in the Faluja area. Sharett reminded Dori of Israel's commitment in the armistice agreement: 'This pledge was part of the first direct agreement between Israel and a neighbouring Arab state, and at stake here is Israel's credibility.'[3]

Sharett was also concerned about Egyptian Zionists who had been imprisoned by the Cairo government. During the armistice negotiations, the Egyptians had made an unofficial promise to release these Jews but Sharett feared that this promise would not be kept if the mistreatment of the Arab civilians at Faluja continued.

But the Foreign Minister believed that there was an even more important reason for the Israelis to avoid any brutality towards the Faluja civilians. He noted that Israel had, 'denied the accusation that she had initiated the expulsion of the Arabs from their homes.' Sharett realized that it was foolish for the Israeli army to employ its usual methods of intimidation on the Faluja civilians in the presence of so many Quaker and UN personnel. He believed that if the neutral observers saw the population of Faluja being mistreated, they would not believe the Israeli denial that the hundreds of thousands of other refugees had been terrorized. Thus Sharett wrote to Colonel Dori: 'Any attempt to dislodge the inhabitants would undermine Israel's credibility and cast doubt on her declarations with respect to the [flight of the] refugees.' The Foreign Minister warned that 'the attempt to stage a "voluntary" mass exit, as it were, was apt to fail since the Arabs would tell of the threats which had impelled them to leave.' In brief, Sharett believed that the removal of a few thousand Arabs from such a visible location was not worth the negative reaction it would cause in Egypt and the international community. Thus the Israeli army relaxed its pressure on the civilians who remained in the Faluja area.

After the armistice agreement with Egypt the other Arab states, Syria, Trans-Jordan and Lebanon also signed agreements with the Israelis. These documents provided among other things, for an indefinite cease-fire, the fixing of the demarcation lines, the withdrawal and reduction of armed forces, the repatriation of prisoners and for the establishment of Mixed Armistice Commissions to supervise the armistice agreements, but the question of the Arab refugees was never addressed directly in the armistice agreements. It was stated in each document that 'civilians who hitherto have been prohibited from passing the fighting lines or entering the area between the lines are henceforth to be prohibited to the same extent from crossing the armistice demarcation line.' By this stipulation the Arab states *de facto* recognized Israel's right to keep out the refugees while the armistice was in force.

Since there was no mention of the status of the refugees in the armistice agreements, there was a need for further negotiations. On 11 December 1948, the United Nations General Assembly established the Palestine Conciliation Commission (PCC) to settle the outstanding problems between Israel and her Arab neighbours. The Commission was empowered to resolve the status of Jerusalem, the borders of Israel, as well as the refugee problem. In the resolution that created the Commission the General Assembly affirmed that 'the refugees wishing to return to their homes and to live in peace with their neighbours should be permitted to do so at the earliest practicable date.'[4] The Commission, which consisted of members from the United States, France and Turkey, realized that the refugee situation was the chief problem between Israel and the Arab states.

Tel Aviv left open the door to a token repatriation of refugees, but only as part of a general peace settlement. The Commission members believed that if the Israelis made an immediate gesture by accepting back a small group of refugees, this would help to bring the Arab states to the negotiating table ready to make concessions of their own. On 24 February, Sharett met with the members of the Commission in Tel Aviv. The American chairman of the Commission, Mark Ethridge, suggested to the Israeli Foreign Minister that the Arab states 'would like to see Israel do or say something about the refugee problem' in order to show 'evidence of their good faith or desire for peace.'[5] Sharett would not agree to accept back even a small group of refugees or make any other gesture or concession on this troubling issue. 'I think the sooner the problem of resettlement in neighbouring countries is tackled seriously and constructively the better it is for all concerned,' he told Ethridge.

On 19 March, the Israelis submitted to the Commission a memorandum which contained a plan to resettle the Palestinians in neighbouring Arab countries. This document ruled out any substantial return of the refugees to Israel. 'The main solution,' according to the memorandum, 'is not repatriation but resettlement elsewhere.'[6] According to the Israelis there was nothing to which the refugees could return. 'During the war and the Arab exodus, the basis of their economic life crumbled away.' Resettlement was urged in Syria, Iraq, and Trans-Jordan because these countries, 'are underpopulated and possess areas suitable for large-scale agricultural development.'

The Israelis urged huge irrigation projects which would be centred near Hananiah Lake and the Jezeral area in Iraq and in the Jordan valley. Christian Arabs might be resettled in Lebanon because there was already a large Christian population in that country. It was suggested that various international agencies might finance the irrigation projects and resettlement effort but it was clear that they expected the United States to shoulder most of the financial burden.

There was, however, a deep division within the Israeli government on the question of refugee resettlement in Arab countries. All of the Zionist hierarchy opposed repatriation of the refugees to Israel but some Israeli leaders such as Sharett and UN Ambassador Abba Eban believed that permanent resettlement of the Palestinians in the Arab countries was an essential step towards the pacification of the Middle East and eventual friendly relations between Israel and her Arab neighbours. They ran into the resistance of Ben-Gurion.[7] The Prime

Minister opposed any resettlement scheme even if it was financed by the United States or other foreign sources. Ezra Dannin worked many months on secret negotiations which gave hope of yielding an agreement that would transfer the Palestinian refugees from camps near Israel's borders to permanent homes in the Arab states. Ben-Gurion would have none of it. Years later Dannin bemoaned, 'Even today I cannot understand why Ben-Gurion opposed the resettlement of the refugees in Arab countries.'

Dannin favoured several projects including a scheme to set up a Palestinian state on the West Bank that would be free from King Abdullah (who was in the process of annexing the West Bank). This independent Palestinian state would have fulfilled the national aspirations of the Palestinians and led to a solution of the refugee problem but Ben-Gurion opposed the scheme.

The most promising proposal during this period was the offer of President Housni Zaim of Syria to take in 300,000 Palestinian refugees for permanent resettlement in his country as part of a comprehensive agreement between Syria and Israel. But Ben-Gurion would not pursue Zaim's proposal. Eban could not understand Ben-Gurion's failure to seize a golden opportunity. 'Why aren't we impressed by the Syrian willingness to absorb the 300,000 refugees,' Eban inquired, 'since their resettlement with American support is of the utmost importance?'

When Dannin pressed Ben-Gurion about the Syrian offer, he replied, 'We will not go into new adventures. Palestinian Arabs have only one role left – to flee.' Several months later Teddy Kollek was on the verge of another breakthrough on Palestinian resettlement in new negotiations. Dannin once again pressed Ben-Gurion to pursue the opportunity vigorously. As Dannin recalled, 'The answer was negative. I shall not repeat the words that he used. It is not to the honour of a man like Ben-Gurion that he spoke like that.' Dannin believed that the Prime Minister lost the opportunity 'to avoid the hostility against us from the camp in which Arafat grew up.'

Moshe Dayan was a member of the Israeli hierarchy who supported Ben-Gurion's intransigent opposition to a permanent solution to the Palestinian refugee issue. According to Dayan, 'The first battle in the process of the establishment of Israel as an independent state is not yet complete, as we have not yet determined whether the territorial boundaries of the state are final.' Dayan favoured 'modifications' in Israel's boundaries, in particular the annexation of the West Bank. He foresaw inter-Arab rivalry and believed that this disunity should be encouraged so that it worked to Israel's benefit since 'possibilities will become available to Israel to change its borders and it is doubtful whether it is worth missing the opportunity.' In April 1949, Ben-Gurion told his aides, 'the issue at hand is conquest not self-defence. As for the setting of borders – it's an open-ended matter. In the Bible as well as in history there are all kinds of definitions of the country's borders so there's no real limit.'

Both Ben-Gurion and Dayan strongly favoured a 'masterplan' that included annexation of the West Bank and Gaza as well as the creation of a puppet Christian buffer state in Lebanon. During the war Ben-Gurion had considered the annexation of the West Bank after a lightning attack in which the Arab population would be driven out. He never gave up this dream.* Ben-Gurion believed that as long as the refugee problem remained unsolved there would be tensions in the region which could eventually be used to ignite a new war of conquest. Ben-Gurion and Dayan tolerated negotiations because they served to disunite the Arabs and placate the Americans but they always saw to it that the Israelis failed to pursue any Arab proposal which might lead to an agreement.

Israeli intransigence was covered with a veneer of reasonableness and willingness to negotiate. The Arabs on the other hand, as the weaker side desired a settlement since they feared Zionist expansionism. However, out of pride and a need to impress their own people, the Arab governments covered their conciliatory position with a tough outer façade. This included

---

*Some years after the war Ben-Gurion told the writer Chaim Guri that he had not annexed the West Bank in 1949 because the Israelis 'either had to use the methods of Deir Yassin to expel hundreds of thousands of Arabs who at the time would not have abandoned their houses and would not have abandoned their houses and would not run away or to accept them in our midst. Such overreaching would have necessarily led to a grave conflict with the Powers . . . But we shall see. History is not yet finished.'[8]

their refusal to sit publicly at the same table with the Israelis who cleverly exploited the tough façade of the Arabs to portray them as the obstacle to peace.

The Palestine Conciliation Commission made a valiant attempt to pacify the Middle East but the refugee problem proved to be a major stumbling block. At the outset, the Arabs took the position that an agreement on this issue had to be reached before a general peace conference could be convened. Publicly they asked that Israel comply with the United Nations resolution of 11 December 1948, which provided for the return of all refugees who desired repatriation. The Arabs realized the urgency of the question since every week thousands of Jewish emigrants were arriving in Israel and settling in the homes and on the land of the Palestinian refugees. Clearly, if an agreement was delayed, repatriation for the Palestinians would become more difficult. Since time was on their side, the Israelis sought to delay a resolution of the refugee issue. They held out hope of a token repatriation but only after the conclusion of a peace agreement in which the Arab states would recognize Israel's control over all the territory conquered by the Zionists during the recent war. The Jewish leaders refused to consider an American proposal that they take back 200,000–250,000 Palestinians.

The Israelis attempted to justify their position on the Palestinian refugee question by claiming that they were not responsible for causing the problem. On 9 April, William Burdett spoke to the Israeli Prime Minister about the Palestinian issue. 'Ben-Gurion emphatically denied that Israel had expelled any Arabs from Israeli territory and with considerable emotion he stated that the creation of the refugee problem was organized by the Arab states or the British or both.'[9] The Israelis emphatically refused to make any concessions. The Arabs, however, agreed to drop their demand that Israel comply with the UN resolution for the return of the Palestinians, before a general conference could be convened. A meeting was arranged for the Arabs and Israelis to meet with the PCC at Lausanne. This was not a formal peace conference but it was hoped that progress could be made on the territorial questions, the status of Jerusalem and especially the issue of Palestinian repatriation and/or resettlement. It was the conciliatory attitude of the

Arabs that made the conference possible. The chairman of the PCC, Mark Ethridge reported to President Truman, 'The Arabs have made what the Commission considers very great concessions, the Jews have made none so far.'[10]

On 29 April, President Truman replied to Ethridge: 'I am rather disgusted with the manner in which the Jews are approaching the refugee problem. I told the President of Israel in the presence of his Ambassador just exactly what I thought about it. It may have some effect, I hope so.'[11] But President Truman's hopes were not realized since the Israelis still refused to change their attitude toward Palestinian repatriation. At the Lausanne Conference, the Israeli delegate, Walter Eytan, denied that Israel had any 'direct or indirect' responsibility for the existence of the Palestinian refugees. He referred to the Arab exodus as a situation that 'in the long run might be considered beneficial and wholesome.'[12]

The Americans wanted the Israelis to agree to a formula whereby they would accept back 200,000–250,000, which was about a third of the refugees, while the remaining half million would be permanently resettled in Jordan, Syria, Lebanon and Iraq. American financial backing was promised for the plan. Truman was determined to force the Israelis to be more flexible on the refugee question, as well as on the issue of the territory they conquered during the war beyond that allotted to the Jewish state under the UN partition resolution. The Americans did not believe that the Israelis should keep all of this occupied territory, which included Lydda–Ramle, Jaffa and parts of the Negev and Galilee.

On 25 May, Ambassador McDonald delivered a stern note in Tel Aviv in which President Truman warned, 'The Government of Israel should entertain no doubt whatever that the US Government relies upon it to take responsible and positive action concerning the Palestine refugees.'[13] Truman warned that if the Israelis failed to change their position on the refugee and boundary questions, 'the United States Government will regretfully be forced to the conclusion that a revision of its attitude toward Israel will become unavoidable.' The State Department suggested to the President a wide range of actions that could be taken by the US in order to put pressure on Israel.

These included revoking the income tax exemption for the United Jewish Appeal and other organizations sending money to Israel, refusing to train Israeli officials in the United States, holding up loans to Israel and lessening support for Israel at the United Nations. Some leverage was applied to the Israelis but not enough to force a change in this intransigent position of the Zionist state. Tel Aviv realized that the Truman administration was too heavily dependent on the American Jewish community to put any really serious pressure on Israel.

The Zionists did, however, make several half-hearted proposals. On 9 June, they offered to annex the Egyptian-controlled Gaza strip and accept the 200,000 refugees living there as citizens of the Jewish state. Since the Israelis refused to offer any territorial compensation to Egypt or give any guarantees that they would allow the Gaza refugees to return to their homes, the Egyptians refused to consider the proposal. As a counter-offer the Arabs requested that the Jews allow the Palestinians who came from Israeli territory not included in the Jewish state under the UN partition resolution to return to their homes. Although not directly stated, the implication of the proposal was that the refugees who came from those areas included in the Jewish state in the November 1947 resolution would be permanently resettled in the Arab states. The Israelis refused the Arab counter-proposal and urged a postponement of any discussion of the refugee question until the other issues at the conference were settled.

In the course of the debate, Dr Walter Eytan referred to the repatriation of the Palestinians as 'a step backward'. The Arabs were enraged by the Israeli gloating over the expulsion of the Palestinians. Fuad Ben Ammoun of Lebanon called the Israeli attitude a denial of the UN charter 'and all of the treaties and conventions and the efforts of jurists and statesmen throughout the centuries in favour of the protection of minorities.'[14] The Lebanese delegate suggested that the Israeli aim was to 'establish a purely Jewish population and set up a theocratic and racial state. On the basis of the world's recent history, however, the Jews should be the first to deny the principle of racism which caused the destruction of six million of their people.' Ben Ammoun decried 'the doctrine of Lebensraum,' which the

Zionist state had carried out by expelling the Palestinians in order to make room for Jewish immigrants.

Many American officials were also critical of the Israeli attitude to the Palestinian refugee question. Mark Ethridge noted that the Jewish position was 'morally reprehensible and politically shortsighted.'[15] In his reports, Ethridge consistently noted that it was Israeli intransigence that was preventing a settlement of the Middle East situation. Ethridge rejected the Israeli claim that they were not responsible for the refugees because the exodus had resulted from a war launched by the Arabs. The American official believed that apart from a general responsibility for the refugees, Israel had, 'particular responsibility for those who had been driven out by terrorism, repression and forcible ejection.'

William Burdett blamed Israeli intransigence on 'the failure of the UN in the past to protect the rights and interests of the Palestinian Arabs by not forcing Israel to comply with various UN resolutions.'[16] Burdett was also critical of Washington for not taking a firm stand in its dealings with Israel. He reported to the State Department that the Israelis were convinced of their 'ability to "induce" the United States to abandon its present insistence on the repatriation of refugees and territorial changes. From experience in the past [Israeli] officials state confidently, "you will change your mind," and the press cites instances of the effectiveness of organized Jewish propaganda in the United States.' (The parallel with recent ineffective American efforts to pressure Israel on the West Bank is striking.)

The Lausanne Conference dragged on for many months with no apparent progress. The Americans continued to press the Israelis to take back 250,000 refugees. Publicly the Arabs insisted that in any agreement the Israelis must comply with the UN resolution for the return of the Palestinians who desired repatriation. Privately, however, the Arabs hinted that they would agree to the permanent resettlement of most of the Palestinians in the Arab world. Everyone involved in the negotiations felt that there was a good chance for a permanent resolution to the Arab–Israeli conflict if the Palestinian refugee problem could be solved.

On 3 August, the Israeli delegation at Lausanne proposed

that the Jewish state would agree to the repatriation of 100,000 refugees under certain conditions. First this group of Palestinians could return if the Arabs recognized Israeli sovereignty over all the territory occupied during the 1948 war. The Israelis made clear that the 100,000 total would include 25,000–30,000 'infiltrators' who they claimed had illegally re-entered Israel since the war. Thus in reality the Israelis were proposing that they would accept back 70,000–75,000 Palestinian refugees, about 10 per cent of the total. The remaining 90 per cent would have to be resettled in the Arab world. Most disturbing was the Jewish insistence that the Israeli government would 'retain full authority to direct the returning refugees to specific localities and to specific economic activities.' In a memorandum submitted to the Lausanne Conference's technical committee on refugees the Israelis stressed, 'the clock cannot be put back,'[17] by which they meant, 'the individual return of Arab refugees to their place of residence is impossible.' The reason given was that the homes, farms and businesses and other Arab property had 'practically disappeared'. The Israelis did not mention that most of the property had been stolen or purposely destroyed by them.

The Arabs considered the Israeli proposal as 'less than token'. There was reason to believe that they were right. Herbert Kunde, the US member of the Lausanne Conference's technical committee on refugees referred to the Israeli offer as a 'sham'. Kunde believed that Israel's failure to present a realistic offer on Palestinian repatriation 'pointed up the great and continuing difficulties that the UN will face in assuring the Arabs in Israel equitable treatment and guaranteeing them basic human rights.'[18]

Burdett reported on 19 August, an incident which he believed 'throws further light on the true value of the proposal to repatriate 100,000 Arabs.'[19] In territory ceded to Israel by Jordan under the armistice agreement, thousands of Palestinians were expelled by the Jews. The Jordanians complained to the UN Mixed Armistice Commission. In the presence of a US military observer, the Jordanian representative on the Mixed Armistice Commission was told by Moshe Dayan that the Jordanians might force the Israelis to take back the Palestinians but 'they would regret it if they returned.' Burdett believed that even if the Arabs agreed to the '100,000 plan', the Israelis would make sure that the Palestinians 'would regret it if they returned.' Like most American officials, Burdett believed that despite any public pronouncements, the Israelis would never carry through a plan for substantial Palestinian repatriation.

Indeed when the '100,000 plan' was announced, there was an outpouring of negative reaction from every newspaper and political party in Israel. The right wing under Menachem Begin predicted dire consequences if the government accepted back even the 10 per cent of the refugees as envisaged under the plan. The left-wing parties in Israel labelled the proposal as a concession to American pressure, which they resented. There was also a great deal of opposition to the plan within the ruling Mapai party. On 13 October, Moshe Sharett met with Lowell Pinkerton, the American Minister to Lebanon, to discuss the Palestinian question. After giving the American diplomat a long lecture 'on Israeli history from Moses to date',[20] Sharett doubted that 'the offer to the PCC to repatriate the 100,000 would be carried out because of the strong reaction from the public and the military chiefs.' Soon after, the Israelis announced that their offer had been withdrawn.

A few refugees were repatriated under the 'Broken Families' plan, which was initiated by the Israelis. At Lausanne, Dr Eytan had indicated that his government would allow a limited number of Palestinians who had members of their immediate family in Israel to re-enter the country. The Israelis were not motivated by humanitarian considerations. Many Palestinians were sneaking across the border to visit or join relatives in Israel, which was creating a serious border problem with incidents occurring almost daily. The Israelis believed that the reunion of families would help to stabilize the border. They were also concerned about thousands of Arab women and children who lacked the support of young men and who thus might be placed on public welfare permanently. None the less the Israelis screened the applications for family reunion very carefully. Indeed, over a ten-year period only about 8,000 Palestinians were allowed to return to Israeli territory. Along with the estimated 25,000–30,000 Arabs who infiltrated back into Israeli territory, they were the only Palestinian refugees to return home.

While the Lausanne Conference was still in session, Secretary of Defence Louis Johnson wrote to the Secretary of State, Dean Acheson, that if the refugee problem was not solved it would 'serve to perpetuate and aggravate conditions of insecurity, unrest and political instability with attendant opportunity for Soviet penetration' in the Middle East. Secretary Johnson's words turned out to be prophetic: the Palestinian refugee problem still remains a major cause of instability in the Middle East and a source of Soviet–American confrontation. Had the problem been solved in 1949, the world would have been spared considerable tension. But despite the negotiations, there was never any chance that the Israelis would have been willing to accept back even a token number of refugees.

The Israeli refusal to consider Palestinian repatriation seriously is not surprising in view of the goals the Zionists had long been pursuing. During the Conference, Dr Farid Zeineddine of Syria commented on the Israeli intransigence on the repatriation issue:

> The Jews are continuing the policy consistently followed by them through all the years that the Palestine problem has been under consideration. From the first they had propounded the theory that the Arab countries had enough land and that Palestine should be evacuated by the Arabs and their place taken by Jews.[21]

The irony of Zeineddine's statement was that Ben-Gurion and Dayan not only opposed the repatriation of the refugees to their homes in Israel but also opposed any permanent resettlement of the Palestinians in the Arab states until Israel had the opportunity to annex the West Bank and Gaza. But the Americans wanted the Israelis to accept a plan that would include resettlement of the majority of the Palestinians in the Arab countries as well as the repatriation of a substantial minority to the Jewish state. The refusal of Israel under Ben-Gurion and Dayan to accept any settlement condemned the Middle East to decades of violence and confrontation.

The Zionists maintained that the Palestinians did not desire repatriation to the Jewish state. Eliahu Epstein, the Israeli diplomatic representative in Washington, told Mark Ethridge that the Arabs, 'when in a majority treated other minorities very well but they did not feel the same way when occupying the minority position themselves.'[22]

But most of the relief workers who actually spoke with the refugees realized that the Palestinians did not desire resettlement in other Arab countries but wanted only to return to their own towns and villages. Howard Wriggins of the AFSC was concerned about the attention being given to resettlement proposals. In a report to his Executive Board, the Quaker official noted, 'there is obviously a great appeal in the idea of a new TVA in the Tigris-Euphrates valley' but 'from the refugees' point of view the only solution they desired is a return to their homes.'[23]

Wriggins wanted the AFSC to counter the effort to portray resettlement as the best solution for the Palestine question. He pointed out that even before the war, the Zionists had tried to sell the idea of resettling the Palestine Arabs in neighbouring countries so as to make room for Jewish immigrants. But Wriggins felt that the scheme would never work since the Palestinians would accept nothing less than repatriation. The best solution he believed was for the Palestinians to be allowed to return home and for them to be compensated for their property which had been destroyed. If Israel would do this as well as assure the Palestinians that they would be safe from 'active persecution by Jewish extremist groups,' he saw no reason why repatriation could not work.

Many other relief workers agreed with him. Ralph Hegnaur of the International Civilian Service reported to his superiors that after working with the refugees, he was certain that the Palestinians, 'believe in their return, they want to believe in it – and their feelings and reason are entirely directed towards this.'[24] Hegnaur noted that the Palestinians were sure that for them, besides repatriation, 'there is no solution but death.'

M. A. Abbasy of the UN spent a great deal of time talking to hundreds of refugees in order to ascertain what they desired for their future. He found that the Palestinians 'wish to return to their homes and land provided their security and safety are guaranteed by the UN and the Arab League.' He noted: 'We have to remember that farmers in this part of the world are very closely tied to the land where they were born.'

On 12 April, Ray Hartsough who had returned to Gaza, reported on the refugees. 'While governments harangue over resettlement questions in international councils, a good many people hereabouts just plain go home – but not to stay.'[25] Of course those refugees who lived in Israeli territory could not go home but some of the refugees from Gaza whose homes were in the no man's land between the Egyptian and Israeli forces risked death from land mines and sniper fire, 'in the hope at least of a momentary glimpse of house, land or relatives left behind.'

As Hartsough drove along the highway leading north, he noticed two columns of civilians, one heading towards their old village in order to visit their former home and the other 'returning to their wretched cave, tent or hovel in and south of Gaza.' The Quaker volunteer was impressed by the sight of the 'camel trains, numbering as many as twenty animals, trudging along in the combination of comedy and disdain which camels always achieve.' Alongside the camels were Arab women, 'with their shawls flowing about their shoulders, walking gracefully with a huge bunch of green stuff on twigs and branches balanced on their heads.'

The journey was not without its dangers. 'The presence of mines was apparent from the dead camels, donkeys and cattle along the highway, but this did not deter the refugees.' Many were killed or wounded by the mines. Hartsough noticed that the refugees warned strangers by pointing to the dangerous areas and shouting, 'boom, boom.'

Hartsough found that as at Faluja, the refugees constantly asked, 'Will we be safe, will our lives be safe?' Once again the Quaker volunteer would attempt to offer assurance and after a few minutes the refugees would turn to him and say 'Just one more question.' Which, as expected, would turn out to be a repeat of the earlier inquiry. The refugees asked every stranger the same questions about when they could go home and whether it would be safe if they did. Hartsough was greatly disturbed by his inability to give a satisfactory reply. 'Not having an answer makes being among these people almost intolerable for a Westerner.'

'Nobody wants anybody,' was the despairing remark of one

refugee. 'We want to go home to our lands,' he told Hartsough. Another refugee, eighteen-year-old Mahmoud Hussain, demanded, 'Let us have a rightful place of our own.' Eight months earlier in August he had fled with his family from their home to Gaza where he ended up in a refugee camp like so many others. He had worked since he was a small boy in his family's orchards and he grew restless from his enforced leisure at Gaza. 'It is too long now since we knew a real life.' Tragically for Mahmoud and hundreds of thousands of other Palestinians, their exile had only just begun.

CHAPTER XII

Theft of a Nation

Thou shalt not oppress a stranger for ye know the heart of a stranger seeing ye were strangers in the land of Egypt.

Exodus 23:9

It was early morning and young Fouzi took his small straw basket to pick figs in his father's orchard in Lydda. Before the war he had frequently begun the day by gathering fruit on his family's land and now with the return of peace he decided to resume the practice. Besides, his family which was now impoverished could use the food.

When he reached the orchard, Fouzi climbed a tree that had beautiful ripe figs. Soon he heard a voice shouting at him. Fouzi turned and saw a guard riding a black horse and wearing a cowboy hat. The guard asked the boy in broken Arabic what he was doing. When Fouzi replied, 'I am picking fruit,' the man became very angry.

'Do you think I am an idiot,' the guard said, 'I see you are picking fruit. Who gave you permission to do that?'

'And since when do I have to be given permission? This is our land and this is my tree,' the boy answered. This made the guard even more angry.

He ordered Fouzi to come down from the tree and insisted that the boy follow him with his basket of figs. Terror-stricken, Fouzi did as he was told. Eventually the boy was put into a car and driven away. He was brought to a police station along with several other boys who had been caught taking figs from the orchard. But when it was discovered that they were Jewish, the other boys were quickly released. A policeman became noticeably hostile when he realized that Fouzi was an Arab. 'Aren't you ashamed to steal, you thief,' he told the boy. 'I didn't steal. It's my orchard – my father's. I went there to pick figs,' was the reply.

'There is no such thing as "ours"! The land belongs to the Jews – do you understand!'

Fouzi was perplexed and angry. He could not understand why his father had never told him that he had sold the land to the Jews. The policeman asked him, 'So whose land is it?' The boy thought it best to concede the point. 'Ours. But I did not know that my father had sold it to the Jews.' Fouzi would never forget the mocking tone of the policeman: 'I told you that the orchard is not yours. Your father did not sell it to the Jews. It belongs to the Jews.'

At that moment Fouzi understood what had really happened to his family, his people and his country.[1]

During the war and immediately afterwards, the wild scramble by the Jews to seize Arab property continued. A study issued in April 1949 by the Knesset's Finance Committee admits that the presence of so much Arab property put 'the fighting and victorious community before serious material temptation.' According to the Israeli report, 'affairs in many areas degenerated without restraint.'[2] Not only were thousands of landholdings seized and occupied but thousands more orchards and vineyards were either uprooted or neglected irreparably by Israelis who wished to use the land for Jewish settlement.

The land of all Palestinian refugees was subject to confiscation, as well as the property of 30,000 Israeli Arabs who were classified as 'internal absentees'. Many of these people had fled only a short distance from their homes or had been absent for only a few days. Even though they had never left Israeli territory and were considered citizens of Israel, their land was subject to confiscation. Many other Israeli Arabs lost their land because they could not prove their ownership. Numerous records had been destroyed in the chaos of war and the transition from British to Israeli administration. There were many cases where Arab residents of Israel lost property which had been in their family for generations.

Some Jews disapproved of their government's policy of seizing the property of the Israeli Arabs. Moshe Smilansky, a member of the ruling Mapai party wrote, 'someday we will have to account for this theft and spoilation not only to our conscience but also to law.'³ But the government had no intention of relenting in its policy. Speaking in the Knesset, Finance Minister Eliezer Kaplan asserted that the question of the seized property was 'a delicate matter' which involved 'national security'.

Arab members of the Knesset protested that the government had even classified as absentee landlords people who the Israeli army admitted had been forcibly transferred after the armistice to other areas for 'security reasons'. The Arab Knesset members asserted that the government had no right to seize the property of legal residents of the country who carried Israeli identity cards. Even the Israeli High Court of Justice ruled in several cases that the government lacked the slightest pretext to seize property of many Arabs. Eventually the government offered monetary compensation for the land of Israeli Arabs but it amounted to a tiny fraction of its real value. Most Israeli Arabs refused to accept the insulting pittance.

The land question was only one of many indignities suffered by the Israeli Arabs. After the armistice agreements were signed about 150,000 Arabs remained in Israeli territory. Over half of them lived in the Galilee with substantial groups in the region known as the 'Little Triangle' adjacent to the Jordanian border. There were also sizeable communities in several other areas including Lydda–Ramle. With the end of hostilities, these people looked forward to a return to normal life. The Israelis promised that the Palestinian minority would be treated as citizens of the Jewish state. But the end of the war did not bring any benefits to the Israeli Arabs.

The Tel Aviv government invoked the 'Defence Emergency Regulations' which had originally been passed by the British in 1945 to cope with Zionist terrorism. During the mandate period the Jews had loudly protested the regulations but now they imposed them in the border regions where most of the Israeli Arabs lived. Under these regulations Arabs in Majdal, Sha'ab, al-Birwa and other towns were expelled from their homes for 'security reasons'. In other Arab areas, police and military personnel were empowered to search any home or business suspected of being used for activities 'inimical to public safety'. Arabs could be searched or arrested on the street without

warrant or expelled from Israel without due process. Under the emergency regulations, police or army personnel could be billeted among the inhabitants at the latter's expense. Martial law could be imposed at the government's discretion. Arabs could not visit another town in Israel without filling out long forms and waiting for permission to travel.

The Israelis justified these measures by claiming that there was always the possibility of renewed conflict with neighbouring Arab countries. But it was clear that the Jews were really attempting to make life as difficult as possible for the Israeli Arabs who were completely docile. The Zionists hoped that the Palestinians would realize that they were not welcome in the new state, which coveted their land and property for Jewish immigrants.

Much larger in extent were the lands of the over 750,000 Arab refugees. Since the Israeli government had no intention of ever allowing any substantial repatriation of refugees much of this land was soon given outright to those who had occupied it during the war. Other portions were given to many of the thousands of Jewish immigrants who were flooding the country. Entire towns that had once been Arab centres were settled by Jews. In the rural areas the situation was the same with scores of kibbutzim and moshavim established on Arab lands. Indeed by 1953, about a third of the Jewish population of Israel was living on property stolen from the Palestinians. According to Zionist propaganda, the new Jewish immigrants were all former concentration camp inmates who had desperately desired the opportunity to come to Israel. But some of the Jews who came to Israel needed a little encouragement to immigrate.

As was their custom on the last day of Passover, about 50,000 Iraqi Jews strolled along the esplanade which ran next to the Tigris river in Baghdad. Usually there was a festive atmosphere during the annual procession which honoured the biblical 'Sea Song'. But this holiday season of 1950, an air of apprehension hung over the Iraqi Jewish community.[4]

The previous month Iraqi authorities had announced that any Jew who wished to emigrate to Israel could freely do so. Police officers had appeared at synagogues and declared themselves ready to answer questions about emigration. Few Jews applied for exit visas, however. Some feared that the offer was a trap to discover Zionists. Although tension was increasing, many others were simply not inclined to leave Iraq where they constituted the most prosperous Jewish community in the Middle East.

At about 9 p.m., the crowd along the esplanade began to thin out as most people headed home for dinner. But there were still a considerable number of people sitting at the Dar al-Beida café, a favourite meeting place for young Jewish intellectuals near the esplanade. Suddenly a small object was thrown from a passing car and exploded on the pavement. Luckily, no one was hurt but there were repercussions throughout the Jewish communities in Iraq. Many felt that Muslim extremists were attempting to murder them. The next morning leaflets were distributed at Baghdad synagogues warning the Jews of the danger of more 'incidents' and advising them to leave the country. Some Jews thought that this was good advice and began to whisper, 'It is better to go to Israel.'

Salman al-Biyat, the investigating judge for South Baghdad became suspicious. The distribution of the leaflets so soon after the bombing led him to believe that there was a conspiracy behind it. Rumours were spreading that the communists were responsible but Biyat was not convinced. Members of his staff arrested two youths whom they suspected of involvement in the plot. The Ministry of Justice intervened, however. The case was transferred to another investigating judge and the two youths were set free.

A second bomb exploded at the United States Information Centre in Baghdad which was frequented by many young Jews. Fortunately, no one was hurt but as a consequence about 10,000 Jews registered for emigration. However, the majority of the 130,000 Iraqi Jews, though greatly concerned, still thought it best to remain in a country where they enjoyed considerable privilege.

But when a third bomb exploded in a Baghdad synagogue killing a Jewish boy and blinding one other person, there was a wild stampede for exit visas. The Jewish community were convinced that their lives were in danger, and that emigration to Israel was essential for their survival. Many paid small fortunes to get out before the March 1951 deadline set by the Iraqi government.

At the last moment the Iraqi government decided to confiscate the property of the departing Jews, in retaliation for the theft of Palestinian property stolen by the Israelis. Thus the wealthy Jews of Iraq came to Israel destitute. They had fled because they believed that if they remained in Iraq they would be slaughtered. But were their fears justified? Several months after the last group of Iraqi Jews departed, the nature of the conspiracy against them became clear.

In June 1951, Yehuda Tagar entered Orosbak, one of the largest department stores in Baghdad. One of the salesmen, a Palestinian refugee, turned white when he saw him. Before the war the Palestinian had been a waiter in Acre, and he was sure that Tagar had been one of his regular Jewish customers. He ran to the police and told them, 'I have recognized the face of an Israeli.' Tagar admitted that he was an Israeli but he claimed that he was in Baghdad to marry an Iraqi Jewish girl. His companion confessed however that they were both members of 'the Movement', a Zionist ring that was operating in Iraq. Gradually the members of 'the Movement' were arrested and a cache of arms and explosives was confiscated. In all fifteen members of the ring were arrested and tried, and two of them were executed for setting off the blast which killed the Jewish boy.

Tagar served ten years in prison and later returned to Israel where he published an account of his exploits. Several other members of 'the Movement' also gave their story to the Israeli press. All their accounts confirm that the bombs had been set off in order to 'encourage' the Iraqi Jews to emigrate to Israel. High-ranking Iraqi officials were involved since they saw an opportunity to confiscate the property of the departing Jews. This evidence makes it clear that the Zionists were not only willing to use terrorist methods to drive out the Arabs from the Jewish state but they did not hesitate to use violence against their fellow Jews who hesitated to emigrate to Israel.

Up until the Second World War, the Zionists had assumed that the Jewish communities of Eastern Europe would provide the human reservoir to colonize Palestine. The Holocaust, of course, destroyed all such plans. Before 1948, few Zionist leaders considered using the Middle Eastern Jews to populate their new state. But with the decimation of the Polish, Hungarian and other East European Jews, the communities in the Muslim countries comprised the largest ready reserve of potential immigrants to Israel.

When the Zionists expelled the Palestinians, they did not realize that the Arab states would retaliate by banishing their Jews. Before the rise of political Zionism, most of the Middle Eastern Jews had lived securely under Muslim rule. Their banishment was certainly not humane but was not nearly as brutal as the expulsion of the Palestinians, many of whom were marched to the frontier at gunpoint. Had the Arabs been as bloodthirsty as they are portrayed in Zionist propaganda, they would not have allowed 650,000 Oriental Jews to emigrate to Israel but would have kept the Jews as hostages in concentration camps until the Palestinians were allowed to return home. Or the Arabs could have murdered the Jews in their midst. Ironically the Zionist conspiracy to terrorize the Iraqi Jews was the most brutal premeditated action taken against any Jewish community in an Arab League state. For the most part the Arab governments prevented any popular outbreaks against the departing Jews. While this massive emigration of Oriental Jews was arriving in Israel, the Palestinians still languished in refugee camps.

It was Christmas when Dr Raymond Courvoisier of UNICEF arrived in Bethlehem with a convoy of twelve trucks loaded with food and medicine. All over the world people were celebrating the birth of Christ but in the place where Jesus was born there was little joy. The French physician found thousands of Palestinian refugees huddled in the caves which surrounded the holy town. Dr Courvoisier observed that in all these caves, 'Seven or eight families live squeezed together. The people sleep on the floor, the majority of whom do not possess mattresses or blankets. Every day infants are born on the stone, the old and the sick die while others suffer because of the lack of water, food and clothing.'[5]

The refugees in Bethlehem ate bread made of black flour which they cooked over fire fuelled by manure. Before the arrival of UNICEF, the refugees scavenged for food all over the countryside, eating whatever scraps they could find. The international volunteers did all they could for people who were 'poor, angry and abandoned'. The Trans-Jordanian government which was in the process of annexing the West Bank was doing all that it could for the refugees but it could not possibly cope with the Palestinians who outnumbered the Trans-Jordanians almost three to one. Egypt sent some aid to the refugees on the West Bank but because of the friction between King Farouk and King Abdullah and the Egyptian preoccupation with the refugees in Gaza, Trans-Jordan received little help from the Cairo government. The chief goal of the UNICEF workers was to save as many of the children as possible, thousands of whom were falling victim to the squalid conditions in the camps all over the West Bank and Jordan.

'Until the end of time, poor people and their families will receive sustenance here.' With these words, according to legend, King Solomon in 900 BC decreed that in Hebron, kitchens would be set up to feed the destitute. In modern times the Arabs had carried on this tradition but the food relief programme had been disrupted by the war. However, as in so many other towns on the West Bank, UNICEF had established a relief centre in Hebron to care for the destitute refugees.

Dr Courvoisier noted that in the ancient city, which dated back from the time of Abraham, the suffering of the refugees was particularly acute. The UNICEF doctor saw numerous refugee children in Hebron lining up for their daily ration of milk. 'They stand there patiently and noisily for hours, holding with their frozen hands a small iron box where they keep their ration card. As soon as the milk is received the small children who are very hungry swallow it greedily.'[6]

The winter of 1948–9 was exceptionally cold, which greatly increased the suffering of the refugees. There was considerable snowfall, which was usually followed by floods. Dr Courvoisier reported that the weather had taken a tragic toll. 'Eight infants died from the cold weather at Ramallah, a small refugee has been washed away by the flood water in Amman and another was frozen to death a few metres from our office.' The weather blocked many roads, preventing the delivery of supplies. There was also considerable spoilage of food stockpiles from the snow and rain. Dr Courvoisier noticed that many of the refugee tents were blown away by the wind.

The spring brought some improvement in the situation of the over 700,000 refugees, but with the coming of summer, their condition once again deteriorated. Herbert Kunde, an American refugee expert, visited five camps in July 1949. He found that, 'Due to overcrowding, lack of privacy and poor or non-existent ventilation it is difficult to isolate contagious cases, especially tuberculosis. The basic calorie diet in this camp is 1,200 per day which is too low to maintain resistance to tuberculosis.' Kunde noted that 'morale is deteriorating due to camp life, lack of work and an extremely strong desire to return home which is expressed on every occasion.'[7]

Indeed, like the refugees at Gaza, the refugees on the West Bank lived for the day when they could return to their homes. In August, a UNESCO mission visited several refugee camps on the West Bank. At the Zerba camp, they were received in complete silence. When the party visited a school tent, they asked the children what they would like to have. They all replied with one voice, 'We don't want anything. We want our country, we want our homes.'[8] Meanwhile a crowd of refugees gathered shouting, 'We want our homes. We want to return to our fatherland.' Everywhere the delegation went, they encountered a similar response. Indeed such sentiments were shared by all of the Palestinian refugees.

It has been claimed by many Zionist historians that the number of Palestinian refugees in 1948 was considerably less than 750,000 and they assert that the total was purposely inflated by pro-Arab agencies. However, an examination of the records of UNICEF and other international organizations who dealt with the refugees immediately after their exodus, reveals that for political and economic reasons the staff who worked with the refugees were under considerable pressure to reduce the number of people eligible for assistance. This suggests that the real total of refugees may have been higher than 750,000.

After careful consideration of all the statistics, demographer Janet Abu-Lughod estimates that there probably were 775,000 (± 50,000) refugees.[9] To this might be added about 80,000 people whose homes before 1948 were on the West Bank or in Gaza but who became destitute when their lands in Israel were seized by the Zionists. We might also consider the Bedouin who after 1948 were no longer permitted to enter their grazing lands in Israel. Thus the UNRWA total of nearly 900,000 Palestinian 'displaced persons' from the 1948 war is probably accurate. Certainly the figure of 750,000 which is generally cited must be considered a reliable minimum total. We can dismiss the claim that there were fewer refugees as just an effort by the Zionists to mitigate the extent of their aggression.

Just as it is not easy to calculate the total number of refugees, it is equally difficult to give an exact figure of how many were expelled, persuaded to leave by the Zionists or left out of fear. Probably roughly equal numbers fall into each category. About a quarter of a million were expelled at gunpoint principally from Lydda–Ramle, Upper Galilee and the Negev region. Another quarter of a million were persuaded to leave by whispering campaigns, threats, sound-trucks and the deliberate bombardment of civilian areas. The remainder of the refugees left out of fear but many of these were influenced by stories of Zionist atrocities.

There can be no doubt that the chief cause of the Palestinian exodus was Zionist terrorism. From the beginning of their movement the Zionists realized that no Jewish state would be possible in Palestine without the displacement of the large, deeply entrenched and prolific indigenous population. For half a century the Zionist leaders considered the best method of removing the Arabs from Palestine. Some Zionists such as Weizmann, sincerely believed that the Palestinians could be removed by negotiation but others like Ben-Gurion realized that force would be necessary.

The 1948 war presented an opportunity for the Zionists not only to create their own nation but according to Sharett to solve 'the most vexing problem of the Jewish state' by expelling the Palestinians.[10] Indeed, the Israeli Foreign Minister was not the only Zionist who believed that the departure of the Palestinians was 'more spectacular than the creation of the Jewish state.' This mass exodus which was of critical importance to the Zionists did not come about by accident. It is no coincidence that Plan Dalet provided for the expulsion of so many Arabs.

But in the early months of the conflict when they were very concerned about world public opinion, the Zionists avoided making their policy of expelling Palestinians too obvious. A subtle approach including whispering campaigns, radio broadcasts and other forms of psychological warfare was used. This was effective because the Palestinians were convinced that they would return in the van of the victorious Arab armies. Later, when the Zionists were in a more secure position they employed more brutal methods against a population that had come to realize that any departure would be permanent. This resulted in the mass expulsions from Lydda–Ramle, Upper Galilee and the Negev.

But Ben-Gurion was careful not to issue written orders for the expulsion of Palestinian civilians. Indeed at Lydda–Ramle, the Israeli leader avoided even verbal orders but instead banished the Palestinians with a wave of his arm. It is hard to imagine that in other areas of the country, the brigade commanders would have initiated the expulsion of tens of thousands of civilians without the approval of Ben-Gurion who served as both Prime Minister and Minister of Defence. Many of these Israeli commanders needed no encouragement, however, since they surely realized that without the expulsion of the Palestinians the viability of a Jewish state would be questionable. According to Ben-Gurion's biographer, Michael Bor Zohar, the Zionist leaders issued an order that Israeli troops abstain from expelling Arabs. Bar Zohar notes, 'all commanders understood that the message was only official'.[11]

The chaos of war has often provided a convenient cover for a wide variety of nefarious activities. It must be realized, however, that many Palestinians were expelled from their homes during periods of truce and that even those villages and towns emptied during military operations rarely resisted the Zionist invaders. Most of these people expected to stay in their homes and left only after the Zionists murdered a group of civilians to show that they would stop at nothing in order to evacuate the town.

While Ben-Gurion and the Israeli High Command were certainly aware that their troops were expelling Arabs, there is no reason to believe that they ordered the massacres that were taking place in so many towns and villages throughout Palestine. These atrocities were almost certainly initiated at the battalion and company level without orders from the High Command. Each battalion and company commander realized that he was expected to expel the Arabs from the territory he conquered; how he accomplished this was up to him. Some commanders were more brutal than others. Israeli units that had suffered casualties were more prone towards brutality than units that had not been bloodied.

Several thousand civilians were killed in the massacres that took place in towns and villages all over Palestine. Deir Yassin was certainly not the only village to be decimated. An even greater number of people died on the forced marches in which thousands of defenceless women, children and old people fled for the border accompanied by Jewish soldiers who used 'warning shots' to keep the civilians moving. We will never know how many children died of heat stroke or how many old people succumbed from exhaustion during the Palestinian exodus. Nor will we ever know the exact total of those who were shot or killed by a land mine while attempting to return to their native village. But they have not been forgotten by their families who still mourn the tragic loss.

Some may argue that the expulsion of the Arabs was justified since the formation of a Jewish state in Palestine would not have been possible without the removal of the indigenous population who owned most of the land and had a huge birth-rate. Ardent Zionists see Israel as necessary for 'Jewish survival' and are willing to overlook any crimes that may have been committed in 1948 by the 'Founding Fathers'. After all Herzl himself had written in his diary, 'He who desires the end, desires the means.'[12]

But was the formation of a Jewish state in Palestine the best alternative to the anti-Semitism of central and eastern Europe? Even the most cursory consideration of contemporary events makes it clear that those Jews who have settled in the United States are much better off than those who emigrated to the 'Promised Land'. Indeed, in recent years over half a million Jews have fled from Israel to the United States, where they enjoy greater physical and financial security. They have been joined by the majority of those Jews who have left Russia, few of whom have chosen to go to Israel. It is no secret that a massive flow of money and military equipment is needed in order to maintain the Zionist enclave in the Middle East. This situation has created a potential flashpoint which continues to exacerbate super power tensions as well as endanger the lives of more than just the three million Jews in Israel.

The founding of a Zionist state in Palestine in 1948 was not a desperate attempt to save millions of lives (from a danger that had already passed) but just one more thinly disguised example of Western exploitation of a Third World people. Would Western opinion have acquiesced in the expulsion of the indigenous population from Palestine if they had been of European descent? This is a moot point since the Zionists would never have been so foolish as to commit such an open transgression against a European people. They were quite aware of the Western prejudice which held Muslim, Arabic-speaking people in such contempt. But the Palestinians have proven to be a more stubborn adversary than most Zionists imagined.

Just as the Holocaust has had a profound influence on the Jewish *Weltanschauung*, so too the catastrophe of their expulsion from their homeland has had a dramatic effect on the Palestinians. Since their diaspora, the Palestinians have not only been physically dislocated but they have been transformed from a mass of largely illiterate peasants into the best-educated and most politically conscious people in the Third World. The terrorism that they suffered during al-Nakba has convinced many Palestinians that their goals can only be achieved by the use of the same brutal methods that were used against them.

While there can be no justification for PLO violence, there is a need to understand the anger and frustration that motivates so many Palestinians. The westerners news media attempt to explain PLO terrorism by describing the Palestinians as a barbaric and fanatic race who are motivated by anti-Semitism. But even those who strongly favour Zionism should make an effort to comprehend the reasons for the Palestinian resentment of Israel. For many members of the PLO, recognition of the

Jewish state would mean acquiescence in the theft of their homeland and the exoneration of those who have murdered so many of their kinsmen. Many Americans may not agree with this attitude, but it is important for them to understand the ordeal the Palestinians have suffered. Indeed, there is no sign that the Zionists of today are any more conciliatory than they have been in previous generations.

Rabbi Meir Kahane and his group have received considerable attention for their programme to expel the Arab population from Israel and the West Bank. A recent survey indicated that 42 per cent of Israeli teenagers approve of the racist rabbi's programme (which includes anti-Arab legislation similar to the Nazi Nuremberg laws). Indeed Kahane's Kach party is expected to increase in the Israeli Knesset after the next election.[13]

Kahane bemoans the fact that not all of the Palestinians were expelled in 1948. He speaks of 'The Demon of Demography' which, even without the annexation of the West Bank, ensures an eventual Arab majority in Israel, because of the high Palestinian birth-rate. The leader of the Kach party fears that with a large Arab population, Israel will no longer be a Zionist state 'by and for Jews' but a Middle Eastern Switzerland in which the language, religion and culture of several ethnic groups would be respected. After all, Kahane claims (perhaps with some justice), that 'Western democracy as we know it is incompatible with Zionism.'

Many Israelis have condemned Kahane and attempted to disassociate themselves from him. They claim that what Kahane is proposing is uncharacteristic of Zionism and could never be carried out by a nation like Israel, which stands on high moral principles. Despite these pious protestations, however, there is no doubt that Kahane's proposal to expel the Arabs represents nothing more than the logical continuation of the Zionist programme and the conclusion of the process which was begun in 1948.

Epilogue

And Essau cried, Is not he rightly named Jacob (that is supplanter)? for he hath supplanted me these two times; he took away my birthright and behold now he hath taken away my blessing.

Genesis 27:36

For the Palestinians the horror of their expulsion from their homeland is compounded by the Western world's acceptance of Zionist myths about 1948. It is a tragic irony that in most accounts of the war, the Zionists are viewed as the innocent victims while little sympathy is given to the Palestinian refugees. The Zionist version of 1948 is constantly being portrayed in English-language books, magazines and newspaper articles as well as in movies and TV programmes that are seen by tens of millions of people. The propaganda about 1948 has helped to perpetuate in the United States and to a lesser extent in Britain the myth that the Palestinians are responsible for their own exile.

Part of the reason for this inaccurate portrayal of 1948 has been the paucity of information. For decades the British, American and Israeli Archives for this period were closed. The invaluable reports of the UN observers in Palestine were kept in the UN Archives, an institution which for many years was known to only a few historians.* Most of the important

---

*In 1980 I announced my discovery of the files of the United Nations War Crime Commission (UNWCC) in the UN Archives (see *New York Times*, 28 March 1980). Shortly afterwards I located the UN observer reports on Palestine in 1948 in the Archives. In 1986 a dossier on Kurt Waldheim was found in the UNWCC files. At present I am writing an account of the cover-up of the Waldheim files by the UN Secretariat as well as numerous governments including the US and Israel. For press coverage of my story see *The Times* (London), 13 May 1986 and *Koteret Rashit*, 21 May 1986.

memoirs of Israeli veterans of 1948 have only recently been published. But even the information on the Palestinian exodus which has been known for decades has been ignored by Zionist historians.

In 1959 and 1960, Erskine Childers and Walid Khalidi separately published excerpts from the CIA and BBC radio transcripts which proved that the Arab broadcasts ordered the Palestinians to remain rather than leave their homes in 1948. But these important radio transcripts are never cited in any of the major accounts on 1948. Similarly the earlier memoirs of Jewish veterans of 1948 such as Arthur Koestler and Leo Heiman who wrote honestly about the expulsion of Palestinians are also missing from histories of the 'War of Independence'.

No widely circulated non-Zionist account of 1948 has appeared in English. In the United States no major company would dare to publish an honest history of the expulsion of the Palestinians since such a book would quickly be forced out of circulation by the powerful Zionist lobby. There is in fact a double standard in both Britain and America since books which deal with Arab 'terrorism' are usually published without protest but someone who writes a book about Zionist atrocities against Palestinians is accused of being 'anti-Semitic'. Such a situation has discouraged many from writing honestly about 1948, thus enabling the Zionists to perpetuate their mythic view of the 'War of Independence'.

The Zionist effort to distort history has included the censorship of any material that revealed their true intentions towards the Palestinians. Thus for many decades an unedited version of Herzl's memoirs was unavailable. When an unabridged version was finally published it contained the Zionist leader's references to the 'expropriation and removal' of the Palestinians. Ben-Gurion's papers were also censored including a 1968 collection of letters. Recently an unedited version of his 1937 letter to his son has been published containing the previously mentioned intention 'to expel the Arabs and take their places.' There are numerous other examples of the censorship of references to the expulsion of Palestinians. Perhaps the most famous case came to light in 1979 when the translator Peretz Kidron leaked the deleted portions of the Yitzhak Rabin and Ben Dunkelman

EPILOGUE

memoirs to the press thus revealing the truth about Lydda–Ramle and Nazareth in 1948. Since Rabin and Dunkelman are retired army officers it was necessary for them to submit their manuscripts to military censors.

Yitzhak Levi who is also a retired army officer had to wait for decades before he was allowed to publish even a censored version of Deir Yassin. But retired army officers aren't the only ones to be intimidated. Joella Har-Shefi was fired from her job as a reporter for *Hadashot* when she attempted to publish an honest investigation article on Dawayma. We do not know how many other people have been silenced but Netiva Ben Yehuda, the Israeli veteran of 1948, is probably right when she says 'this country is filled with stories that won't be told.'[1]

Ben Yehuda makes it clear, 'you can't rely on the Israel State Archives.' Many important files dealing with the Palestinian exodus such as the Office of Adviser on Arab Affairs and a large part of the documents from the Ministry of Minorities are closed. According to the Assistant Director of the Israel State Archives 'about 2 per cent' of the material from the files which are supposed to be open has been censored. Despite the obvious gaps in the material from the Israel State Archives, many recent Zionist historians make little effort to supplement their research with documents from the more trustworthy American, British and other foreign archives.

There is also an effort to keep any serious discussion of 1948 off Israeli TV. Thus in 1979 when Israeli television showed a dramatization based on S. Yizhar's 'Story of Hirbet Hiz'ah' (see page xix), there were complaints from the government and threats of dismissal against those responsible. The press pointed out that Yizhar's story was supposedly fiction but most people in Israel know that such events were standard procedure in 1948.

It is common knowledge in Israel that most Palestinians were forcibly expelled. Israel is a small country and most people have relatives, friends and neighbours who served in the war. Almost every Israeli is familiar with stories about how the Arabs were driven out but few residents of the Jewish state are apologetic. 'They would have done the same to us' is the familiar refrain. The only regret most Israelis have about 1948 is that the job was not completed by the occupation of the West Bank and Gaza with the total expulsion of all Palestinians from 'Eretz Yisrael'. The Zionist attitude toward atrocities against Arabs is similar to what nineteenth-century Americans thought about the massacre of native Americans. ('The only good Indian is a dead Indian.')

What concerns Zionist propagandists most is not what Israelis think about 1948 but what the British and even more importantly what the American public is told about the exodus of the Palestinians. A major cornerstone of Zionist propaganda is the myth that they are and always have been the innocent victims of Arab 'terrorism'. The Zionists monitor movies and TV very carefully to make sure that only the approved version of 1948 is portrayed.

The Hollywood movie *Exodus* (which is frequently shown on American TV) is based on the novel by Leon Uris that gives the standard Zionist line of the 'War of Independence'. Both the book and film portray a mythical struggle by Zionists against both anti-Semitic British and bloodthirsty Arab hordes. The Uris book refers to 'the absolutely documented fact that the Arab leaders wanted the civilian population to leave Palestine as a political issue and a military weapon.'[2] In the film we actually hear (conveniently in English) the mythic radio broadcasts in which the Palestinians are ordered to leave by their leaders who are inspired by Nazi advisers. The Haganah, gallantly headed by Paul Newman, makes a persistent but futile attempt to persuade the Palestinians to remain but the hapless Arabs are terrorized into leaving by 'the Mufti's Gang' who are carrying out a cynical and diabolic scheme. It is of course unthinkable that Hollywood could ever produce an honest film about 1948.

An accurate account of the Palestinian exodus is not permitted even in a documentary on American TV. Thus in 1986, when the Public Broadcasting System (PBS) scheduled a 90-minute presentation on the Arab–Israeli struggle which attempted to give both sides of the conflict, the Zionists forced the cancellation of the showing of the documentary in many cities despite the fact that the programme had already been paid for. The documentary contained two films which attempted to give

EPILOGUE

the Zionist and then the Palestinian view of the Middle East situation. The Zionists were particularly eager to stop the entire 90-minute programme because they did not wish the American people to see among other things a sequence which contained the testimony of survivors from the Deir Yassin and Dawayma massacres. As the Palestinian scholar Edward Said has noted, 'If you need a virtual thought police to champion a cause, something is wrong.'[3]

In Britain more diversity of opinion in the Middle East is permitted but the Zionists make every effort to cover up the truth. As recently as September 1986, British TV viewers were presented with Kenneth Griffith's *The Light: A Life of David Ben-Gurion*. There were many inaccuracies, especially regarding the Palestinians. Fortunately Griffith was roundly criticized by the British press. On 11 September, *The Listener* noted its disapproval of Griffith's 'juvenile and closed-minded bias'. However, shortly afterwards British TV showed *Pillar of Fire*, an Israeli-made series that repeats the usual myths about the creation of the Jewish state in 1948. With the wealth of new evidence it may eventually be possible to have a documentary about 1948 on British TV which is accurate.

The Israeli cover-up of the truth about the Palestinian exodus is not over. In view of the implications, the Zionists will never admit that the expulsion of hundreds of thousands of innocent Arab civilians was in any sense premeditated. The censorship of books, TV programmes and the closing of historical records is likely to continue. But perhaps the extent of the Zionist effort to conceal so much of the evidence relating to 1948 is the best proof of what really took place.

Sources

Abbreviations for Document Collections and Archival Sources

AFSC	American Friends Service Committee Archives (Philadelphia)
B	Ben-Gurion Archives (Sde Boker)
BD	Ben-Gurion's Diary (published in Hebrew)
BBC	BBC Monitoring Service, British Library (London)
CIA	CIA Foreign Broadcast Information Branch, Library of Congress (Washington)
Cmd.	British Parliamentary Command Papers
CZA	Central Zionist Archives (Jerusalem)
DFPI	*Documents on the Foreign Policy of Israel*
FRUS	*Foreign Relations of the United States*
GA/OR	*United Nations General Assembly: Official Records*
GB-PD	British Parliamentary Debates
HHA	Aharon Cohen Papers, Hashomer Hatzair Archives
ISA:FM	Foreign Ministry Files, Israel State Archives (Jerusalem)
ISA:MM	Minorities Ministry, Israel State Archives (Jerusalem)
JA	Jabotinsky Archives (Tel Aviv)
MEC	Middle East Centre, St Anthony's College (Oxford)
NA	US State Dept. Files, National Archives (Washington D.C.)
PDD	*Political and Diplomatic Documents of the Jewish Agency, 1947–48*
PRO:CAB	Cabinet Papers, Public Record Office (London)
PRO:CO	Colonial Office Papers, Public Record Office (London)
PRO:FO	Foreign Office Papers, Public Record Office (London)
PRO:WO	War Office Papers, Public Record Office (London)
RICR	*Revue Internationale de la Croix Rouge*
SC/OR	*United Nations Security Council: Official Records*

SOURCES

UNA	United Nations Archives (New York)
UND	United Nations Documents, UN Library (New York)
UNICEF	UNICEF, Historical Division (New York)
UUL	Uppsala University Library (Uppsala, Sweden)
WD	Weitz Diary (published in Hebrew)
WNRC	Washington National Record Center (Suitland, Maryland)
WP	*Weizmann's Papers and Letters*

Prologue

1. UNA 13/3.3.1, box 10. Report of the 'Special Investigating Team for the Negev'.
2. DFPI, vol.II, no. 31.
3. UNA 13/3.3.1, box 10. 'Negev Report'.
4. UNA 13/3.3.1, box 10. 'Negev Report'.
5. ISA:FM A/21/2401.
6. BD, 10 November 1948.
7. MEC: Thames Interviews, box II, file 5.
8. *Davar*, 6 September 1979.
9. UNA 13/3.3.1, box 11, *Atrocities September – November*.
10. NA 867 N.01/11–1648.
11. Tom Segev, *1949: The First Israelis*, p. 26.
12. AFSC Palestine 1948, General Reports.
13. DFPI, vol. I, no. 442.
14. Robert Goldston, *The Sword of the Prophet*, p.176. 'Many Arabs were encouraged to leave by their own leaders who promised that they would be able to return.' Martin Gilbert, *The Arab–Israeli Conflict*, p. 47.
15. Benny Morris, articles in *Studies in Zionism*, September, 1985; *Middle Eastern Studies*, January 1986; *Middle East Journal*, Winter 1986. More significant are the articles by Yoram Nimrod in the left Zionist newspaper, *Al Hamishmar* (5 April, 11 April, 24 April, 7 June, 14 June 1985). Nimrod has some important material on the attitude of the Israeli government toward the exodus but his analysis of the Arab attitude suffers from his failure to use many non-Israeli sources.
16. Interview with Meir Pa'il.

Chapter I: Land Without a People

1. CZA Executive Proceedings, 12 June 1938.
2. CZA Executive Proceedings, 12 June 1938.

3. *Jewish Chronicle* (London), 13 August 1937.
4. PRO:FO 371/20808.
5. MEC:Thames Interviews, box I, file 9.
6. BD, vol. IV, p. 299.
7. CZA Minutes of the Population Transfer Committee, 22 November 1937.
8. CZA Arab Transfer Sub-Committee, 5 December 1937.
9. CZA Arab Transfer Sub-Committee, 1 December 1937.
10. CZA Executive Proceedings, 12 June 1938.
11. Theodore Herzl, *The Complete Diaries* I, p. 88.
12. Amos Elon, *Herzl*, p. 58.
13. Michael Selzer, *The Aryanization of the Jewish State*, p. 37.
14. Shlomo Avineri, *The Making of Modern Zionism*, p. 153.
15. Theodore Herzl, p. 88.
16. Avineri, p. 123.
17. Moshe Menuhin, *The Decadence of Judaism*, p. 52.
18. Esco Foundation for Palestine, *Palestine: A Study of Jewish, Arab and British Policies*, vol. I, p. 107.
19. PRO:CAB 24/24.
20. Howard M. Sachar, *A History of Israel*, p. 164.
21. Walter Laqueur, *A History of Zionism*, p. 213.
22. Redcliffe N. Salaman, *Palestine Reclaimed*, pp. 175–6.
23. Joseph Schechtman, *The Jabotinsky Story: Fighter and Prophet*, p. 324.
24. Avineri, p. 180.
25. William Ziff, *The Rape of Palestine*, p. 373.
26. Vincent Sheean, *Personal History*, p. 358.
27. PRO:CO 733/163.
28. Cmd. 3530, p. 36.
29. GB-PD *Commons*, vol. 248, col. 751.
30. David Ben-Gurion, *My Talks With Arab Leaders*, p. 16. See also Sachar, p. 182.
31. Edwin Black, *The Transfer Agreement*, p. 380.
32. Schechtman, p. 217.
33. Mahatma Gandhi, *My Non-Violence*, p. 70.
34. Chaim Weizmann, *Trial and Error*, p. 419.
35. WD II, p. 181.
36. Schechtman, p. 324.
37. WP:B2, p. 372.
38. Chaim Weizmann, p. 535.
39. WP:B2, p. 428.
40. WP:B2, p. 441.

41. FRUS:1943 IV, p. 776.
42. WP:B2, p. 507.
43. PRO:FO 371/3541.
44. MEC: Philby Papers, box 10.
45. *Manchester Guardian*, 24 April 1944.
46. *Palestine Post*, 11 May 1944.
47. John Snetsinger, *Truman, the Jewish Vote and the Creation of Israel*.
48. Cmd. 6808, p. 20.
49. Richard Crossman, *Palestine Mission*, p. 132.
50. Robert John, *Palestine Diary* II, p. 42.
51. Frederick Morgan, *Peace and War*, p. 245.
52. Lenni Brenner, *Zionism in the Age of the Dictators*, p. 267.
53. Bernard L. Montgomery, *The Memoirs of Field-Marshal Montgomery*, p. 419.
54. PRO:FO 371/61878.
55. John, p. 201.
56. NA 501BB Pal/12–947.
57. John, p. 206.
58. PRO:FO 371/20816.
59. CZA Executive Proceedings, 7 June 1938.
60. Richard Meinertzhagen, *Middle East Diary*, p. 191.
61. George Antonius, *The Arab Awakening*, p. 412.
62. A heavily censored version of this letter was included in a collection of Ben-Gurion's correspondence published in 1968. The uncensored version has recently become available. Shabtai Teveth, *Ben-Gurion and the Palestinians*, p. 189.

Chapter II: Plan Dalet

1. *New York Times*, 3 December 1947.
2. Nicholas Bethell, *The Palestine Triangle*, p. 354.
3. *New York Times*, 14 December 1947.
4. MEC: Cunningham Papers, box 2, file 3.
5. MEC: Cunningham Papers, box 2, file 3.
6. *Haaretz* supplement, 17 November 1978.
7. Marion Woolfson, *Prophets in Babylon*, p. 123.
8. SC/OR:S/676, 16 February 1948.
9. David Ben-Gurion, *Be'hilahem Yesrael*, p. 69.
10. ibid., p. 127.
11. BBC report #43, p. 63.
12. PDD, no. 129.
13. L. R. Banks, *Torn Country: An Oral History*, p. 110.

14. CZA S–25/9679.
15. BD, vol. I, 19 December 1947.
16. *Hadashot*, 11 January 1985.
17. PDD, no. 12.
18. Interview with Meir Pa'il, 17 January 1986.
19. Nataniel Lorch, *The Edge of the Sword*, p. 87.
20. UND Palestine Commission Reports, A/AC21/9, p. 7.
21. Ronny Gabbay, *A Political Study of the Arab–Jewish Conflict*, p. 66.
22. *Al Hamishmar*, 5 April 1985.
23. PDD, 239.
24. John, p. 384.
25. Segev, p. 45.
26. Gabbay, p. 66.
27. CZA S–25/9679.
28. CZA S–25/8184.
29. Harry Levin, *Jerusalem Embattled*, p. 61.

Chapter III: Deir Yassin

An important source for this chapter is an interview with Meir Pa'il. See also his previous testimony in Banks, pp. 55–8, 65–8, and *Yediot Aharonot*, 4 April 1972.

1. *Koteret Rashit*, 13 May 1986.
2. JA 1/10–4K.
3. JA 1/10–4K.
4. MEC: Thames Interviews, box II, file 4.
5. *Koteret Rashit*, 13 May 1986.
6. MEC: Thames Interviews, box II, file 4.
7. MEC: Thames Interviews, box I, file 19.
8. PRO:FO 371/68504.
9. JA 1/10–4K.
10. Dr de Reynier: *A Jerusalem au drapeau flottait sur la ligne de feu*, pp. 69–74.
11. Larry Collins and Dominique Lapierre, *O Jerusalem*, p. 290.
12. JA 1/10–4K.
13. PRO:CO 733/477/5.
14. UNA 13/3.1.0.
15. Menachem Begin, *The Revolt*, p. 226.
16. *Koteret Rashit*, 13 May 1986.
17. JA 1/10–4K.
18. PRO:CO 733/477/5.

Chapter IV: The Haifa Tragedy

1. CIA report of 13 April, II, p. 5.
2. FRUS vol. 5, part 2, p. 817.
3. BBC report #47, p. 71.
4. Sami Haddawi, *Palestine: Loss of a Heritage*, foreword by Millar Burrows, p. vii.
5. Banks, p. 112.
6. Letter from the Archbishop to Erskine Childers in Ibrahim Abu-Lughod, *The Transformation of Palestine*, p. 197.
7. A British military report of 2 January 1948 noted, 'Haganah attacks on Balad al-Sheikh, 14 Arabs killed including 10 women and children, 11 Arabs seriously wounded.' PRO:WO 275–67.
8. BBC report #44, p. 65.
9. CIA report of 4 March, II, p. 2.
10. BBC report #40, p. 62.
11. CIA report of 29 March, II, p. 5.
12. PRO:FO 371/68505.
13. Arthur Koestler, *Promise and Fulfilment*, p. 207.
14. Leo Heiman, 'All's Fair. . . ', *Marine Corps Gazette*, June 1964.
15. MEC: Thames Interviews, box II, file 4.
16. MEC: Thames Interview, box I, file 8.
17. WNRC:RG84 Haifa 1948–840.4.
18. Jon and David Kimche, *A Clash of Destinies*, p. 219.
19. BBC report #48, p. 65.
20. CIA report of 26 April, II, p. 4; see also BBC report #47, p. 60. Despite the conclusive evidence of Kaukji's attitude, Mattityahu Shmuelevitch, a spokesman for the Likud party stated 'the flight of the Arabs. What caused that was that Kaukji issued a call to them to leave their homes. . . Those are the historical facts and it's very easy to certify them.' Banks, *op. cit.*, p. 67
21. PRO:FO 371/68544.
22. PRO:FO 371/68505.
23. PRO:FO 371/68505.
24. Kimche, p. 123; see also *Jewish Observer* (London), 11 September and 18 September 1959.
25. PRO:FO 371/68544.
26. WNRC:RG84 Haifa 1948–800.
27. FRUS 1948, vol. V, part 2, p. 838.
28. PRO:FO 371/68505. General Stockwell later stated that the Jews wanted to keep the Palestinians in Haifa because, 'they were all Christian Arabs' who ran 'water works, roads, a tremendous lot'. MEC: Thames Interviews, box I, file 19.

29. PRO:FO 371/68454.
30. Banks, p. 114.
31. MEC: Thames Interviews, box II, file 4.
32. MEC: Thames Interviews, box I, file 19.
33. MEC: Thames Interviews, box I, file 8.
34. R. D. Wilson, *Cordon and Search: With 6th Airborne Division in Palestine*, p. 194.
35. UNA 13/3.1.0., box 4.
36. CZA 45/2 meeting of JAE, 6 May 1948.
37. HHA 10.95.10(5).
38. *Hadashot*, 19 October 1986.
39. *Al Hamishmar*, 7 June 1985.
40. *Al Hamishmar*, 5 April 1985.
41. ISA:MM 303/41.
42. WNRC:RG84 Haifa 1948–800.
43. PRO:FO 371/68373.
44. PRO:FO 371/68547.
45. BBC report #48, p. 60.
46. PRO:FO 371/68370.
47. PRO:FO 371/68370. On 5 May, a Zionist agent reported 'American military attaché in Damascus informs me that Arab politicians are unwilling to send forces to Palestine but mob enthusiasm which they roused for volunteer army now turning against them, urging them to send Arab [regular] forces.' PDD, no. 458.
48. FRUS 1948, vol. 5, p. 915.
49. FRUS 1948, vol. V, part 2, p. 383.
50. PRO:CAB 127/341.
51. NA 867N.01/4–1248.
52. Levin, p. 87.
53. Kenneth Bilby, *New Star in the Middle East*, p. 28.
54. Ben-Gurion, p. 69.

Chapter V: The Fall of Jaffa

1. Banks, p. 125.
2. MEC: Thames Interviews, box II, file 1.
3. BBC report #40, p. 62.
4. CIA report of 19 February, II, p. 3.
5. CIA report of 14 March, II, p. 3.
6. Begin, p. 455.
7. PRO:WO 275–66.
8. MEC: Thames Interviews, box I, file 19.

9. PDD, no. 436.
10. MEC: Thames Interviews, box II, file 1.
11. CIA report of 26 April, II, p. 3.
12. BBC report #49, p. 70.
13. de Reynier, p. 210.
14. MEC: Thames Interviews, box I, file 1.
15. MEC: Gurney Diary, 2 May 1948.
16. Begin, p. 467.
17. Banks, p. 124.
18. MEC: Thames Interviews, box II, file 5.
19. PRO:WO 275–66.
20. MEC: Gurney Diary, 2 May 1948.
21. MEC: Thames Interviews, box II, file 1.
22. John, p. 339.
23. UUL 431, box 1.
24. MEC: Gurney Diary, 5 May 1948.
25. CIA report of 6 May, II, p. 6.
26. MEC: Gurney Diary, 2 May 1948.
27. John, p. 347.
28. Lorch, p. 111; see also, Banks, *op. cit.*, p. 123.
29. Lorch, *op. cit.*, p. 111.
30. MEC: Thames Interviews, box I, file 6.
31. Begin, p. 450.

Chapter VI: The City of Peace

1. Frank Epp, *The Palestinians*, p. 47.
2. CIA report of 17 May, II, p. 5.
3. BBC report #49, p. 71.
4. The American publisher of Bertha Vester's book *Our Jerusalem*, deleted this passage but the full text was published in Beirut in 1962. Ibrahim Abu-Lughod, *The Transformation of Palestine*, p. 186.
5. Levin, p. 160.
6. Collins and Lapierre, pp. 103–4.
7. CIA report of 29 April, II, p. 7.
8. BBC report #48, p. 63.
9. CIA report of 26 April, II, p. 3.
10. CZA: S25/4013.
11. Correspondence with author.
12. *Koteret Rashit*, 13 May 1986.
13. CZA: S25/824551.
14. de Reynier, p. 129.

15. AFSC: Palestine 1948 Correspondence.
16. WRNC: RG84, Jerusalem *Refugees*.
17. John, p. 347.
18. CIA report of 30 March, II, p. 7.
19. Banks, p. 132.
20. Pablo de Azcarate, *Mission in Palestine*, p. 211.
21. Banks, p. 187.

Chapter VII: The Road to Safed

1. Amina Musa's story of a Zionist attack on Kabri is verified by General McNeil, a retired British officer who had large landholdings in Galilee. On 21 May, he wrote in his diary: 'Every house in Kabri demolished, Faris Sirhan's big new house was the first to go up. He is a member of the Arab Higher Committee in Damascus.' MEC McNeil Papers, Diary 1948.
2. PRO:WO 275/66–60294.
3. WNRC:RG84 Haifa 1948–840.4.
4. UNA 13/3.3.1, box 11.
5. Dan Kurzman, *Genesis 1948*, p. 165.
6. CIA report of 6 May, II, p. 4.
7. CIA report of 5 May, II, p. 1.
8. BBC report #40, p. 66.
9. Uri Avnery, *Israel Without Zionism*, p. 224.
10. Koestler, p. 215.
11. PRO:FO 371/68507.
12. *Koteret Rashit*, 27 February 1985.
13. Yigal Allon, *Book of the Palmach* (Hebrew), II, p. 286.
14. WD, vol. III, p. 256.
15. BBC report #50, p. 57.
16. FRUS 1948, vol. 5, part 2, p. 983.
17. PRO:FO 371/68507.
18. UNA 13/3.3.1, box 13.
19. HHA 10.95.13(1).
20. Benny Morris, 'The Causes and Character of the Arab Exodus from Palestine', *Middle East Studies*, January 1986, p. 18.
21. ISA:FM 2570/6.
22. BA Correspondence 15 July 1948.
23. Dunkelman removed the Nazareth episode from the manuscript of his book before publication of his memoirs but ghostwriter Peretz Kidron released it to the press. Not surprisingly the anti-Arab racist Meir Kahane (*They Must Go!*, pp. 240–41) blames Dunkelman for the large Arab population in Galilee. Kahane was

SOURCES

not the only one displeased with Dunkelman's action. According to Ben-Gurion's official biographer, Michael Bar Zohar, when the Israeli Prime Minister visited Nazareth and saw many Arabs, he angrily told Chaim Laskov, 'What are they doing here?' *Hadashot*, 19 October 1986.
24. Epp, *The Palestinians*, p. 51.

Chapter VIII: The Lydda Death March

1. Reprinted in *Palestine Post*, 13 July 1948.
2. Kenneth Bilby, *New Star in the Near East*, p. 43.
3. Banks, p. 253. Raja'i Buseilah, 'The Fall of Lydda 1948: Impressions and Reminiscences', *Arab Studies Quarterly*, Spring 1981, pp. 137–8.
4. CIA report of 12 July, II, p. 4.
5. Ben-Gurion, p. 129.
6. Fouzi al-Asmar, *To Be an Arab in Israel*, p. 15.
7. Interviews by the author with Raja'i Buseilah and Saba A. Saba; see also, *London Economist*, 21 August 1948, Dana Adams Schmidt, *Armageddon in the Middle East*, pp. 160–61.
8. MEC: Thames Interviews, box II, file 5.
9. Sami Haddawi, *The Palestinian*, p. 33.
10. Haddawi, p. 41.
11. Segev, p. 71.
12. BD, II, p. 589, 15 July 1948.
13. MEC: Thames Interviews, box II, file 1.
14. MEC: Thames Interviews, box II, file 5.
15. Count Folke Bernadotte, *To Jerusalem*, p. 200.
16. FRUS 1948, vol. 5, part 2, p. 1295.
17. WRNC:RG84 Jerusalem 1948, *Refugees* report of 29 July.
18. *Al Hamishmar*, 24 April 1985.
19. Benny Morris, 'Operation Dani and the Palestinian Exodus from Lydda and Ramle', *The Middle East Journal*, January 1986, p. 82.
20. ISA:FM 25/64/5.
21. WNRC:RG84 Jerusalem 1948, *Refugees* report of 12 August.

Chapter IX: The Troubled Truce

1. Report of UN investigators, testimony of survivors and other documents are in UNA 13/3.3.1, box 7, case 10. See also the letter of 3 August 1948 in UUL #431, box 1.
2. Interview with Joseph Argaman.
3. Statement in *Al Hamishmar*, 3 December 1985.

4. RICR, August 1948.
5. UNA 13/3.3.1, box 7, case 10.
6. BA Mapai Protocols, 4 April 1948.
7. WD III, p. 293.
8. BD II, p. 477.
9. ISA:FM 2564/19.
10. CIA report of 11 June, p. 6.
11. DFPI, vol. I, no. 189.
12. Ben-Gurion, p. 164.
13. HHA 10.95.11(1).
14. ISA:FM 2466/2.
15. FRUS 1948, vol. 5, part 2, p. 1151.
16. FRUS 1948, vol. 5, part 2, p. 1158.
17. Bernadotte, p. 189.
18. UNA 13/3.3.0, box 3. In an undated memorandum marked 'Points for discussion with Mr Shertok on Refugee Problem', Bernadotte mentions other categories of Arabs who might be allowed to return home. These include: those in Israeli-controlled territory, citrus farmers, urban people for whom employment is available, rural people whose villages are intact and special humanitarian cases. UUL #431, box 1.
19. FRUS 1948, vol. 5, part 2.
20. SC/OR supplement 108(s/949), p. 109.
21. DFPI, vol. 1, no. 352.
22. ISA:MM 304/8.
23. ISA:MM 304/8.
24. Asmar, *To be an Arab in Israel*, p. 21.
25. ISA:MM 304/8.
26. FRUS 1948, part 2, p. 989.
27. ISA:MM 309/2.
28. ISA:MM 309/2.
29. UNA 13/3.3.0, box 52.
30. FRUS 1948, vol. 5, part 2, p. 1308.
31. UNA 13/3.3.0, box 10.
32. Joel Migdal, *Palestinian Society and Politics*, p. 157.
33. Bilby, *op. cit.*, p. 107.
34. RICR, September 1948.
35. ISA:FM 2566/13.
36. ISA:FM 2570/11.
37. ISA:FM 2444/19.
38. BD, vol. II, p. 652.
39. BD, vol. II, p. 655.

40. ISA:FM 2570/11.
41. UND A/648, p. 1.
42. UNA 13/3.3.0, box 10.

Chapter X: Operation Hiram

1. UNA 13/3.3.1, box 11, *Atrocities September–November*.
2. Epp, p. 51.
3. Nazzal, *The Palestinian Exodus in Galilee*, p. 73.
4. UNA 13/3.3.1, box 11, *Atrocities September–November*.
5. Nazzal, *op. cit.*, p. 89.
6. UNA 13/3.3.1, box 11, *Atrocities September–November*.
7. ISA:FM 2578/11.
8. SC/OR: S/1071, p. 11 (5 November 1948).
9. Segev, pp. 56, 275.
10. NA 867N.01/11–1648.
11. UNA 13/3.3.1 box 11, *Atrocities September–November*.
12. UNA 13/3.3.1 box 11, *Atrocities September–November*.
13. PRO 371/68679.

Chapter XI: There Could Have Been Peace

1. AFSC: Palestine 1949, Faluja file.
2. AFSC: Palestine 1949, Faluja file.
3. DFPI, vol. II, no. 418.
4. GA/OR Resolution 194III (11 December 1948).
5. DFPI, vol. II, no. 400.
6. DFPI, vol. II, no. 443.
7. *Al Hamishmar* 14 June, 1985, contains much information based on the testimony of Ezra Dannin. See also Segev, pp. 6, 15–18.
8. *Davar*, 24 October 1986.
9. FRUS 1949, vol. VI, p. 903.
10. FRUS 1949, vol. VI, p. 905.
11. FRUS 1949, vol. VI, p. 905.
12. UNA Record of the PCC at the UNA meeting at Lausanne, 3 May 1949 (files in process at the UNA).
13. FRUS 1949, vol. VI, p. 1073.
14. UNA Record of PCC at the UNA meeting at Lausanne, 17 June 1949 (files in process at the UNA).
15. FRUS 1949, vol. VI, p. 1125.
16. FRUS 1949, vol. VI, p. 1205.
17. UNA Memorandum by the Economic Division of the Israeli Foreign Ministry, 28 July 1949 (files in process at the UNA).

18. FRUS 1949, vol. VI, p. 1277.
19. FRUS 1949, vol. VI, p. 1314.
20. FRUS 1949, vol. VI, p. 1425.
21. UNA Lausanne meeting 1 June 1949 (files in process at UNA).
22. FRUS 1949, vol. VI, p. 709.
23. AFSC Palestine 1949, Geneva Letters.
24. AFSC Palestine 1949, Work Camps file.
25. AFSC Palestine 1949, Reports from Gaza.

Chapter XII: Theft of a Nation

1. Fouzi al-Asmar, *To Be an Arab in Israel*, p. 27.
2. Gabbay, p. 349.
3. Sachar, p. 387.
4. David Hirst, *The Gun and the Olive Branch*, pp. 155–64; *Documents from Israel*, pp. 127–9.
5. UNICEF B–165, report of 31 January 1949.
6. UNICEF B–165, report of 28 February 1949.
7. UNA Report of the PCC Technical Committee on Refugees, 4 July 1949 (files in process at UNA). The Israelis did not accept the UN estimate of the number of refugees claiming that there were between 550,000–600,000. For a discussion of this dispute from an Israeli perspective, see Amitzur Ilan, *The War of Independence* (Hebrew), pp. 79–81.
8. UNICEF B–166, report of 31 August 1949.
9. Janet Abu-Lughod, 'The Demographic Transformation of Palestine' in Ibrahim Abu-Lughod, *The Transformation of Palestine*, pp. 153–161. See also UNICEF B–166.
10. DFPI, vol. I, no. 189.
11. *Hadashot*, 19 October 1986.
12. Theodore Herzl, *Diaries* III, p. 77.
13. *New York Times*, 5 August 1985; Meir Kahane, *They Must Go!*

Epilogue

1. *Koteret Rashit*, 27 February 1985.
2. Leon Uris, *Exodus*, p. 553.
3. Edward W. Said, *After the Last Sky*, p. 140.

Acknowledgements

Many who assisted me in the research for this book cannot be publicly acknowledged because of possible retaliation by the Israeli government and the American Zionist lobby. Among those who can be acknowledged, a special place belongs to Professor Israel Shahak of the Hebrew University of Jerusalem, to whom this book is dedicated. In particular, I greatly appreciate the use of the large number of newspaper and magazine articles on 1948 from his collection which proved to be a major source for my words. Ilan Hazouth, a doctoral candidate in linguistics at Amherst University was unusually competent both as translator and research assistant.

In Britain, I am greatly indebted to Taylor Downing, director of Flashback Television Ltd who gave strong support. Professor Noam Chomsky of the Massachusetts Institute of Technology has been a constant source of encouragement. Without his involvement it is doubtful that this book would ever have been completed.

Archivists and librarians in Europe, Israel and the United States have been extremely helpful, including the staffs of the Central Zionist Archives and the Israel State Archives, who courteously made available all declassified material in their collections. Special thanks go to Alf Erlandson and his staff at the United Nations Archives in New York who helped me find many important documents on Palestine in 1948, after I had located the United Nations War Crimes Commission files in 1980.

Index

Abdullah, King of Trans-Jordan, 78, 117, 131
Abu Gush, 47
Abu-Lughod, Janet, 203
Acre, 119
Allon Yigal, 127–8
Almadi, Mahmud, 139
American Friends Service Committee (AFSC), 175, 191
Antonius, George, 32
Arab Higher Committee (AHC), 19, 37–8, 43, 60, 66, 152–3
Arab Legion, 118
Arab Liberation Army (ALA), 38, 62, 66, 93, 107, 109, 114, 163–4, 167
Arab National Committee, 60
Argaman, Josef, 141–2
al-Arif, Arif, 135
al-Asmar, Fouzi, 128–30, 149–51, 194–5
Auni, Abdul Hadi, 18
Avnery, Uri, 113
Azcarate, Pablo, 102–3
Azouri, Naquib, 10
Azzam, Abdul Rashman Pasha, 147

Bahnan, Fuad, 95–6
Baruch, Colonel, x
Bar Zohar, Michael, 205
Bauer, Yehuda, 93
Beersheva, xi
Begin, Menachem, 2, 34; Deir Yassin, 55; Jaffa, 89, 94; opposes repatriation of refugees, 189
Beisan, 116
Beit Jann, 169
Ben Ammoun, Fuad, 186
Ben-Gurion, David, viii–xi, 2, 4, 17–18, 24, 32–3, 38, 40–1; Plan Dalet, 45; Haifa, 76; Jaffa, 91; proclaims the Jewish State, 117; Lydda-Ramle, 127; refugees, 144, 156–7, 182–3, 190, 205, 210
Ben Porat, Yeshayahu, 37
Ben Yehuda, Netiva, 114–15, 126–7
Bernadotte, Count Folke, 120, 135, 141, 145–7, 157–61, 171
Bevin, Ernest, 79
Bilby, Kenneth, 89, 126, 154–5
Biltmore Programme, 22
al-Bi'na, 168
Block, Hans, 18
British Broadcasting Corporation (BBC), xvii
Buber, Martin, 12

Bunche, Ralph, 171
Burdett, William, 171, 184, 187–9
Burrows, Millar, 59
Buseilah, Raja'i, 129–30

Caesarea, 141
Campbell, Sir Ronald, 67
Carmeli Brigade, 119
Central Intelligence Agency (CIA), xvii
Chamoun, Camille, 29, 118
Childers, Erskine, xvi
Churchill, Winston, 20
Cizling, Aharon, xiv, 133
Cliento, Sir Raphael, 58
Cohen, Aharon, 75
Cohen, Benzion, 48
Courvoisier, Raymond, 201–3
Crossman, Richard, 25
Cunningham, Sir Alan, 35–6, 41

Dannin, Ezra, 136, 144, 155, 182
Daoud, Hanna, 164
Daoud, Markos, 164
Dawayma, xii–xiv, 212
Dayan, Moshe, 76, 126, 160, 183
De Greer, Gerald, vii–x
Deir al-Assad, 168, 169
Deir Yassin, xviii, 47–57, 102, 104, 107, 112, 133, 183, 206
Deleque, Father, 91
Descoudenes, Dr P., xiv
Dix, Richard, 71
Dori, Yaacov, 39, 179
Druse, 110, 122
Dunkelman, Ben, 124

Eban, Abba, 170
Eichmann, Adolf, 27
Elabun, 163–6
Ennab, Basil, 87
Ethridge, Mark, 181, 185
Eytan, Walter, 185, 189

Faluja, xi, 175–8
Farouk, King of Egypt, 202
Fuller, W. V., 92

Gandhi, Mahatma, 19
Gerah, Captain, 178
Ghalyon, Mahmoud Abu, xii
Ghazal, 139–40
Ghuweir, 109
Glass, Dr D. V., 25
Golani Brigade, 116
Goldmann, Dr Nahum, 23, 80
Gordon, A. D., 6
Grinberg, Reuven, 56
Grunich, Fred, 171
Grusenberg, Senator O. O., 12
Gumri, Wadi, 96
Guri, Chaim, 183
Gurney, Sir Henry, 29, 87, 92

Ha'Am Ahad (né Asher Ginzberg), 8
Habash, Dr George, 131
Ha'Cohen, David, 157
Hadashot, 212
Haddawi, Sami, 98–9
Hadi, Auni Abdul, 18
Haganah, 19, 36, 39; aids terrorists, 48; POWs, 83
Haganah Radio, 58, 85, 88, 91
Haifa, 58–81, 151–3
Haikal, Yusef, 89
Hajjar, Yusuf Ahmad, 111
Hanegbi, Major Michael, vii–x
Har-Shefi, Joella, 211
Hartrough, Ray, 175–8, 192
Hassan, Abu, 132–4
Hebron, 15
Hegnaur, Ralph, 191
Heiman, Leo, 64, 210
Henderson, F. P., 169
Hentig, Otto von, 27

INDEX

Herzl, Theodore, 5–7, 210
Hirbet Hiz'ah, xix
Horowitz, D., 156
Hoskins, Colonel Harold, 23
al-Huneiti, Muhammad Hamad, 60
Hurley, General Patrick, 22
Hushi, Abu, 75
Hussaini, Haj Amin (Grand Mufti of Jerusalem), 19, 66, 84

Ibn Saud, King of Saudi Arabia, 21, 23
International Civilian Service, 191
Iraq el Menskiya, 176
Irgun, xviii, 27–8, 36; in Jaffa, 85–9, 91, 93
Izzam, 139–40

Jaba, 139–40
Jabotinsky, Vladimir, 5, 12–13, 21
Jaffa, 82–94
Jewish Agency, 1–5, 43, 71, 76, 80, 100
Jewish National Fund, 143
Jifna, 155
Jish, 171
Johnson, Louis, 190
Joseph, Dov, 160

Kabri, 105–6
Kahane, Meir, 208
Kaplan, Eliezer, 196
Kardosh, Mansour, 124, 167
Katamon, 98–100
Katzenelson, Berl, 2
al-Kaukji, Fawzi, 66, 163
al-Khadra, Abed, 113
Khalidi, Wadi, 210
Khamis, Fayiz, 109
Khayat, Victor, 67

Kidron, Peretz, 210
Kimche, Jon, 65
Kirkbride, Sir Alex, 78
Koestler, Arthur, 58, 64
Kollek, Teddy, 182
Koussa, Elias, 67–9, 152–3
Kunde, Herbert, 188
Kuwatly, President, 69

Lajjun, 169
Laskov, Chaim, 123–4
Lausanne Conference, 187–8
Levi, Yitzhak, 47, 99, 211
Levin, Harry, 45–6, 80
Levy, Shabtai, 68, 70, 76
Lippincott, Aubrey, 70, 77
London Economist, 129
Lorch, Nataniel, 41
Lotsky, A., 44
Luke, Sir Stephen, 3
Lundstrom, Agee, 159
Lydda, 94, 126–38

Ma'ari, Mustafa Ahmad, 59
Machnes, Gad, 36
Majd al-Kurum, 172
Mapai Party, 2, 38, 74
Mapam Party, 75, 145, 156
Marchal, Captain, F., 108
Marinburg, Yehuda, 52
Marriott, Cyril, 63, 68, 71
Marshall, George C., 118
McDonald, James A., 146, 185
McMillan, Sir Gordon, 51
Meinertzhagen, Richard, 32
Meir, Golda, 74
Menuhin, Moses, 8
Miller, A. L., 101
Moeri, Dr Emil, 173
Mohn, Paul, 143, 178
Montagu, Edward, 9

Montgomery, General Bernard, 79
Montzkin, Leo, 11
Morgan, General Frederick, 26
Morris, Benny, 120, 136
Moyne, Lord, 27
Murray, Sir Horatius, 51, 86–7, 88
Musa, Amina, 105–6

Nablus, 72, 96
Namier, Professor Lewis, 21
Nazareth, 123

Negev, 29
Newman, Paul, 212
Notestein, Dr Frank, 25

Operation Charmetz, 85
Operation Gideon, 116
Operation Hiram, 163, 173
Operation Matateh, 108, 112
Operation Ten Plagues, x
Oren, Major, 176

Pa'il, Meir, xviii, 48–50, 56–7
Palestine Conciliation Commission (PCC), 180, 184
Palestine Liberation Organization (PLO), 27, 135, 207
Pallemans, A., 172
Palmach, 115
Peel Commission, 3
Perrossier, Commandant, 166
Petah Tikva, 34
Petite, Lieutenant, 119
Philby, St John, 21
Pinkerton, Lowell, 189
Plan Dalet (D), 34–46, 123
Plehve, Wenzel von, 6
Public Broadcasting System (PBS), 212

Qadurah, Faujz, 113

Rabin, Yitzhak, 127–8, 130, 137
Ramallah, 133
Ramle, 127, 132–4
Red Cross, 88, 100, 129, 135, 140–3, 155
Revisionists, 21
Reynier, Jacques de, 52–4, 56, 88
Roplogle, Delbert, 175–6
Rupin, Arthur, 11

Sa'ad, Farid, 67
Saba A. Saba, 129
Safed, 113–15
Said, Edward, 214
Salame, Hassan, 84
Sammour, Mohammed Aref, 50
Sartre, Jean-Paul, 82
Sasson, Elias, 122, 144, 170
Semiramis Hotel, 98
Serot, Colonel, 159
Shaltiel, David, 47
Shamir, Yitzhak, 27, 160
Shammout, Ismail, 131
Sharett (Shertok) Moshe, xv, 17–18, 39, 143–9, 155–6, 176, 179, 181, 189
Sharq al-Adna, 97
Shaw Commission, 15
Sheean, Vincent, 14
Sherban, Abdullah, 110
Shimoni, Yaacov, 122, 155, 170
Shishakli, Abed, 114
Shitrit, Belchor, 76
Silwan, 54
Simpson, Sir John Hope, 16
Smilansky, Moshe, 195
Sore, Colonel, xiii
Staton, Charles N., 169
Stern, Abraham, 26

INDEX

Stern Gang, xviii, 26, 36, 47–8, 62, 83, 126
Stockwell, Hugh, 63, 79

Tagar, Yehuda, 200
Taha Bey, xi
Tahatmuni, Issam, 116
Tel, Major Abdullah, 102
Thon, Yaacov, 4
Tiberias, 107–8
Toledano, Shmuel, 82–3, 89
Toubi, Tawfik, 72
Truman, Harry, 161, 185

United Nations Educational, Scientific and Cultural Organization (UNESCO), 203
United Nations International Children's Emergency Fund (UNICEF), 157, 202
United Nations Mixed Armistice Commission, 180
United Nations Palestine Commission, 74
United Nations Relief and Rehabilitation Agency (UNRRA), 26
United Nations Special Committee on Palestine (UNSCOP), 28–31
Uris, Leon, 212
Ussishkin, Menahem, 1–2

Vaag, Yaacov, 50
Van Wassenhove, Warrant Officer, xiii
Varshitz, Yosef, 60
Vermeulen, Colonel, ix–x
Vesta, Berta, 97

Waddy, John, 65, 73
Weingarten, Mordechai, 103
Weingarten, Rivka, 103–4
Weitz, Joseph, 4, 143–4
Weizmann, Chaim, 21, 32
Welles, Sumner, 23
Wheller, Keith, 126
White Paper (1939), 20
Williams, Colonel, 177
Wilson, R.D., 73
Wissman, Leo, 103
Woodhead, Sir John, 3–4
Wriggins, Howard, 191

Yadin, Yigal, 39
Yaffe, Abraham, 124
Yehidya, 34–5
Yiftach Brigade, 112
Yizhar, S., xix, 212

Zafrullah Khan, Sir Mohammed, 31
Zaim, Housni, 182
Zangwill, Israel, 11
Zeineddine, Dr Farid, 190
Zeuty, Captain E.J., 163–4
Ziff, William, 13–14